Supply Chain Management

Beiträge zu Beschaffung und Logistik

Reihe herausgegeben von

Michael Eßig, München, Universität der Bundeswehr, Neubiberg, Germany

Wolfgang Stölzle, Universität St. Gallen, St. Gallen, Switzerland

Wolfgang Kersten, Institut Logistik & Unternehmensführung, Technische Universität Hamburg, Hamburg, Hamburg, Germany

Industrielle Wertschöpfung wird immer komplexer. Der steigende Wettbewerbsdruck zwingt zu differenzierten Angeboten, gleichzeitig nimmt der Kostendruck zu. Unternehmen können diesen gestiegenen Anforderungen nur gerecht werden, wenn sie neben der Optimierung eigener Produktion besonderen Wert auf die Gestaltung effektiver und effizienter Netzwerke legen. Supply Chain Management befasst sich mit unternehmensübergreifenden Wertschöpfungsaktivitäten von der Rohstoffgewinnung bis zur Endkundendistribution. Die Schriftenreihe sieht sich dabei besonders den lange vernachlässigten betriebswirtschaftlichen Teildisziplinen Beschaffung und Logistik verpflichtet, die als Treiber des Supply Chain Management gelten.

Tim Brandl

Managing Contract Manufacturing Relationships

A Design Science Approach to Client-Applied Management Practices

Springer Gabler

Tim Brandl
St.Gallen, Switzerland

The University of St. Gallen, School of Management, Economics, Law, Social Sciences and International Affairs hereby consents to the printing of the present dissertation, without hereby expressing any opinion on the views herein expressed.
St. Gallen, October 24, 2022
The President:
Prof. Dr. Bernhard Ehrenzeller

ISSN 2627-292X ISSN 2627-2938 (electronic)
Supply Chain Management
ISBN 978-3-658-41358-3 ISBN 978-3-658-41359-0 (eBook)
https://doi.org/10.1007/978-3-658-41359-0

This Springer Gabler imprint is published by the registered company Springer Fachmedien Wiesbaden GmbH, part of Springer Nature.
The registered company address is: Abraham-Lincoln-Str. 46, 65189 Wiesbaden, Germany

Vorwort

Die vorliegende Dissertation entstand im Rahmen meiner dreijährigen Forschungstätigkeit am Institut für Supply Chain Management der Universität St. Gallen (ISCM-HSG). Während dieser Zeit am Institut durfte ich zahlreiche Projekte im Supply Chain Management mit dem Fokus «Contract Manufacturing» betreuen, die mir in Zusammenarbeit mit verschiedenen Praxispartnern immer neue Einsichten in die Thematik gestatteten. Auf diese Weise konnten jederzeit die wissenschaftliche und praktische Perspektive auf das Forschungsvorhaben reflektiert und für die Arbeit miteinander vereint werden.

Zahlreiche Wegbegleiter haben zum Erfolg meiner Promotionszeit beigetragen. Deshalb möchte ich im Folgenden meine Dankbarkeit zum Ausdruck bringen.

Allen voran gilt mein besonderer Dank meinem Referenten Prof. Dr. Wolfgang Stölzle (ISCM-HSG). Seine Betreuung unter dem Motto «fördern und fordern», gestattete mir jegliche Freiheiten in der Zusammenarbeit und stellte doch sicher, dass ich niemals die Orientierung verlor. Des Weiteren bedanke ich mich bei Prof. Dr. Erik Hofmann (ISCM-HSG) für die Übernahme des Ko-Referats. Seine Impulse regten mich stets an neue Blickwinkel und Methoden auszuprobieren und meinen Horizont zu erweitern.

Ein grosser Dank gilt ebenfalls allen Praxisvertretern, die Einblick in ihre Perspektiven gegeben haben. Dazu zählen neben zahlreichen Interviewpartnern auch Repräsentanten von Unternehmen, die mich über die volle Zeit des Doktorats in verschiedenen Projekten begleitet und unterstützt haben. Ihr wertvolles Feedback hat dazu beigetragen, stets den eigenen, wissenschaftlichen Blickwinkel zu hinterfragen und nie die Sichtweise der Praxis aus den Augen zu verlieren. Im gleichen Atemzug sind die wissenschaftlichen Mentoren zu nennen, die in fortlaufenden

Diskussionen im Rahmen von Konferenzen und des Doktoratsstudiums, Fundament und Methodik kritisch hinterfragten und die Arbeit durch wertvolle Impulse voranbrachten.

Besonders bedanken möchte ich mich auch bei meinen Kollegen und Freunden in und rund um St. Gallen. Da ich eigens für das Doktorat in die Schweiz gezogen bin, sind sie in den letzten drei Jahren zu einer Ersatzfamilie geworden, die mich durch alle Höhen und Tiefs des Doktorats begleitet hat. Dies betrifft insbesondere, unabhängig vom Geschlecht, einen Kern «überragender Typen» die zu guten Freunden geworden sind, sowie alle weiteren wissenschaftlichen und nicht wissenschaftlichen Angestellten des ISCM-HSG. Darüber hinaus geht ein besonderer Dank an die Werkstudierenden und Praktikanten, die mir in schwierigen Zeiten den Rücken freigehalten haben um die verschiedenen Aufgaben im Doktorat und am Institut zu bewältigen. Ohne euch alle, wäre diese Dissertation nicht möglich gewesen.

Gleichzeitig möchte ich mich bei meinen Freunden aus der Heimat bedanken, die wiederholt aus zeitlichen Gründen zurückstecken mussten. Der Rückhalt, den ich von ihnen in dieser Zeit erfahren habe ist unvergleichlich. Einen besonderer Dank gilt meiner Familie, die mich auf jeglichen Wegen, selbst wenn diese Neuland waren, mein ganzes Leben lang begleitet und bedingungslos unterstützt hat. Euer Vertrauen und eure uneingeschränkte Unterstützung haben mich stets motiviert und inspiriert. Euch sei daher diese Arbeit in tief empfundener Dankbarkeit gewidmet.

St. Gallen
im Oktober 2022

Tim Brandl

Zusammenfassung

Contract Manufacturing hat sich seit der ersten Outsourcing-Welle branchenübergreifend als Grundpfeiler der globalen Supply Chains etabliert. Markenführende Unternehmen haben sich seitdem verstärkt auf die Kundenorientierung konzentriert und ihre Supply Chains auf den Endverbraucher ausgerichtet. Im Gegenzug haben Auftragsfertiger sich weiterentwickelt und die Markenführer in vielen operativen Bereichen der Supply Chain, wie Produktion, Logistik und Werkstoffkunde, übertroffen. Infolgedessen gehen Klienten Auftragsfertigungsbeziehungen nicht mehr ein, um Fertigungstätigkeiten auszulagern, sondern um ihre Produktentwürfe unter Einsatz der hochentwickelten Fähigkeiten von Auftragsfertigern umzusetzen. Die zunehmende Integration des Auftragsherstellers bedeutet für den Klienten eine enorme strategische und operative Abhängigkeit, da die eigenen Produkte extern durch das Liefernetzwerk des Auftragsfertigers hergestellt werden. Das Beziehungsmanagement muss folglich die Koordination der Fertigung über Unternehmensgrenzen hinweg vor dem Hintergrund fortlaufender Beziehungsdynamiken ermöglichen.

Diese Dissertation befasst sich mit dem Management von Auftragsfertigungsbeziehungen durch den Einsatz von Managementpraktiken seitens des Klienten. Dabei wird die theoretische Perspektive der Transaktionskostentheorie und der Relationship Velocity-Perspektive eingenommen. Die Dissertation untersucht Auftragsfertigungsbeziehungen erstens auf angewandte Managementpraktiken, zweitens auf die Bewertung von Managementbedürfnissen, drittens auf managementrelevante Beziehungsdynamik und viertens auf die gezielte Anwendung und Anpassung von Managementpraktiken.

Die Forschungsergebnisse weisen auf die Notwendigkeit einer systematischen Harmonisierung der kommerziellen und sozialen Beziehungsebene zwischen Klienten und Auftragsfertigern hin. Zudem erfordert die Beziehungsdynamik eine regelmäßige Neubewertung der wirtschaftlichen und sozialen Eignung. Zu diesem Zweck sollte die Beziehung zeitlich gegliedert werden, um eine gezielte Zielerreichung zu ermöglichen. Die Dissertation trägt zum Verständnis des Managements von Auftragsfertigungsbeziehungen bei und leitet aus den Ergebnissen Empfehlungen für die Praxis ab.

Summary

Contract manufacturing has established itself as a cornerstone of global supply chains across industries since the first wave of production outsourcing. Since then, brand-leading companies have focused on customer centricity and geared their supply chains towards the end consumer. In turn, contract manufacturers have developed their capabilities and surpassed the brand leaders in many areas on the value chain's supply side, such as production, logistics, and materials science. As a result, clients no longer enter into contract manufacturing relationships to outsource manufacturing activities but to implement their product designs with the advanced capabilities of contract manufacturers. The increasing integration of contract manufacturers means an enormous strategic and operational dependency for the client, as the client's products are manufactured externally by the contract manufacturer's supply network. Consequently, relationship management must enable the coordination of manufacturing across company boundaries against the backdrop of continuous relationship dynamics.

This dissertation[1] addresses the relationship management of contract manufacturing relationships through the client's use of management practices. It adopts the theoretical lenses of transaction cost economics and the relationship velocity perspective. To this end, the dissertation examines contract manufacturing relationships, first for applied management practices, second for management needs assessment, third for management-relevant relationship dynamics, and fourth for the purposeful application and adjustment of management practices.

---

[1] Excerpts from this dissertation were pre-published in: Brandl T., Müller, A. & Stölzle, W. (2022). Excellence in Management of Contract Manufacturing Relationships. Cuvillier. Göttingen

The research findings indicate the need for systematic alignment of client companies and contract manufacturers at commercial and social relationship levels to enable effective coordination. Furthermore, the dynamics of contract manufacturing relationships require a regular reassessment of the commercial and social fit. To this end, the relationship should be temporally partitioned to ensure targeted goal achievement. The findings contribute to the understanding of contract manufacturing relationship management by addressing the research gap in the literature. Furthermore, the dissertation derives recommendations for practical application from the results.

Contents

Abbreviations

3PL	Third-party logistics
4PL	Fourth-party logistics
AT	Agency theory
CM	Contract manufacturing
CMO	Contract manufacturing organization
CMR	Contract manufacturing relationship
COGS	Cost of goods sold
CRM	Customer relationship management
DC	Dynamic capabilities
EDI	Electronic data interchange
ESM	Electronic supplementary material
IOR	Inter-organisational relationship
JDM	Joint design manufacturing
JV	Joint ventures
KAM	Key account management
KPI	Key performance indicator
ODM	Original design manufacturing
OEM	Original equipment manufacturer
PBV	Practice-based view
RA	Relationship age
RACI	Responsible, Accountable, Consulted, Informed
RBV	Resource-based view
RG	Research gap
RLC	Relationship life cycle
RMV	Relationship marketing view
RO	Research objective

RQ	Research question
RV	Relational view
RVP	Relationship velocity perspective
S&OP	Sales & operations planning
SA	Strategic alliances
SCM	Supply chain management
SM	Service management
SRM	Supplier relationship management
TCE	Transaction cost economics
WMS	Warehouse management system

List of Figures

List of Tables

1 Introduction to Contract Manufacturing Relationships

This dissertation deals with the management of contract manufacturing relationships (CMRs). The first chapter introduces the topic by pointing out the relevance of CMRs and governance in contemporary supply chains. First, Section 1.1 looks at the subject from a managerial perspective, while Section 1.2 outlines the theoretical relevance of the topic. Next, based on the practical challenges and the academic research interests, section 1.3 establishes the research objectives of the thesis. Finally, section 1.4 brings together the preceding considerations and presents the structure of the paper as it proceeds.

1.1 Managerial Relevance

Contract manufacturing (CM) is a supply chain management (SCM) arrangement by which a company subcontracts one or more stages of manufacturing activity to external parties (Han, Porterfield, & Li, 2012; Morschett & Donath, 2011). The subcontracted activities can entail individual production steps, cover the entire manufacturing process, and involve further *'manufacturing-related processes'* (Sousa & Voss, 2007, p. 975), such as product design, fulfilment, or aftermarket services.

Prevalence of contract manufacturing

CMRs are observed across industries but are particularly relevant in high-tech sectors such as pharmaceuticals, automotive, energy, electronics, telecommunication, aerospace, textiles, and defense (Essig, Hofmann, & Stölzle, 2013; Han

T. Brandl, *Managing Contract Manufacturing Relationships*, Supply Chain Management, https://doi.org/10.1007/978-3-658-41359-0_1

et al., 2012; Handley & Gray, 2013). Supply chains in these industries are experiencing a gradual shift toward an ever larger share of value-added provided by contract manufacturers (Kaiser & Obermaier, 2020). As a result, the depth of value added by brand-owning companies has decreased across industries in recent decades. For example, in the electronics and fashion industries, CM accounts for more than 50% of the cost of goods sold (COGS) (Tsay, Gray, Noh, & Mahoney, 2018).

In 2020 contract manufacturers were responsible for assembling nearly half of electronic products around the globe (New Venture Research, 2021). CM affects low-cost or 'no-name' products and world-renowned brands likewise. For example, *'Hewlett-Packard no longer manufactures printers, Cisco no longer manufactures routers, and Apple no longer manufactures iPhones'* (Morschett & Donath, 2011, p. 213). Concerning Apple, Bloomberg estimates the COGS share accounted for by the top three contract manufacturers at 77%, with Hon Hai Precision Industry Co. Ltd. (Foxconn) alone accounting for nearly 60% of COGS (Bloomberg L.P., 2022). Experts estimate that electronics CM can benefit from geopolitical tensions, geographic diversification of supply chains, and growing cross-industry demand for electronic products and achieve continued growth (Mordor Intelligence, 2021b).

Meanwhile, CM accounts for a third of COGS in generic drugs in the pharmaceutical industry, with an even higher share in innovative products (Boston Consulting Group, 2019). As a result, by 2018, the manufacturing capacity of contract manufacturers accounted for 43% of global manufacturing output in the pharmaceutical industry (IQ4I Research, 2019). Moreover, recent data shows that contract manufacturers are increasing their manufacturing capacities, and client companies are preparing to expand their reliance on CM (Accenture Life-Sciences, 2019). As a result, market researchers anticipate stable and sustained growth in the pharmaceutical CM market (Tsay et al., 2018). For the U.S. drug market, contract manufacturers are expected to take over up to three-quarters of manufacturing and related processes in the long run (Han et al., 2012).

Other industries are less transparent about their reliance on CM. For example, CM is a sensitive issue in the food industry because it carries a reputational risk for client companies regarding quality and marketing (Just Food, 2019). Similar motivations are plausible for industries with high competition between brand-name products, such as the automotive industry and clothing, which have also been shown to rely on contract manufacturers (Essig et al., 2013). In this context, the media nicknamed the CM industry *'stealth manufacturing'* in the early 2000 s for its lack of public visibility (Lüthje, 2002, p. 229). As a result, there is little accurate data on market share, but estimates suggest that 20–30% of beverages sold in the U.S. are filled by contract manufacturers (BMC, 2020). However, based on the present data, experts forecast the CM market in the food industry to nearly double between 2021 and 2026 (Mordor Intelligence, 2021a).

- *Managerial characteristic 1 (MC_1)*: With further growth expected, CM is deeply embedded in the supply chains of the global economy across industries, although its presence is little known and, in some cases, actively hidden from end consumers.

Relevance of contract manufacturing for client companies
While contract manufacturers traditionally took over core manufacturing processes, they have begun to forward-integrate and provide further contract services in manufacturing-related areas (Tsay et al., 2018; Zhang, Pawar, Shah, & Mehta, 2013). Consequently, the actual set of subcontracted activities may vary substantially in specific CM agreements, encompassing research, product design, process planning, raw materials procurement, fulfilment, distribution, and even repair services or aftersales handling (Lüthje, 2002). In this concern, CM differs significantly from traditional manufacturing outsourcing. In traditional outsourcing, the outsourcing companies' primary purpose is to externalize excess processes to develop internal core competencies. Therefore, the outsourced operations are not considered decisive for the company's success and are managed at arm's length by the purchasing department. However, in CM, the objective is to integrate external competencies to gain a competitive advantage (Chan & Chung, 2002).

Beyond traditional cost savings concerns, contract manufacturers contribute to integral aspects of client companies' business models through technology and market access, risk sharing, economies of scale, licensing, regulatory protection, and further complementary skills (Morschett, 2003; Nassimbeni, 1998). In practice, this can be observed as contract manufacturers actively position themselves as partners who offer holistic supply chain solutions as strategic partners and 'all-in-one' service providers (Essig et al., 2013; Tsay et al., 2018). For example, through its 'end-to-end-solution' model, as depicted in Figure 1.1, the electronic contract manufacturer Flex covers the entire supply chain, including design, manufacturing, inventory management logistics, e-commerce fulfilment, and aftermarket services (Morschett & Donath, 2011). In addition, Flex excels in network design and location planning, offering its customers adequate industrial parks with streamlined access to low-cost labor and sales markets (Essig et al., 2013).

Likewise, one of Flex's main competitors in CM, Foxconn, considers itself a service provider for supply chain coordination rather than a manufacturer of clients' products (Denicolai, Strange, & Zucchella, 2015). The rationale for this forward integration of contract manufacturers draws on economies of scale and scope. While brand-owning companies concentrate on innovation and customer orientation, contract manufacturers actively pursue a vertical integration strategy of the physical supply chain, which allows them to cooperate with client companies on an equal footing (Lüthje, 2002; Morschett & Donath, 2011).

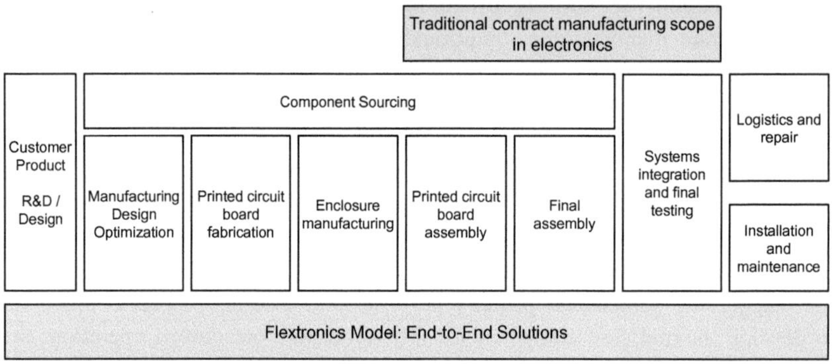

Figure 1.1 The Flextronics Model: End-to-End Solutions[1]

As a result, CM has become deeply embedded in affiliated companies' operations, and, in extreme cases, the contract manufacturer operates nearly the entire physical supply chain (Lüthje, 2002). Therefore, SCM with CM requires the collaborative coordination of business processes and functions such as design, production planning, and distribution channels (Chan & Chung, 2002). Since the alignment of interests across business functions and companies is decisive for collaboration, CM has to be handled at the top management level (Chan & Chung, 2002). Consequently, CM is regarded as a potential *'sustainable competitive advantage'* (Zhang et al., 2013, p. 1094) in specific industries, such as electronics and pharmaceuticals.

In return, inadequate management of CMRs can negatively affect client companies' overall performance (Ittner, Larcker, Nagar, & Rajan, 1999; Pernot & Roodhooft, 2014). According to recent studies, over 60% of managers see the

[1] Adapted from Morschett and Donath (2011, p. 220).

inability of external supply chain partners to meet economic, social, and environmental demands as the most significant reputational risk to their company and identify the management of integrated partners as a strategic corporate priority (KPMG, 2020). This development leads to the second managerial characteristic of CMRs.

- *Managerial characteristic 2 (MC_2)*: Contract manufacturers integrate themselves into the supply chains of brand-owning companies and support vital functions and aspects of their business model, significantly influencing their customer's business success.

Challenges

Despite CM's growing relevance, there is strong evidence that a significant share of CMRs fails to meet performance goals (Dekker, 2004; Meira, Kartalis, Tsamenyi, & Cullen, 2010; Wiengarten, Pagell, & Fyness, 2013). For example, German toy manufacturer Margarete Steiff GmbH returned finished goods manufacturing to the company after six years because of the high expenses of auditing contract manufacturers' compliance with social and environmental standards (Foerstl, Kirchoff, & Bals, 2016). The Margarete Steiff case is one of a series of other instances. In a survey of third-party management executives, one-third of respondents stated that suppliers and service providers were responsible for massive business disruptions in their supply chains in the previous three years (Deloitte, 2016). It is noteworthy that despite solid governance frameworks, respondents have little confidence that relationship management is implemented effectively through tangible operational processes, practices, and technical support systems (Deloitte, 2016).

More accurately, studies underline that outsourcing of operations represents a paradox since it is one of the last decades' most widely used management practices and simultaneously the least satisfying tool for managers (Rigby & Bilodeau, 2015). While back shoring activity has declined steadily since the mid-2000 s, high-tech industries with a high penetration of CM, such as electronics and pharmaceuticals, remain dynamic with above-average outsourcing and reintegration activities (Dachs, Kinkel, Jäger, & Palčič, 2019; Kinkel, 2014).

Studies show that linking production with research and development across partners to achieve innovation remains a complex task in these industries (Dachs et al., 2019). Furthermore, managers name lack of access to real-time manufacturing and inventory data and process standardization at the interface of CMRs as barriers to agile and efficient supply chains (Accenture LifeSciences, 2019).

In addition, a recent survey in the pharmaceutical industry reveals that the top operative challenges cited by practitioners are judged very differently by client companies and CM organizations (CMOs), pointing to conflicts of interest and lack of communication (Accenture LifeSciences, 2019). As a result, while 80% of pharma executives state their companies pursue strategic partnerships with contract manufacturers, only 25% consider their attempts successful (Boston Consulting Group, 2018).

These figures can be understood more clearly when considering the trend of coopetition[2], a term describing the contemporary competition between cooperating firms in CMRs (Chen, Wang, & Xia, 2019). For example, IBM and Motorola had to cut back their relationship with Acer and BenQ, respectively, when the contract manufacturers entered into direct competition with their client customers through brand building (Liu, Chen, & Chen, 2011). Coopetition is driven by mainly two trends: On the one hand, the market becomes more fragmented as brand-owning companies begin to provide CM services to optimize in-house manufacturing capacities, even for their competitors. Intel is an example of such a practice in electronics, while Fisker Automotive offers secondary CM services for other OEMs (Han et al., 2012). On the other hand, mainstream contract manufacturers, like the Chinese electronics market leader Flex, offer their in-house-developed products in the low-cost segment to end consumers or license them to their customers (Morschett & Donath, 2011). Moreover, Flex is actively pursuing a strategy to increase its leverage against customers by acquiring competitors and integrating the physical supply chain on the one hand and limiting customer share on the other (Morschett & Donath, 2011). In cases of coopetition, management needs to closely monitor knowledge management to protect intellectual property (Dekker, 2004).

Consequently, shared goals and values necessary for close collaboration become challenging to achieve and susceptible to relationship dynamics. However, because changing integrated suppliers is complicated and involves operational, financial, and legal risks, client companies tend to replace contract manufacturers only in pressing cases (Pernot & Roodhooft, 2014). Moreover, the reluctance to switch contract manufacturers is reinforced because social partnerships develop within long-term, integrated business relationships and influence purely economic-rational motives (Nassimbeni, 1998). Therefore, especially in CMRs with critical strategic importance, where alignment of objectives is paramount, it is necessary to continuously adjust management practices (Meira et al., 2010). Furthermore, due to the various internal stakeholders involved

[2] *Coopetition* is a compound of *cooperation* and *competition.*

in implementing and changing of management of integrated third parties, the management of CMRs requires transparent and effective governance processes (KPMG, 2020).

- *Managerial characteristic 3 (MC_3)*: Due to their complexity and dynamic nature, the management of CMRs is crucial to client companies to mitigate performance losses and failures in the supply chain.

Consequently, it can be concluded that appropriate management of CMR is a highly relevant issue for practitioners. Moreover, the paradox between the prevalence of CM despite its mixed results and the enormous dissatisfaction of managers raises the question of appropriate practices for managing CMRs. Figure 1.2 summarizes the drivers for managerial relevance of the management of CMRs.

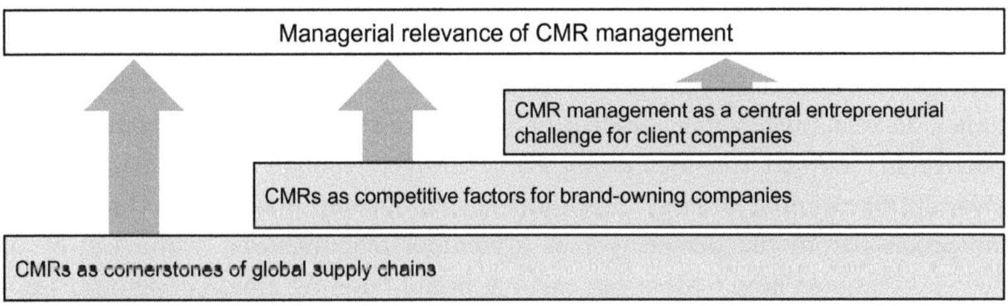

Figure 1.2 Managerial relevance of CMR management

1.2 Theoretical Relevance

In the pursuit of mapping all relevant aspects of CMR management, this dissertation draws on several research streams in the sense of an interdisciplinary research project. The research topic finds its firmest roots in SCM, with service management, operations management, and strategic management as additional relevant research streams. Section 2.5 details the research streams mentioned above and their contribution to the research project.

Mentzer et al. note that SCM includes *'a strategic orientation toward cooperative efforts to synchronize and converge intrafirm and interfirm operational and strategic capabilities into a unified whole'* (2001, p. 7) and that the *'key to such coordination is an orientation toward closer relationships with suppliers'* (2001,

p. 2). Consequently, outsourcing and subcontracting have been prevalent topics in the SCM literature since the term gained popularity in the 1990 s. Essig et al. (2013) conclude that managing interfaces and controlling contract manufacturers become a core competency of brand-owning companies when subcontracting their manufacturing. However, research on the management of outsourced operations in SCM and management of CMRs has been comparably scarce (Busi & McIvor, 2008). Research on outsourcing in supply chains centers around antecedents, performance outcomes, management, and the make-or-buy decision (Han et al., 2012; Tsay et al., 2018). In addition, research concerning the management of outsourced activities, primarily relationship management, project management, and control, does not differentiate between outsourcing of manufacturing, logistics, or other activities (Embleton & Wright, 1998; Stouthuysen, Slabbinck, & Roodhooft, 2012; Tsay et al., 2018)

Complementary, dedicated studies on CMRs rarely cover relationship management in favor of other aspects. For example, Sousa and Voss (2007) and Fredriksson (2011) examine how seemingly decoupled processes and factory layouts are affected by CMRs. Their studies highlight the widespread impact of CMRs on the internal organizations of involved companies. On the other hand, studies on relationship management of CMRs are found primarily from the perspective of contract manufacturers. For example, Noonan and Wallace (2003, 2004, 2006) examine strategy development, relationship planning, and the selection process from the perspective of a contract manufacturer, while Liu et al. (2011) investigate how CMOs can excel at brand-building amid coopetition from their customers.

Studies from the OEM's perspective reflect the lack of distinction between establishing the relationship and its management, with the term *'management'* enjoying a broad interpretation. Even influential studies often focus on outsourcing management and limit the view of CM management to success factors (Busi & McIvor, 2008). For example, Embleton and Wright emphasize the importance of change management for manufacturing outsourcing and limit their recommendations on relationship management to *'a procedure must be implemented to enable management to monitor and evaluate adherence to the outsourcing contract'* (1998, p. 102). Furthermore, studies on interfirm collaboration, on the one hand, show that managers misinterpret management efforts before entering CMRs, and on the other hand, relationships begin to stagnate over time without continuous management (Agarwal, Aggarwal, & Singh, 2015; Palmatier, Houston, Dant, & Grewal, 2013). In addition, the perceived shift from cost minimization objectives in outsourcing decisions to value optimization requires greater management attention to CMRs, which has not yet been expressed in academic work (Denicolai et al., 2015). Thus, the observed shift provides an opportunity for research as it contradicts the influential view of transaction cost economics (TCE) that high-frequency, strategic, and specific transactions are more efficient when designed in a vertically integrated form (Stölzle, 1999). In this context, Stölzle (1999) emphasizes the need for adequate concepts, methods, and instruments to manage outsourcing arrangements efficiently. Busi and McIvor go even further and state *'that scientific generation of knowledge specific to outsourcing is still at an embryonic stage compared to more mature disciplines'* and that research on CMRs *'is lagging behind practice'* (2008, p. 186).

- *Theoretical shortcoming 1 (TS_1)*: Research on CMR is mainly concerned with the preconditions and outcomes of CM. Existing management research is limited to the selection process and physical relocation rather than relationship management. Moreover, recent operational developments and CM practices are neglected or contradict theoretical assumptions.

However, research outside of SCM also addresses issues concerning the relationship management of CMRs. For example, CMRs are frequently found as cases in research on managing interorganizational relationships (IORs). IORs cover various interfirm relationships such as buyer-supplier relationships (Palmatier et al., 2013; Pernot & Roodhooft, 2014), joint ventures (Kamminga & van der Meer-Kooistra, 2007), service relationships (Stouthuysen et al., 2012), strategic alliances (Lamminmaki, 2008), interfirm projects (Chakkol, Selviaridis, & Finne, 2018) and company carve-outs (van den Bogaard & Speklé, 2003) as an umbrella term.

Fields contributing to this interdisciplinary topic include operations management (Tsay et al., 2018), supply chain management (Essig et al., 2013), service management (Simon, Scheidl, Campos, & Matana, 2021), and strategic management (Isidor, Steinmetz, Schwens, & Kabst, 2014; Kamminga & van der Meer Kooistra, 2007).

Drawing from the literature that regards CMRs as a case for relationship management, several emerging topics can be observed: The relevance of dynamics throughout the relationship (Busi & McIvor, 2008; Mandjak et al., 2021; Pernot & Roodhooft, 2014), collaborative management of integrated interfaces (Chao, Iravani, & Savaskan, 2009; Narayanan & Narasimhan, 2014; Ülkü, Toktay, & Yücesan, 2007), coopetition, opportunism and knowledge transfer (Chen et al., 2019; Handley & Angst, 2015; Handley & Benton, 2012a; Mandjak et al., 2021), (informal) control (Luo, Liu, Zhang, & Huang, 2011; Meira et al.,

2010; Stouthuysen et al., 2012, 2017) and the relationship power balance (Gray, Tomlin, & Roth, 2009; Handley & Benton, 2012b, 2012a).

While these studies contribute to understanding specific aspects of managing CMRs, they do not advance the research field of CM. A significant issue is the lack of comparability of findings due to differences in field-specific terminology, methodology, and understanding of crucial questions chosen to support the contribution to respective fields. The differences in interpretation begin with blending specific concepts such as outsourcing and offshoring. They are further reflected in undeclared normative baseline assumptions about subcontracted activities, relationship objectives, internal capabilities, and the scope of the management process, all of which influence the management of CMRs. However, by documenting the heterogeneity and complexity of CMR, these studies underscore the need for research on CMR management (Dekker, 2004). Findings from research on various IORs can provide valuable insights but need to be reviewed for applicability in CMRs. Section 2.6 addresses the in-depth positioning of CMRs against other relevant types of IORs.

- *Theoretical shortcoming 2 (TS_2)*: Although CMRs are a much-frequented subject in the literature on relationship management of IORs, few studies from this field contribute to a consistent CMR knowledge base as CMRs are not covered as research objects as case studies.

Consequently, while substantial research addresses CMRs and manufacturing outsourcing, the management of CMRs does not have a consistent knowledge base. Therefore, control of CMRs lacks basic assumptions that can be developed through research and tested against perceived trends in the literature (Palmatier et al., 2013) and practice (Busi & McIvor, 2008; Denicolai et al., 2015; Tsay et al., 2018). As a result, knowledge transfer between research and practice stagnates due to the lack of tangible findings. Thus, the management of CMRs can be considered a gap in the literature. Figure 1.3 presents the theoretical shortcoming of CMR research to reveal the theoretical relevance of the research topic.

1.3 Research Objectives

This dissertation's research objectives (RO_n) arise from the presented managerial relevance and the theoretical shortcomings of research on CMR management. The research objectives are loosely connected, meaning they may build on each other or provide different perspectives on the research phenomenon. After a detailed

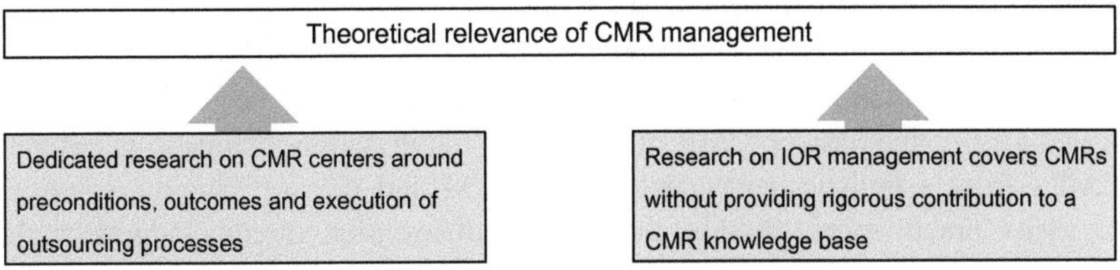

Figure 1.3 Theoretical relevance of CMR management

analysis of the existing literature, substantive research questions are derived in Section 2.8.

Figure 1.4 gives an overview of the considerations on managerial relevance and theoretical shortcomings of the management of CMRs graphically and presents the research objectives of this dissertation. The research objectives are described in detail in the following paragraphs.

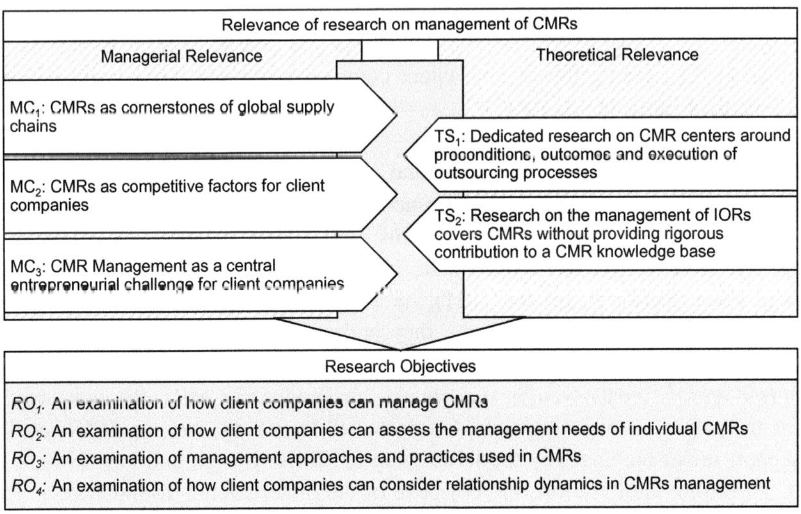

Figure 1.4 Research objectives of the dissertation

- *RO_1:* An examination of how client companies can manage CMRs.

Firstly, RO_1 contains the main objective of the dissertation project. Without a dedicated knowledge base on CMR management, the dissertation aims to investigate CMRs from a holistic perspective within SCM and develop tangible solutions to assist practitioners. In this context, the dissertation directly addresses the theoretical shortcomings identified by Busi & McIvor (2008).

In light of the multitude of challenges in managing CMRs and the fluid crossover of different relationship concepts on the actor level of the supply chain, the need arises for companies to determine the actual management needs for CMRs on an individual basis (Dekker, 2004). In addition, Agarwal et al. (2015) point out the risk of performance losses in business relationships if the management needs are misjudged. However, so far, the literature has only addressed specific aspects of CMR management and has not discussed an approach to holistically analyzing the management needs of CMRs. This shortcoming includes the particular tasks and areas of the relationship that need to be managed and the relative importance of these elements in various CMRs. Hence, the second research objective of this dissertation can be expressed as follows:

- *RO_2:* An examination of how client companies can assess the management needs of individual CMRs.

Practitioners must address the individual challenges of their CMRs with appropriate actions, dubbed management practices. However, while existing literature often discusses methods and mechanisms of relational management or control, there is little knowledge about CMRs in particular and concrete actions taken in practice (Stölzle & Brandl, 2021). As a result, management practices are not named in the literature, neither are they presented in detail, nor is their applicability evaluated. As a result, there is little transparency about how companies pursue specific goals or address particular challenges in CMRs. By understanding the management practices used, a dedicated knowledge base on CMRs could support understanding why the failure rate of CMRs is high and how to reduce it. Therefore, the third research objective of the dissertation is formulated.

- *RO_3:* An examination of management approaches and practices used in CMRs.

Lastly, the dynamics of CMRs are eminent (Mandjak et al., 2021; Mentzer et al., 2001; Pernot & Roodhooft, 2014; Varoutsa & Scapens, 2018). Therefore, the management of CMRs needs to be adaptable to developments in the relationship, which require different management practices (Agarwal et al., 2015). However, the triggers for changes in management requirements are still uninvestigated in the literature. Furthermore, there are no conclusive results on how CMR management can consider these dynamics. Consequently, the dissertation will address this theoretical shortcoming as its fourth research objective.

- *RO_4:* Examining how client companies can consider relationship dynamics in CMR management.

After outlining the dissertation's research objective, the next chapter adequately presents the thesis structure to address RO_1 to RO_4.

1.4 Thesis Structure

The dissertation is structured into six chapters to meet the intended research objectives. While Chapter 1 serves as a comprehensive introduction to CMR management from practical and theoretical perspectives and concludes with the research objectives, an overview of the further sections of the dissertation is presented in the following paragraphs.

Chapter 2 deals with the theoretical fundament of CMR management. Section 2.1 introduces the applied literature review approach for the dissertation. Section 2.2 defines CMR management and delimitates it from adjacent terms to provide a common terminological foundation. Next, Section 2.3 looks into the drivers and objectives for companies to employ contract manufacturers in their supply chains. The challenges of managing CMRs in supply chains are then addressed in Section 2.4. Section 2.5 consolidates the knowledge from the previous sections and provides a research map that depicts the research context. Analyzing the research map, Section 2.6 positions CMRs in the research field of IOR management, highlighting distinctive features. Next, the research gaps are outlined in Section 2.7. Finally, Section 2.8 concludes Chapter 2 and presents the dissertation's research questions.

Chapter 3 outlines research access to the research question derived from Chapter 2. First, Section 3.1 develops a theoretical positioning of the dissertation. Next, the research design is established by applying the selected theories in Section 3.2. Third, Section 3.3 combines the research questions and design within the research framework. Finally, Section 3.4 introduces the research methodology.

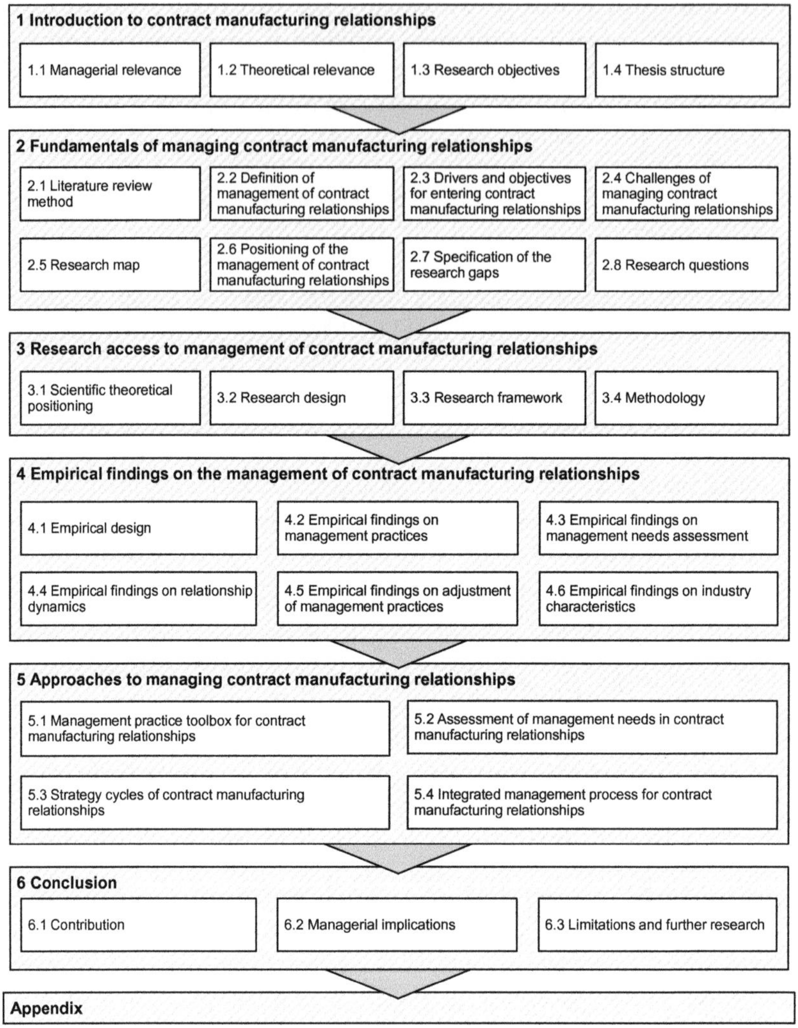

Figure 1.5 Visualization of the dissertation structure

Chapter 4 contains the empirical design and findings of the dissertation project. The data collection approach is laid out first in Section 4.1. Then Sections 4.2 to 4.5 present the practical insights gained into the respective research questions RQ_1 to RQ_4. Finally, Section 4.6 outlines further relevant insights from the explorative research design.

Chapter 5 presents the findings on the management of CMRs. First, along with the introduced research questions, Section 5.1 presents an artifact that comprehensively encompasses and outlines the identified CMR management practices. Second, Section 5.2 proposes an approach to assessing an individual CMR's management needs. Third, Section 5.3 maps the management-relevant relationship dynamics of CMRs. Finally, drawing on the insights from sections 5.1 to 5.3, an integrated management process for adjusting management practices to relationship dynamics is outlined in section 5.4. The artifact comprises the assessment of management needs, the detection of necessary changes in the management approach, and the management practices to be applied to CMR.

Chapter 6 concludes the thesis by summarizing the contributions of the dissertation in section 6.1 and the managerial implications in section 6.2. Finally, section 6.3 reflects on the research project by discussing limitations and providing suggestions for further research.

The *electronic supplementary material (ESM)* contains detailed profiles of the investigated management practices and excerpts from the interviews' questionnaires.

The structure of the thesis is visualized in Figure 1.5.

2 Fundamentals of Managing Contract Manufacturing Relationships

This chapter introduces the topic of CMR management from a theoretical perspective and lays the foundation for the dissertation. First, Section 2.1 presents the applied literature review approach to establish the theoretical foundation. Second, Section 2.2 defines and delimitates the topic of CMR management and the scope of this dissertation. Third, Section 2.3 brings forth the drivers and objectives that shape the management of CMRs. Fourth, Section 2.4 describes the challenges in managing CMRs. Fifth, Section 2.5 aggregates and visualizes the research field in the research map. Sixth, Section 2.6 positions the management of CMRs among other mature research streams that cover the management of IORs. Seventh, Section 2.6 analyses the present literature and specifies relevant research gaps. Lastly, Section 2.8 derives the research questions of the dissertation project.

2.1 Literature Review Method

Literature reviews are essential to define and explore the knowledge base of a research project in literature (vom Brocke et al., 2015). According to Durach, Kembro, and Wieland, they *'provide the opportunity to critically reflect, compare, and discuss prior study findings triangulating through the different perspectives and contexts'* (2017, p. 76). Hence, they are conducted at the beginning of the research process to deliver a theoretical foundation by identifying research gaps, means for contribution, and appropriate theoretical framing (Denyer & Tranfield, 2009).

Literature reviews in SCM pose particular challenges since the field is interdisciplinary (Essig et al., 2013) and lacks a unified theoretical foundation (Defee,

T. Brandl, *Managing Contract Manufacturing Relationships*, Supply Chain Management, https://doi.org/10.1007/978-3-658-41359-0_2

Williams, Randall, & Thomas, 2010). Durach et al. (2017) acknowledge the difficulty of reviewing supply chain literature due to its various perspectives, such as the frame of the unit of analysis and the stakeholder perspectives. The aspects mentioned above risk that relevant knowledge is overlooked or misinterpreted. Therefore, a systematic and transparent approach to the literature review is pivotal to ensuring the rigor of the theoretical foundation of the dissertation project (vom Brocke et al., 2015).

Durach et al. (2017) lay out the potential biases in supply chain literature reviews and recommend countermeasures in the review process. These recommendations are included in the literature review process, which follows the framework of vom Brocke et al. (2015). Engel and Ebel (2019) adapted the approach at the University of St. Gallen and provided a detailed guideline for the literature review.

Based on a concept-centered approach, the two main elements of the research topic, *'contract manufacturing'* and *'management of IORs,'* were reviewed to identify significant intersecting literature (Watson & Webster, 2020). Applying the framework of vom Brocke et al. (2015), the process was iterative due to the increasing number of labels and overlapping concepts in content, presented in Section 2.2. The keywords for the two primary elements of the research topic were continuously refined until a saturated collection of literature was available. In alignment with the research process's explorative nature, the approach encompassed four databases as sources, including various publications from the supply chain field and broader management literature. The review sought a representative sample of publications since the ambiguity of labels in the interdisciplinary supply chain fields made comprehensive coverage unviable. As a technique, a keyword search was employed and enriched with forward and backward searches and the platform *Connected Papers*, which identifies similar publications through co-citation and bibliographic coupling. The publications for these in-depth searches were identified using the criteria of context and perspective outlined by Durach et al. (2017).

The following steps can thus describe the applied approach to reviewing the literature:

Step 1: The selection of appropriate keywords marked the first step of the process. Since both areas of interest, CM, and (relationship) management, are associated with various labels across research fields, multiple keywords were used in iterative reviews. Following the explorative stance of the dissertation, even broader synonyms and overlapping terms, such as outsourcing, were included. Furthermore, since CM features heavily in the literature on the theory of the firm and vertical (dis-) integration, keywords for both topics were applied in conjunction to produce relevant results. Finally, the search was restricted to identifying the keywords in the publications' titles, abstracts, and keyword lists to ensure the relevance of the identified publications.

Step 2: Driven to produce a representative sample of the literature on CMR management, four different databases Scopus, Web of Science, EBSCO Host, and Emerald Insight, built the source for the literature review to cover the publications on supply chains and management sufficiently. In addition to books and journal entries, conference proceedings were considered to cover emerging topics and explorative publications.

Step 3: The keywords were modified to increase the search scope systematically. The main objective was not to overlook relevant literature due to diverging terminology (vom Brocke et al., 2015). Therefore, alternative keywords were collected in advance and enhanced through emerging jargon in the identified papers. Concerning the lack of a unified terminology, publications with overlapping concepts were also included and evaluated based on the authors' interpretation.

Step 4: The identified publications were screened and evaluated in a multistep process. First, duplicates and papers which were not written in either German or English were excluded. Second, the abstracts and research designs were screened for relevance following the publication's authors' understanding of CM and the context and perspective of the topic. Finally, publications that did not cover relationship management or took an actor's perspective were not selected.

Step 5: Finally, the selected papers were analyzed thoroughly based on their content, methodology, and theoretical access. The results of the analysis constitute the remainder of Chapter 2. Concerning the sources of bias in supply chain literature (Durach et al., 2017) and the review process itself (vom Brocke et al., 2015), the literature review's result cannot be exhaustive but aims to be representative instead.

Figure 2.1 gives an overview of the results from the literature review. It has to be noted that other tested keywords such as *"external manufactu*,"* *"manufactu* service,"* *"manufactu* subcontract*,"* and *"relationship management"* did not add any new relevant publications to the knowledge base and were therefore left out of the visualization.

	Databases							
	Scopus		Emerald Insight		Web of Science		EBSCO	
Search Strings	Hits	Relevant	Hits	Relevant	Hits	Relevant	Hits	Relevant
("contract manufactur*") AND ("management")	224	26	21	5	58	4	18	6
("contract manufactur") AND ("supplier")	137	19	16	6	63	12	41	13
("manufactu* outsourc*") AND ("management")	40	6	5	1	32	6	5	0
("manufactu* outsourc*") AND ("supplier")	27	6	4	0	16	5	17	7
Sum per Database	428	57	46	12	169	27	81	26
Total number of relevant literature selected from 724 screened papers	With Duplicates:	122	+	F/B Screening	6		=	72
	Without Duplicates:	53		Connected Papers	13			

Figure 2.1 Quantitative results of the literature review

Compared to the number of hits, the low ratio of relevant publications derives from the broad choice of keywords to extensively cover existing literature. Furthermore, despite forward and backward screening, no significant research stream on managing CMRs could be identified. Aside from a few recurring authors, such as Noonan and Wallace (2003, 2004, 2006) and Handley (2015; 2012b, 2012a; 2013, 2015), publications remained fragmented in scope, perspective, and terminology.

Those two examples reveal another pattern in the knowledge base on the management of CMRs. The literature is divided into publications that address CM as a stand-alone topic and research papers that address other research topics and incorporate findings from CM cases into the empirical design. For example, Noonan and Wallace (2003, 2004, 2006) focus on CMRs as a dedicated topic from the perspective of the contract manufacturer. Conversely, Handley covers quality and risk-related research topics in outsourced operations, encompassing logistics, manufacturing, and IT cases (2015; 2012b).

The distinction between dedicated and case-based literature is significant because only stand-alone studies of CMR management can be expected to ensure the generalizability of results across CMRs and thus provide scientific rigor. This limitation in terms of context and perspective in the supply chain literature has been described by Durach et al. (2017). For this reason, in the knowledge base analysis, the distinction between dedicated knowledge for managing CMRs and more fundamental knowledge from managing IORs, including CMRs, must be made.

2.2 Definition of Management of Contract Manufacturing Relationships

This chapter presents the author's understanding of the management of CMRs with particular attention to boundary concepts and their delimitation. Thus, the chapter addresses the diversity of context and perspective in the supply chain literature that Durach et al. (2017) presented.

Following Essig et al., '*Supply Chain Management is the cooperative coordination of [...] material, information, and finance-flows in company networks through the establishment of integrative, cross-functional leadership and execution process to realize competitive advantages [...]*' (2013, p. 41). The frame of reference of SCM comprises three fundamental perspectives: Network, relationship, and actor levels (Essig et al., 2013). The following paragraphs outline the relevant terminology along the supply chain perspectives to derive a common understanding of the management of CMRs.

Network level

The network level of the supply chain comprises at least three independent organizations involved in value creation. Therefore, the right decisions must be set at the network level regarding the players involved and the distribution of tasks to achieve an appropriate economic benefit for all partners (Essig et al., 2013).

The theoretical basis of CM stems from academic discussions on the firm's boundaries and the degree of vertical integration, which is explained in particular by transaction cost economics (TCE) (Tsay et al., 2018). CM describes the production of goods in a supply chain by a company under the product ownership of another company (Han et al., 2012). Hence, since CM involves the separation of product ownership and production steps across companies (Morschett & Donath, 2011), it is associated with substantive asset specificity making it a hybrid form of transaction (Williamson, 2008). Consequently, CM is a field of action in the governance of supply chains (Essig et al., 2013). It is regarded as a design practice of SCM, changing the firm's boundaries in the supply chain and setting constraints for the value creation management due to interorganizational interfaces (Handley & Gray, 2013; Kaiser & Obermaier, 2020). However, while CM is associated with the focal company's decision to disintegrate vertically, CMOs are seen actively integrating the supply side outside the focal company's boundaries and establishing themselves as specialists in operations at eye level (Lüthje, 2002).

This development makes it more challenging for scholars to position CMR among other hybrid forms of governance of supply chains. For example, a popular notion in literature is that CM is a form of manufacturing outsourcing (Han et al., 2012; Sousa & Voss, 2007). According to Meira et al. (2010), outsourcing is a process whereby a company subcontracts activities previously carried out internally to external parties. Outsourcing is associated with three key characteristics which are not entirely transferable to CM: First, the activities in question were previously carried out internally. Second, outsourcing results in a fragmented supply chain. Third, an ongoing IOR with the service provider emerges (Denicolai et al., 2015). While the lasting relationship with the CMO is evident in CM, the subcontracted processes need not have been operated by the client company previously. For example, in the pharmaceutical industry, it is common to in-license products to optimize the portfolio without having manufactured them before or after the license acquisition (Glowik, 2017). Consequently, manufacturing outsourcing is only one possible origin of CMRs.

Furthermore, contrary to supply chain fragmentation, Lüthje (2002) and Han et al. (2012) consider CM a form of network integration driven by the objective of joining capabilities for competitive advantage. Thus, there is some overlapping of the concepts but decisive differences. Outsourcing is about a shift in operational responsibility, comparable to licensing as a change of ownership and offshoring as a switch of location (Denicolai et al., 2015).

Chan and Chung define a contract manufacturer as *'a provider of goods and services working collaboratively with other providers of goods and services as a networked business partner'* (2002, p. 118), emphasizing self-determined collaboration and equal footing. Han et al. (2012) refine that the client company is the owner of the design and product, and the CMO supplies labour, capacity, and know-how. Their refinement holds three meaningful aspects of CM: First, CMRs bring together complementary capabilities to manufacture specific products that both partners cannot manufacture alone. Second, detailed application knowledge allows CMOs to execute complex customer-specific processes along the entire supply chain, as seen in the example of Flextronics (see Figure 1.1), as a mature business partner (Lüthje, 2002). Third, according to Asanuma (1989), the lens of ownership can provide a defining perspective.

Ownership of the product designs distinguishes CM from original design manufacturing (ODM), where the manufacturer owns the plans and only provides customer customization services (Lüthje, 2002). In ODM, the manufacturer decides whether customers may exclusively brand the products under their trademark (*private label*) or whether the product is available to various buyers and their respective brands (*white label*) (Silva, Souza, & Machado, 2020). The third ownership-based form is joint design manufacturing (JDM), in which designs are jointly owned by the brand company and the manufacturer (Tsay, 2014). Even though collaborative development is becoming more important in CM, in JDM, the manufacturer can safeguard licenses and demand royalties as a product shareholder (Weber, 2003). Taking these aspects into account, the author's understanding of CM is as follows:

Contract manufacturing is a supply chain concept in which a design-owning company collaborates with an independent manufacturing partner to access external capacities and capabilities needed to deliver its designs to the market.

Figure 2.2 summarizes the discussion through a framework containing the most relevant terms in the manufacturing service debate. Turnkey, consignment, and tolling refer to the procurement responsibility in external manufacturing and will be described in the remainder of this section. The framework shows that the most distinctive aspects of CM are the client's design ownership and its separation from manufacturing responsibility. Furthermore, CM includes complete and mixed manufacturing responsibility by the service provider, producing heterogeneous CMRs based on the scope of the agreement. For example, Nordigarden et al. (2014) point out that CM is often used alongside internal production and classify CMRs on a scale between dominant internal and external manufacturing.

However, aside from manufacturing capacity, favorable economic conditions and access to specialized knowledge remain integrating factors of supply chains under CM (Imrie, 1994). Considering that outsourcing is not a prerequisite for CM, client companies, despite design ownership, do not necessarily possess manufacturing know-how and aim to access it through CM.

Dyer and Singh (1998) note that complementary resources, such as design and manufacturing knowledge, create higher value in collaborations because both partners rely on each other to deliver the finished product. As a result, knowledge-driven CM, in particular, is strategically important to strengthening supply chain competitiveness at the network level. However, the integration of complementary know-how in CM poses challenges for network coordination: First, the governance structure of supply chains derives from the ownership of critical resources, which in the given case would be decentralized, resulting in an intransparent power balance (Essig et al., 2013). Second, complementarity causes interdependency of processes, requiring extensive communication and interlocked decision-making (Thompson, 1967). The client company and CMO need to address these challenges at the relationship level of the supply chain.

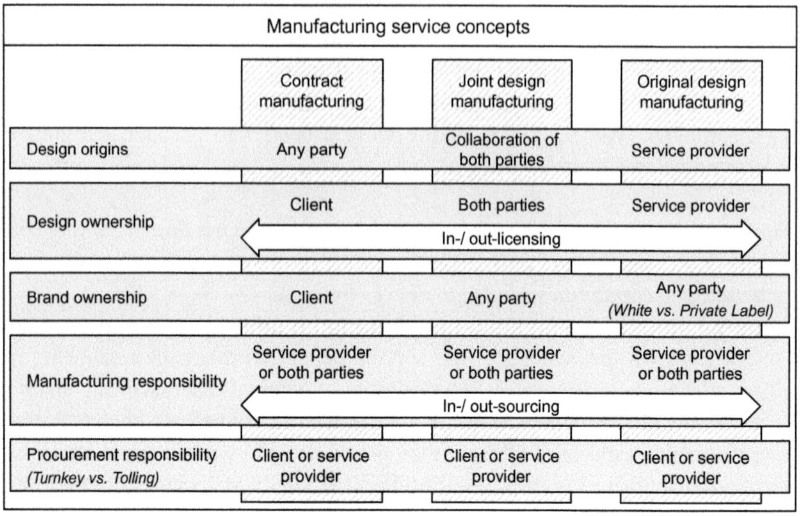

Figure 2.2 Classification of manufacturing service concepts

Relationship level

The relationship level consists of two companies, which form a dyad. Depending on the degree of integration, the dyad is frequently named *'quasi-firm,'* emphasizing the need to manage the relationship like an independent company (Essig et al., 2013, p. 109). The emerging relationship between client and service provider in CM is called a *contract manufacturing relationship* (Brandl, 2021, p. 104). Given the diverging supply chain perspectives, the CMR is a supplier relationship from the standpoint of the client company but a customer relationship from the CMO's perspective (Trumpfheller & Hofmann, 2004). Moreover, CMRs are primarily vertical business relationships. Still, they can also represent horizontal or diagonal arrangements if the partners are in 'coopetition' or subcontract logistics-related processes (Trumpfheller & Hofmann, 2004).

Although the definition of CMR only covers the dyad, the network level's supply chain configuration significantly affects the relationship, making it necessary to include the extended supply chain in the management scope (Mentzer et al., 2001). For example, the CMO and the client company may share customers or work with competing companies, resulting in coopetition that requires management practices to protect intellectual property and market shares (Liu et al., 2011).

Furthermore, depending on the agreement, for example, considering *turnkey* (procurement by the CMO) or *consignment* or *tolling* (procurement by the client company), it may be necessary to control or coordinate with the sub-supplier in CMR management (Tsay, 2014, p. 98). In addition, in-licensing can produce similar effects, requiring the inclusion of third parties to adjust processes and products (Glowik, 2017).

To draw value from the CMR, the stakeholders must manage the relationship (Tsay et al., 2018). Following Stölzle, *'from a business perspective, relationship management refers to the coordination of objectives, guiding principles, and individual measures for the long-term selection, planning, management, and control of business relationships'* (1999, p. 8). A business relationship in a supply chain comprises the flow of *goods*, *information*, *finance*, and *social* and *regulatory exchanges* within the scope of relationship management (Essig et al., 2013, p. 300). The performance of a relationship is measured against the strategic goals established before entering the relationship, so the specific objectives and management practices can be diverse (Trumpfheller & Gomm, 2004).

Relationship management design moves between an aggressive philosophy focused on efficiency and competition and resource-intensive collaborative approaches (Essig et al., 2013). Moreover, collaborative approaches are more relevant in integrative and long-term business relationships where a fit of guiding principles partly substitutes complex controls (Trumpfheller & Hofmann, 2004). Zhang et al. (2013) show that depending on whether the client derives value from the CMO's efficiency or complementary capabilities, both relationship philosophies can shape CMRs. Furthermore, inherent relationship dynamics require constant adaptation of relationship governance or a sufficient degree of freedom to cover the changed circumstances (Denicolai et al., 2015). Trust and commitment are essential for stable business relationships because they reflect the relationship partners' belief in generating benefit through cooperation relative to the effort required (Trumpfheller & Gomm, 2004). Hence, at the relational level of SCM and CMRs, social theories, such as Social Exchange Theory (SET), are often invoked as explanatory approaches in addition to TCE (Lambe, Wittmann, & Spekman, 2001).

Actor level

The actor level considers the company as an individual part of a dyad or supply network and the internal company decisions and activities in this context (Essig et al., 2013). A CMR comprises a company that receives manufacturing services for its product design and another company that provides it (Morschett & Donath, 2011).

The literature refers to several names of the 'client' or 'buying' companies in a CMR (Tsay, 2014). First, one term already used in this dissertation is the *'brand-owning'* or *'brand-leading company'* (Brandl, 2021, p. 104). In the tradition of the automotive industry, the term *'original equipment manufacturer'* (OEM) is also frequently used (Han et al., 2012, p. 159). Another manufacturing-related name is *'manufacturing company'* (Kim, 2003, p. 63). Ownership-based naming seems the most appropriate terminology from a content perspective but is inaccurate because CMOs also distribute their propriety brands. Therefore, the dissertation will primarily rely on the name of the *client* or *client company* as a distinctive feature of the company roles in CMRs.

The terminology for describing the company providing the manufacturing service is even more diverse, including *'contract manufacturer'* (Van Weele & Eßig, 2017, p. 455), *'contract manufacturing organization'* (Johnson, 2005, p. 22), *'manufacturing service provider'* (Sousa & Voss, 2007, p. 975), *'external manufacturer'* (Ferretti, Mazzoldi, Zanoni, & Zavanella, 2017, p. 222), *'toll manufacturer'* (Rumer, 1994, p. 23), and *'subcontractor'* (Tsay, 2014, p. 5). In addition, certain terms are specific to different industries: In the clothing industry, for example, contract manufacturers are often referred to as *'contract factories'* (Knight & Greenberg, 2002, p. 543). In the chemical and pharmaceutical industries, CMO is the most common label (Pollak, 2011), while the consumer electronics industry mainly uses *'electronic manufacturing service providers'* (Morschett & Donath, 2011, p. 213). Finally, the terms *'co-packer'* and *'co-manufacturer'* are the most common in the food industry due to the origins of CMOs as packaging service providers (Brady, Seidman, & Morris, 2009, p. 4). However, to cover different industries and be consistent with the presented understanding of CM, the author will refer to the service provider as a contract manufacturer or CMO throughout the dissertation. Since providing CM services can be a secondary income for companies, companies would not necessarily label themselves as CMO. Thus, the contract manufacturer or CMO does not refer to the company but the role in the CMR. Client and CMO are labels relative to the observed CMR. Outside the agreement, both parties can take over the roles of client and contract manufacturer in other CMRs.

As Tsay et al. (2018) noted, CMRs require management by its stakeholders to integrate individual business goals into the relationship. Both parties, the client company and CMO perform management activities to enable collaboration and ensure their objectives in the relationship are respected individually. According to Daft, management consumes resources intending to influence the performance of the relationship in a desired way by *planning*, *organizing*, *leading*, and *controlling* the conducted activities (2010, p. 6). The specified activities performed in the management process are called *'management practices,'* which are a *'defined activity or set of activities that a variety of firms might execute'* (Bromiley & Rau, 2014, p. 1249). In the context of dyads, literature also speaks of *'governance mechanisms'* applied by a company to steer the relationship (Bowen & Jones, 1986, 430). In outsourcing and supplier management, the more restricted term *'control mechanism'* can be found (Kang, Wu, Hong, & Park, 2012, p. 1195). Because the balance of power in CMRs can fluctuate and the scope of management extends beyond control, the dissertation will employ the term management practices.

A company can deploy management practices in collaboration with its counterpart or as an active hedge against opportunism. However, a one-size-fits-all approach to relationship management falls short. Instead, the company must determine specific management practices individually while carefully considering network, product, and market requirements (Trumpfheller & Hofmann, 2004). Due to the integrative nature of the relationship, the CMR produces multiple interorganizational interfaces and internal stakeholders the parties need to coordinate through aligned organizational forms (Stölzle & Brandl, 2021). Hence, management practices might not only be directed at the relationship but also

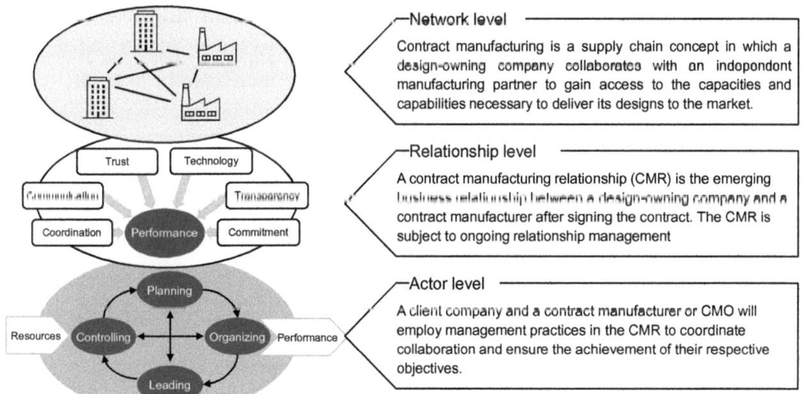

Figure 2.3 Positioning of contract manufacturing in supply chain management[1]

[1] Adapted from Essig et al. (2013, p. 45); Daft (2010, p. 6); Trumpfheller and Gomm (2004, p. 308).

facilitate internal coordination within the companies (Trumpfheller & Gomm, 2004).

In concluding this chapter, Figure 2.3 summarizes the most crucial defining terminology of the management of CMRs across the supply chain perspectives as a frame of reference.

2.3 Drivers and Objectives for Entering Contract Manufacturing Relationships

The value contribution of SCM to the company's success is multidimensional and comprises the superordinate categories of *effectiveness*, *efficiency*, and *risk* (Essig et al., 2013, p. 369). Effectiveness refers to maximizing the level of service perceived by the customer, e.g., through higher availability, flexibility, and product quality. Efficiency describes the increase in process efficiency, e.g., by improving production and transport costs, lead times, and material cost structure. Risk, lastly, aims to minimize capital commitment in terms of fixed assets, inventories, and payment cycles. However, it is sometimes problematic to fully harmonize these sub-goals, which often leads to conflicting objectives that SCM tries to resolve. Figure 2.4 illustrates the relationship between SCM sub-goals.

IORs have always been means for companies to benefit from economies of scale, risk sharing, and access to new technologies (Nassimbeni, 1998). Moreover, as technology advances and global markets become increasingly dynamic, complex supply chains require in-depth knowledge, prompting specialization at each stage of the value chain and driving the need for interorganizational collaboration (Morschett, 2003; Nassimbeni, 1998). The CM sector grows in this environment because it allows companies to achieve better supply chain performance by covering all targets in the *'magic triangle'* through cost-efficient manufacturing, capacity without investments in assets, and specialized skills (Imrie, 1994, p. 571). Whereas cost efficiency was the primary motive in the past, modern CMRs typically target increased customer value and reduced supply risk (Handley & Gray, 2013). Kang et al. refer to a movement in the triangle from *'efficiency-seeking'* to *'innovation-seeking'* CM, enabling client companies to deliver more innovative products to market in a shorter time (2014, p. 179). Furthermore, end-to-end solutions for CM, including the whole physical supply chain, are emerging, effectively covering all performance targets of SCM simultaneously (Denicolai et al., 2015).

The following paragraphs outline how CMRs support client companies in covering the objectives of the SCM target triangle.

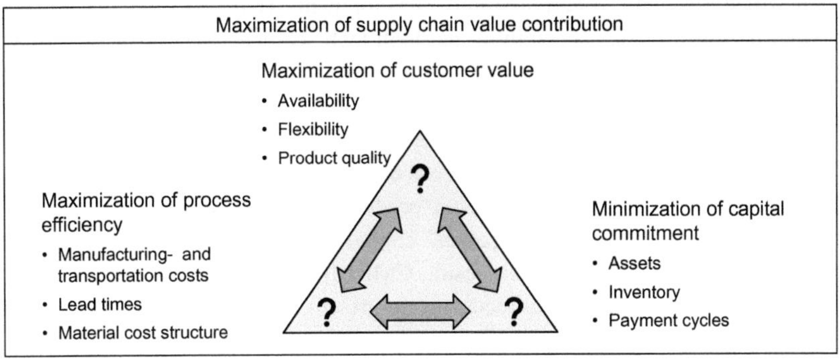

Figure 2.4 Target triangle of supply chain management[2]

- *Maximization of process efficiency*: Entering CMRs enables client companies to reduce the transaction costs of delivering their product to the customer through economies of scale, scope, and skill (Essig et al., 2013). CMOs achieve economies of scale and scope by bundling the combined production volume of multiple customers to obtain more favorable purchasing terms, utilizing capacity efficiently, and allocating fixed costs for equipment and administration via cost degression (Morschett & Donath, 2011). As a result, client companies benefit from CMRs by offering the same products to their customers at a lower cost per unit (Handley & Gray, 2013). Since the final products in CM are customer-specific, economies of scale relate to earlier production stages in the manufacturing process. In contrast, economies of scope arise in the final manufacturing stages when resources can be shared with other manufactured products. Consequently, especially the latter becomes challenging to achieve in CMRs with highly customized products reducing the potential value created by economies of scale and scope. However, the third source of process efficiency CMRs unlock is economies of skill (Essig et al., 2013). Lüthje (2002) explains process efficiency in CMRs with the vertical specialization of the client company and the CMOs. Both parties develop and apply unique capabilities to their respective tasks in the value chain and achieve higher worker productivity by specialization (Han et al., 2012). Combined with offshoring, CMRs can additionally profit from lower labor and transportation costs.
- *Minimization of capital commitment*: Market dynamics lead companies to avoid capital commitments for production or logistics facilities to remain flexible

[2] Adapted from Essig et al. (2013, p. 369).

in situations with uncertain future development (Han et al., 2012). Shorter product life cycles, especially in the high-tech segment, mean that investment in manufacturing capacities must be amortized in a shorter period (Morschett & Donath, 2011). In addition, they entail that products must be brought to market as quickly as possible, as they can only be marketed within a limited time frame. CMOs address these needs of brand-owning companies by offering strategically located state-of-the-art production facilities, staff, and required licenses, reducing client companies' capital commitment and time-to-market (Handley & Gray, 2013). As a result, CMRs form especially in industries that experience the following aspects: strong growth, high volatility, short product life cycles, or highly regulated and expensive capacities, such as electronics, food, pharmaceuticals, or clothing (Han et al., 2012). Finally, CMRs reduce capital tied up in inventory, as CMOs are better suited to harmonize demand and leverage excess inventory across customers (Morschett & Donath, 2011).
- *Maximization of customer value*: Whereas the specialized capabilities of CMOs were primarily used for cost improvements before the turn of the millennium, their positive effect on customer value has been increasingly recognized and sought after in recent years. Several scholars have observed co-specialization in the CM sector, with brand-owning companies focusing on product innovation, design, and marketing and CMOs acquiring advanced skills in operations (Han et al., 2012). For example, client companies' access to CMOs' logistics network, fulfillment, manufacturing, and material know-how has increased customer value through value-added services, delivery, and product quality (Han et al., 2012; Morschett & Donath, 2011). Consequently, CMRs contribute to customer value beyond freeing up research budgets by integrating complementary capabilities to implement and improve designs through superior processes and material knowledge (Mandjak et al., 2021).

The current development of CM can be linked to the fact that CMRs increasingly cover all performance objectives of supply chains and even partially integrate them to resolve conflicting objectives. For example, client companies can achieve high process efficiency by economies of scale without investments in large-scale facilities. In this capacity, CMRs succeed because they overcome a major shortcoming of traditional outsourcing: The separation of research and development activities and manufacturing, decreasing innovativeness in the long run (Dachs et al., 2019). However, the leading manufacturing and materials expertise of CMOs enables continuous and collaborative improvement in designs in the manufacturing process and external stimulus from outside the company. Consequently, the re-integration of the physical supply chain and consolidation of know-how across manufacturing stages and customers has been coined the main success factor of CMOs in electronics (Lüthje, 2002).

Furthermore, global supply chains have become so complex that collaboration has become necessary to balance out and implement performance targets in SCM (Lüthje, 2002). Some leading CMOs have recognized the potential and are positioning themselves as end-to-end service providers for the entire physical supply chain, from procurement to after-sales services, to take performance achievement and balancing off their clients' hands (Denicolai et al., 2015). However, even if this development could revive the discussion concerning virtual organizations, a fundamental trend in this direction has not yet been discovered (Picot et al., 2020).

Still, further growth of CM as a self-reinforcing process is likely as brand-owning companies increasingly align their business model with customer needs. If the emerging gap in manufacturing expertise between clients and CMOs is not closed, the dependency on the CM business model will further grow.

2.4 Challenges of Managing Contract Manufacturing Relationships

The cross-company coordination of production and logistics represents a central challenge in SCM. In an interorganizational context, conflicts of interest, a lack of trust, and little knowledge of the processes involved are much more pronounced than within a single company (Essig et al., 2013). In addition, no formal hierarchies exist across company boundaries that can balance out conflicts of interest as a neutral authority. Both sides must therefore solve problems collaboratively and contractually to protect their interests. In turn, the contract design depends on the companies' negotiating power. However, due to the complexity and dynamics in supply chain relationships, the suitability of contracts as a coordination tool is limited (Essig et al., 2013).

Furthermore, the reliance on legal arrangements for coordination can be interpreted as a sign of mistrust, which in turn decreases the flexibility of the CMR in reacting to internal and external changes (Wiengarten et al., 2013). Due to the separation of product ownership and operational manufacturing responsibilities, these SCM challenges are particularly salient for CMRs. As a result, 30–50% of CMRs do not achieve their performance potential (Wiengarten et al., 2013).

Safeguarding

First, client companies face several issues to safeguard against when establishing CMRs. Quality assurance across companies is a primary management challenge in CMRs because the product and quality assurance procedures are new to the CMO (Handley & Gray, 2013). However, since the client owns and markets the products, the CMO's failure to adhere to standards can harm the company's brand image and cause regulatory and financial damage (Handley & Gray, 2015). As a result, client companies in highly regulated or brand-sensitive industries, such as food, pharmaceuticals, or clothing, must take extraordinary measures to ensure that products reaching consumers are not objectionable. The safeguarding needs are so great in offshore CMRs that client companies in the clothing industry set up their quality assurance organizations in addition to the CMO's internal quality control (Essig et al., 2013). Alternatively, to avoid high safeguarding costs, a sound joint alignment of goals, values, and capabilities is necessary to enable trust-based self-monitoring (Handley & Gray, 2013).

However, high development costs and shorter product life cycles lead competitors to increasingly enter CMRs with each other for mitigation of risk and capital commitment (Chen et al., 2019). In coopetitive CMRs, one partner typically avoids investing in assets at the early or late stages of the product life cycle, while the other partner seeks to utilize excess capacity (Han et al., 2012). In addition, CMOs that cover the entire value chain of their clients are stepping into developing private brands and competing with their clients' (Morschett & Donath, 2011). Coopetition poses a new risk to principals in CMRs that goes beyond the passive loss of knowledge in process control but involves appropriating intellectual property by potential competitors. Wang et al. (2013) find that the complexity of CMR management increases significantly when the client and CMO are engaged in multiple buyer-supplier relationships with each other simultaneously. The phenomenon of coopetition is a vibrant topic in economics, but the challenges it poses for relationship management have barely been addressed in operations management research (Wang et al., 2013).

While the pooling manufacturing jobs by CMOs to achieve economies of scale, scope, and skill is a key advantage of CM, it also carries significant risks. Pooling risk refers, on the one hand, to the risk of intellectual property flowing off to competitors outside direct coopetition whose production is placed in the same CMO plant (Sanders, Locke, Moore, & Autry, 2007). On the other hand, the concentration of capacity in a CMO leads competitors to compete for market share and supply share making their strategies more visible and potentially leading to supply bottlenecks by amplifying the bullwhip effect (Sanders et al., 2007).

Due to the CM market dynamics with frequent capacity acquisitions, in-, and outsourcing activities, the client company must rely on the CMO's capacity planning capabilities to offset the firm level of planning uncertainty (Tsay et al., 2018). Consequently, the gained strategic flexibility by low capital commitment results in an operational loss of flexibility, depending on the CMO's capacities (Essig et al., 2013). Furthermore, this dependency can become strategically relevant if the CMO provides crucial complementary knowledge, which is paramount to the client company's customer value (Sanders et al., 2007). Consequently, in managing the CMR, the client company must safeguard against these risks by enabling and aligning with the CMO to provide the desired service results. However, CMOs might consider alignment and integration with particular client companies unattractive to their business model. Concerning their revenue risk, certain CMOs are actively diversifying their customer base and limiting clients' revenue share to avoid co-dependency (Morschett & Donath, 2011). CMO commitment as a safeguard is often built through personal relationships between companies. Still, given the workforce dynamics, this safeguard is risky, so commitment beyond contractual obligations must be institutionalized in the CMR (Varoutsa & Scapens, 2018).

Adaptation

Beyond safeguarding CMR, adaptation is another challenge. According to Häkkinen (2008), efficient and effective coordination across companies constitutes a primary issue in managing CMRs. In addition, the client company's vision to steer the CMO *'as an extension of their business'* incorporates several challenges (Häkkinen, 2008, p. 15). For example, subcontracting manufacturing through a CMR creates interfaces in the partnering companies' sales and operations planning cycles, requiring mutual adjustment of both companies' processes (Fredriksson, 2011). Furthermore, considering parallel production of the same product at the client's and the CMO's site, capacity and quality management are additionally linked to ensure consistent utilization and product quality (Nordigården et al., 2014). In addition to process interfaces, CM connects companies and organizations beyond the purchasing and sales departments across the operational functions with oversight through the top management (Chan & Chung, 2002). However, contrary to internal business processes, conflicts of interest cannot be solved through hierarchy, requiring compatible business cultures and a shared understanding of the partners' business models (Trumpfheller & Hofmann, 2004).

However, substantial heterogeneity in the scope, objectives, and partner characteristics of CMRs hinders the development of universal best practices for the mutual adjustment of clients and CMO (Sanders et al., 2007). Moreover, contrary to routine, heterogeneity makes it difficult to transfer knowledge between CMRs, which slows adjustment and diminishes the CMR's ability to quickly achieve performance targets (Handley & Gray, 2015). Moreover, managers often underestimate the effort and adjustment time required, leading to dissatisfied performance expectations for the CMR (Agarwal et al., 2015). Handley and Gray (2015), therefore, suggest that client companies must develop and apply in-depth knowledge for designing and implementing relationship management to meet an individual CMR's requirements

However, since CMRs are inherently dynamic, the complex alignment must be adapted over time to avoid performance loss making the relationship unstable (Denicolai et al., 2015). In knowledge management in CMRs, an initial natural exchange of expertise, for example, is followed by saturation, after which improvement and innovation management must be systematically advanced (Mandjak et al., 2021). From a product life cycle perspective, changes in production quantities, procurement channels, sales markets, organizational structures, and product versions may require the adaptation of performance metrics and coordination procedures (Chen et al., 2019). Similarly, building trust can replace formal controls in favor of greater efficiency and partner engagement at the social relationship level, or a loss of confidence could necessitate the opposite (Varoutsa & Scapens, 2018). Furthermore, the balance of power in the CMO shifts in favor of the CMO over time after the contract is signed, making adjustments and renegotiations of the agreement more difficult (Denicolai et al., 2015). As a result, client companies often find their engagement in CMRs failing to meet expectations when the CMO holds substantial power over the relationship (Häkkinen, 2008). Long-term studies of CMRs in this context show that clients seek to offset this trend by locking in the CMO to create bilateral dependency (Denicolai et al., 2015).

Performance evaluation

Finally, a significant challenge of managing CMRs is measuring the arrangements and CMOs success through sound performance evaluation. While the performance of the manufacturing process can be easily measured using established metrics, the intangible service of process execution is often vague and tied to expectations that are challenging to quantify (Busi & McIvor, 2008). For example, improved availability and unit costs in CMRs can only be achieved jointly through aligned ordering procedures and acceptance and return guarantees making individual partners' contributions challenging to measure (Ülkü et al., 2007). Furthermore, the lack of accessibility and understanding of the CMO's internal processes makes it difficult for client companies to accurately interpret performance metrics, which can strain collaboration in the long run (Busi & McIvor, 2008). Hence, uncertainty in the CMO's performance evaluation is a significant challenge, as emerging intangible relationship objectives, such as innovation, require systematic coordination and performance measurement (Revilla & Villena, 2012).

Finally, the proportionality of the expense of performance evaluation in CMR must be considered. Performance control in CMRs is costly and requires resources (Häkkinen, 2008). Nevertheless, due to the lack of influence and accessibility of the CMO's operational processes, it cannot assure performance through corrective action. Instead, concerning the safeguarding challenge, the performance evaluation must assess the sustainability and progression of CMRs (Foerstl et al., 2016).

Hence, the management of CMRs is exceptionally challenging, as it faces, on the one hand, the general challenges of interorganizational relationships but also, on the other hand, specific problems based on CMR characteristics. Overall, the envisioned image of CMOs, although increasingly partners at eye level, are to be managed as an extension of internal operations, faces several challenges regarding coordination and alignment. Secondly, the heterogeneity of CMR requires a thorough understanding of the relationship to develop a tailored management approach to achieve situational goals efficiently.

2.5 Research Map

Reviewing the literature on the management of CMRs, the most influential research fields concerning the research topic can be depicted in a research map. The research map helps anchor the research topic in the literature and gives an overview of the relevant research streams that the dissertation project wants to address. Figure 2.5 provides a comprehensive overview of the relevant research fields and streams, showing that CMR management lies at the intersection of two research streams: CM and the management of IORs. Furthermore, these research streams intersect with multiple research fields, resulting in a fragmented knowledge base on CMR management. The four corresponding research fields are *operations management*, *supply chain management*, *strategic management*, and *service management.* SCM arguably is the most impactful as SCM researchers contribute to both relevant research streams concerning CMR management.

The different fields and their connection to the research topics are briefly summarized below. Then, the research streams are analyzed in the following chapters to carve out the research gaps in CMR management.

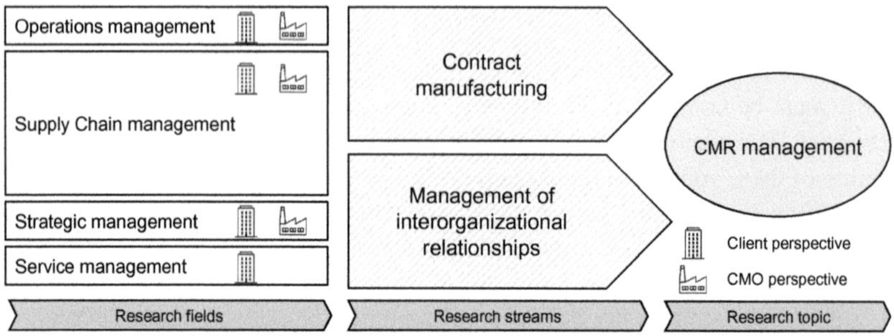

Figure 2.5 Conceptual background for CMR management

Operations Management

Slack, Brandon-Jones, and Johnston define operations management as '*the activity of managing the resources which are devoted to the creation and delivery of services and products* (2013, p. 6). Subsequently, operations management deals with the impacts of CMRs on manufacturing, for example, factory layouts (Sousa & Voss, 2007) and production program planning (Fredriksson, 2011). Thus, the research field provides a perspective on the corporate interfaces affected by CM and their involvement in CMR management. However, operations management offers no comprehensive insights into IOR management between the partnering companies.

Supply chain management

Already introduced in Section 2.2, SCM constitutes the primary research field for managing CMRs contributing to the two corresponding research streams.

On the one hand, SCM regards CM as a design practice at the network level, defining the degree of vertical integration (Essig et al., 2013). In this context, research focuses on the make-or-buy decision and the outcomes of CM (Tsay et al., 2018). Thus, SCM provides valuable insights into the context and objectives of CMRs. On the other hand, CMRs are referenced in the research stream of *supply chain relationship management,* encompassing both the concepts of *supplier relationship management* (SRM) and *customer relationship management* (CRM) (Trumpfheller & Hofmann, 2004, p. 72). Consequently, SCM literature offers frameworks and management practices for systematic supplier portfolio management, development, and performance control (Trumpfheller & Gomm, 2004).

Service Management

Service management covers various types of services as a research field (Bryson, Sundbo, Fuglsang, & Daniels, 2020). Sampson and Froehle highlight service's '*intangibility, heterogeneity, simultaneity (inseparability), perishability, and customer participation*' (2006, p. 334). In this context, service management literature has focused on outsourced business processes such as logistics from the client's perspective, with a strong focus on selection and performance management (Simon et al., 2021). Hence, service management holds information regarding the nature and challenges of interorganizational service relationships.

Strategic management

According to Nag, Hambrick, and Chen, '*strategic management deals with the major intended and emergent initiatives taken by general managers [...] to enhance the performance of firms*' (2007, p. 944). Examples of such interorganizational initiatives within the strategic management literature encompass *strategic alliances* (SA) (Isidor et al., 2014, p. 141) and *joint ventures* (JM) (Kamminga & van der Meer-Kooistra, 2007, p. 133). Strategic management connects with the increasingly strategic notion of CM, integrating the client company's and CMO's complementary capabilities. Furthermore, the literature on SAs and JVs contributes to the research on managing IORs focusing on strategic alignment and safeguarding (Isidor et al., 2014). Consequently, strategic management is relevant for understanding and coordinating joint value creation in CMRs.

To conclude, the subject of CMRs considers and draws insights from various research fields and streams. Therefore, literature from these streams needs to be analyzed to define research gaps in this dissertation project.

2.6 Positioning of the Management of Contract Manufacturing Relationships

Section 2.2 highlighted that CM evolves dynamically between different established concepts, sometimes with significant overlap. Consequently, relationship management of CMRs intersects with the existing literature on the management of different IORs. However, literature has provided multiple partly conflicting approaches to define and delimitate different types of IORs, resulting in a fragmented understanding of the matter (Cropper, Ebers, Huxham, & Ring, 2009; Sanders et al., 2007). Therefore drawing on the presented drivers, challenges, and literature streams of CMRs, this chapter aims to carve out the relevant peculiarities regarding the management of CMRs and other types of IORs.

Analyzing the diverse approaches to characterizing IORs for management purposes in literature, Tangpong et al. have identified *power dependence* and *relationalism* as the key attributes guiding researchers in their classification (2015, p. 154). Power dependence adheres to dynamics, control, and opportunism in the relationship, while relationalism focuses on cooperative efforts and integration (Tangpong et al., 2015). Both attributes express the degree of interdependence at the strategic and operational levels of IORs, characterizing the complexity of coordination between business partners (Thompson, 1967). The following paragraphs will outline the management requirements of CMRs utilizing Tangpong et al.'s (2015) findings.

As previously introduced, the trend toward the complementary provision of knowledge in CMRs has tremendous effects on relationship management (Essig et al., 2013). The ability to create higher value through collaboration reflects the dependency on the partner to generate the envisaged returns from the CMR (Dyer & Singh, 1998). As described in Section 2.3, CMRs can not only enhance supply chain performance but also create new customer value, elevating the CMO from a service provider to a crucial business partner with significant bargaining power. Therefore, Mandjak et al. consider CMRs unique because the manufactured products have *'two owners,'* not in a legal sense but in a capability sense (2021, p. 13). Power in a business relationship refers to the *'capability of one of the partners to control another one's intentions, decisions, behavior, and actions'* (Morsy, 2017, p. 36). As a result of the increasing dependency on CMOs' capabilities, client companies are losing the traditional power dominance and ability to control the CMR single-handedly.

Furthermore, CMOs can often customize and market their services to various potential customers. At the same time, the client company has limited options to adjust the manufacturing requirements of their product designs to increase the potential supplier base (Zhang et al., 2013). Morschett and Donath (2011) even observe that some CMOs are pursuing a strategy to diversify their customer base by limiting order quantities and actively expanding their market power. Häkkinen further remarks that in CMRs, even *'satisfactory partnerships are dominated by the supplier'* (2008, p. 17). Due to the trend towards complementary resources, clients and contract manufacturers are highly interdependent, with CMOs increasingly occupying a position of power (Morsy, 2017). Consequently, the clients are significantly dependent on the CMOs, but no general statements about the reverse relationship can be made.

Investigating the relational attributes of CMRs, Nassimbeni's (1998) work on network structures and coordination can provide valuable insights. CMRs could traditionally be regarded as supply relationships since their main objective was operational synergies generated through integrating material flows in the operating core of the partnered companies (Nassimbeni, 1998). However, recent developments show an increasing relevance of technological synergies facilitated through the deliberate exchange of skills and expertise comparable to joint ventures (Nassimbeni, 1998). Takeishi (2001) shows that leveraging technological synergies between relationship partners requires joint coordination and creates a dynamic environment. Furthermore, the duality of operative and functional integration involves broad areas of the partnering organizations, causing strong operational interdependency (Nassimbeni, 1998). Therefore, the term *'coordination'* serves as a critical distinguisher since the management of CMRs requires operative coordination of joint value creation. For example, integrating sales and operations planning, quality management, and product and process improvement in parallel production emphasize the emerging coordination needs (Nordigården et al., 2014).

Consequently, CMR management goes beyond the management of the relationship interfaces and oversees the integration of complementary capabilities in the manufacturing process. Several studies support the degree of complementarity of capabilities as an indicator of relationalism in collaboration (Kang et al., 2014; Zhang et al., 2013). Suppose a client company contracts a CMO to achieve higher efficiency in operations. In that case, it could theoretically sustain itself, the CMR holds low relationalism and the managerial focus is on transaction output. On the other hand, if the CMO provides complementary capabilities to value creation, there is significant integration and relationalism led by a common understanding. Malmi and Brown (2008) point out the substantial relationalism in such arrangements since the high degree of integration make the control of all interfaces impractical, requiring a high degree of self-governance under the strategic alignment of interests. Thus, Häkkinen argues that CMRs with complementary capabilities fall under Eccles' (1981) concept of quasifirms with strong organizational ties, which need to be steered through socialization and alignment of goals due to limited governance ability by a single party (Häkkinen, 2008). In summary, CMRs can experience either low or high relationalism according to the relevance of the CMO for value creation.

Based on these premises, CMRs can be classified according to Tangpong et al.'s (2015) typology of IORs. Tangpong et al. (2015) distinguish eight different types of IORs based on the attributes of relationalism, buyer dependence, and supplier dependence, with the latter two describing power dependence. Four of these eight IORs are characterized by high client dependence on the supplier, as described for CMRs in the previous paragraphs. However, in the absence of detailed evaluations of the dependence of CMOs and relationalism, no other relational forms can be excluded.

Figure 2.6 illustrates the procedure. The four relevant IORs and the attributed client's challenges following Tangpong et al. (2015) are described below.

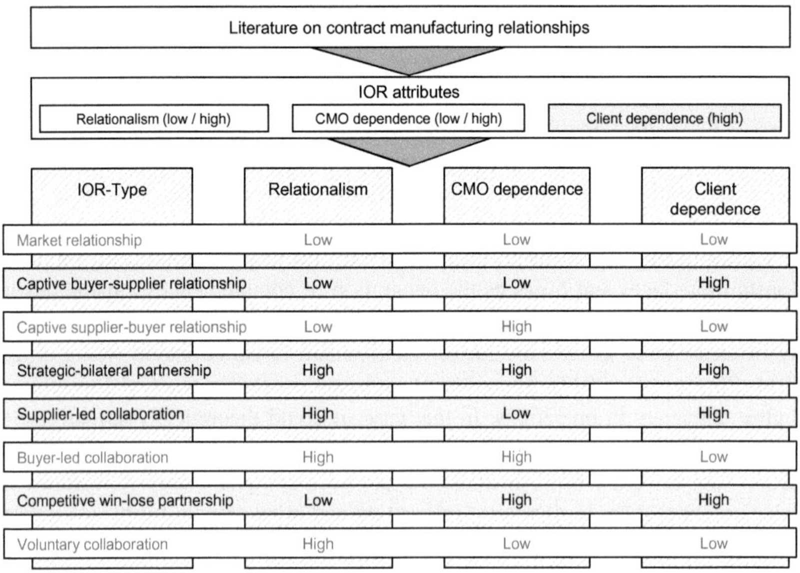

Figure 2.6 Positioning of CMRs among IORs[3]

- *CMR as a captive buyer-supplier relationship*: The client aims to leverage the supplier's capabilities and secure access to critical resources. Within an arms-length relationship, management activities from the client-side focus on output controls and safeguarding against the CMO.

[3] Adapted from Tangpong et al. (2015, p. 166).

- *CMR as a strategic-bilateral partnership*: Both parties are deeply committed to the CMR and manifest this by aligning strategies, investing in the relationship, and actively adjusting their interfaces to enable joint value creation on eye level. Relationship management focuses on intensive communication and collaboration along the manufacturing process, while self-governance promotes control.
- *CMR as a supplier-led collaboration*: The client aims to leverage the supplier's capabilities collaboratively and secure access to critical resources. The client company shapes relationship management toward behavior control and promotes integration to bind the CMO to the CMR.
- *CMR as a competitive win-lose partnership*: Both parties meet on eye level in an arms-length relationship to optimize their operations. Relationship management focuses on output controls and safeguarding against the opportunism of the CMO.

Consequently, the management of IORs must address several relationship management challenges to cover CMRs comprehensively. The main challenges can be summarized through the governance problems of transaction cost economics (Rindfleisch & Heide, 1997).

- *Safeguarding requirements*: Client companies must safeguard dedicated investments into adjusted interfaces or the CMR. Furthermore, reliance on the CMO's capabilities to deliver its product to the market makes it necessary to limit opportunism and keep the CMR stable, and the CMO committed to secure access to critical capabilities.
- *Adaptation requirements*: The combination of significant integration of interfaces, long relationship duration, and complex switching procedures with limited control over eye-level CMOs requires trust-based flexible and synched management structures to minimize adaptation needs and costs. The consequence is a significant need for transparency and communication to share information.
- *Performance evaluation requirements*: Limited visibility into CMO operations of arms-length CMRs requires meaningful output controls, while superior know-how by the CMO limits evaluation by the client. In the latter case, the CMR requires a significant degree of trust-based self-governance through aligned goals.

Thus, the core challenge of managing CMRs can be narrowed down to the limited ability to oversee and control the manufacturing process. The main difficulties arise from the little oversight in non-integrated CMRs and the limited understanding of the process in integrated CMRs, which causes strong dependency on the CMO. Consequently, the particular management challenges may vary significantly between individual CMRs.

After positioning CMRs among IORs, the following chapters review the relevant research streams on IOR management to assess their fit with the identified management challenges of CMRs. Based on the identified fields of literature in the research map (see Section 2.5), these are *supplier relationship management* (SRM), *customer relationship management* (CRM), service management (SM), *management of strategic alliances* (SA), and *management of joint ventures* (JV).

2.6.1 Supplier Relationship Management

SRM concerns a company's *'supply-side side interfaces with suppliers'* and covers the *'design, development and control of supplier interfaces on all network levels'* (Trumpfheller & Hofmann, 2004, p. 70). Hence, it aims to meet the performance goals by appropriately designing the relationship's *coordination, communication, commitment*, *technology*, *transparency*, and *trust* (Trumpfheller & Gomm, 2004, p. 308). In this context, it also covers integrated approaches to joint planning and development measures with suppliers (Essig et al., 2013).

SRM has been the primary knowledge base to explain and design the management of CMRs in literature so far. However, many scholars have identified limits to the explanatory power of SRM in the context of CM. For example, Tsay (2014) expresses the difficulty of SRM to adjust from the supply of goods to the management of integrated services. In addition, Häkkinen identifies further contrasting views of SRM and management of CMRs, regarding *selection criteria, manufacturing process, pricing, schedules, quality expectations, product innovation,* and *information transfer* (2008, p. 68). Trumpfheller and Hofmann (2004) confirm this view from the SRM perspective and state that complex service relationships as integrated logistics must be distinguished from the management of vertical supplier relationships. According to Hayes et al. (1988), a process philosophy contrasting a focus on outputs and products is paramount to enabling value creation from manufacturing. However, procurement and SRM lack a deeper understanding of manufacturing processes. SRM, as a discipline, aims to optimize the focal company's supply-side interfaces following a clear separation of tasks between buyer and supplier (Trumpfheller & Hofmann, 2004). In CMRs, this relates to the difficulty of measuring CMO performance while integrating processes and coordinating the value creation process jointly due to performance ambiguity (Kang et al., 2014). Specifically, SRM lacks approaches to strategic alignment, leveraging complementary knowledge, joint operational coordination, and knowledge sharing commonly found in strategic management because it aims to optimize the purchasing transaction.

The second significant limitation of SRM toward CMRs is the management of supplier-dominated relationships. Häkkinen (2008) finds that even in strategic partnerships, CMOs hold more ex-post power than the client company. However, SRM builds on an advantage in negotiation power or knowledge by the client company and leads to unsatisfactory results in outsourcing relationships (Cox, 2001). From the SRM perspective, supplier-dominated relationships depend on the supplier's goodwill and lead to the exploitation of customer companies (Tangpong et al., 2015). Therefore supplier-dominated relationships must be avoided. Due to the aim to design supplier relationships across all supply chain levels, SRM counters unfavorable relationships through an optimized supply design, e.g., by dual sourcing or insourcing on the network level (Essig et al., 2013). Specific recommendations of SRM for locked-in client companies, such as building safety stocks, are scarce and often fall short of practice requirements in CMRs (Caniëls & Gelderman, 2007).

Thus, SRM provides various impulses for managing CMRs and dealing with the *adaptation governance problem* exceptionally well, as it has expansive knowledge of creating adaptive and standardized supplier interfaces. However, SRM fails to address the *performance evaluation problem* of highly integrated processes and intangible results. Furthermore, SRM lacks management practices to *safeguard* investment into the relationship by strategical alignment with the CMO in favor of more suitable supply network designs. Figure 2.7 summarizes the findings on SRM.

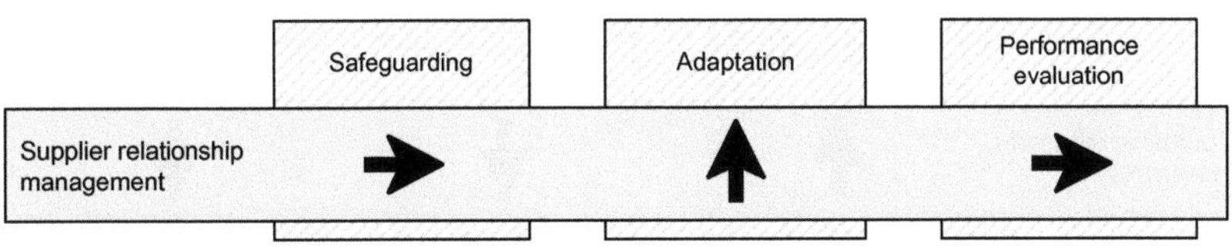

Figure 2.7 Explanatory power of SRM for managing CMRs

2.6.2 Customer Relationship Management

CRM is *'a customer-oriented corporate strategy which (...) attempts to build up and consolidate profitable customer relationships in the long term through holistic and differentiated marketing, sales and service concepts'* (Trumpfheller & Hofmann, 2004, p. 70). Strongly influenced by the relationship marketing literature, CRM enhances the role of behavioral aspects in managing business relationships (Das, 2009). In marketing, CRM is seen as an approach that enables a consistent customer orientation of the entire company (Leußer, Hippner, & Wilde, 2011). As a core element of SCM, CRM breaks down functional silos and supports a customer-oriented process view of value creation (Mentzer et al., 2001). In this capacity, CRM strongly influences SRM, of which it is the counterpart (Essig et al., 2013).

The underlying concepts of CRM that encompass a long-term focus on the relationship, partner orientation, a weaker bargaining position, and the necessity for strategic alignment address CMR management challenges complementary to SRM (Leußer et al., 2011; Zupancic & Belz, 2006). The key account management concept of CRM, for example, has been adapted to companies' supply sides to adjust interfaces to crucial suppliers systematically and minimize the risk of them leaving the relationship (Trumpfheller & Gomm, 2004; Zupancic, 2008). CRM consequently provides impulses for the inter-and intraorginazational coordination of value creation in CMRs and alignment with the CMO (Zupancic, 2008).

Moreover, because CRM assumes a weaker power position relative to the partner than SRM, it is open to a less deterministic return on relationship management investments accepting external dynamics as drivers of uncertainty (Leußer et al., 2011). However, CRM also struggles with performance evaluation of integrated value creation and dominantly targets internal processes' performance control of the relationship interface (Zupancic & Belz, 2006).

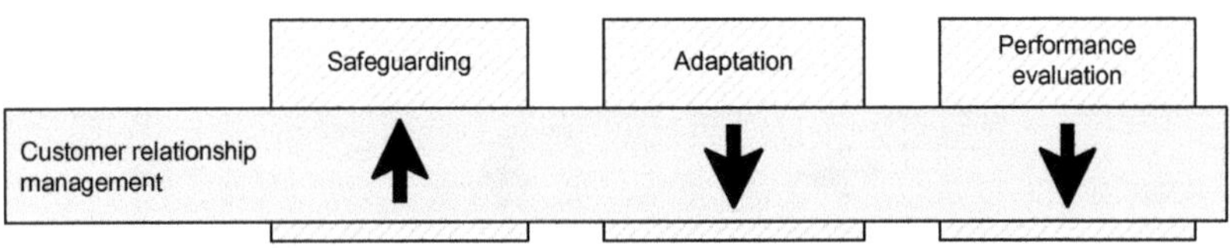

Figure 2.8 Explanatory power of CRM for managing CMRs

Altogether, CRM is complementary to the contribution of SRM to managing CMRs. The *safeguarding problem* of CMRs is addressed in more vital terms, actively aiming to commit the dominant power partner to the relationship. However, while CRM suggests a more ambiguous *performance evaluation*, the evaluation of partner performance in CM is absent. Concerning the *adaptation problem*, CRM aims for more robust integration and adjustment toward the CMO, resulting in higher adaptation costs. Figure 2.8 recaps the explanatory impulses of CRM.

2.6.3 Service Management

SM covers the entire field of the service business and addresses the management of outsourced service operations (Bryson et al., 2020). In the supply chain context, SM focuses on logistics as *'the process of handling and managing supply chains, including designing supply chains'* (Bryson et al., 2020, p. 203). Furthermore, SM literature paints similar characteristics and challenges to managing outsourced logistics operations to CM (Cooper & Gardner, 1993). For example, the management of third- (3PL) or fourth-party (4PL) logistics is considered *'problematic'* due to a lack of mutual understanding, unrealistic expectations, and intangibility of results (Selviaridis & Spring, 2007, p. 134). Hence, SM literature proposes to complement the limitations of formal management in highly individual service relationships with informal expectation management and strategic alignment (Bryson et al., 2020; Selviaridis & Spring, 2007; Stouthuysen et al., 2012). However, the main focus of overcoming relationship challenges in SM lies in proper service provider selection, information sharing, and performance management (Selviaridis & Spring, 2007). In relationship management, SM leans heavily on the more mature fields of SRM and strategic management (Eggert, Böhm, & Cramer, 2017; Selviaridis & Spring, 2007).

Despite the positive fit with the management characteristics of 3PLs and 4PLs, the SM literature has significant drawbacks regarding CMRs. SM primarily refers to outsourcing business processes that are not part of the customer's core competencies and are not directly related to value creation and production (Bryson et al., 2020). Therefore, the relevance of the covered operations for the client is comparatively low and only includes CMRs resulting from efficiency-oriented outsourcing arrangements (Chan & Chung, 2002). Hence, SM does not address the *safeguarding problem* sufficiently since the service provider handles no strategically important investments or intellectual property. Furthermore, integration between clients and service providers is operations-focused and less expansive, dealing with a considerably lower *adaptation problem*. However, SM combines approaches to *performance evaluation* from SRM and strategic management, which can depict formal and informal aspects of complex services. Figure 2.9 visualizes these conclusions.

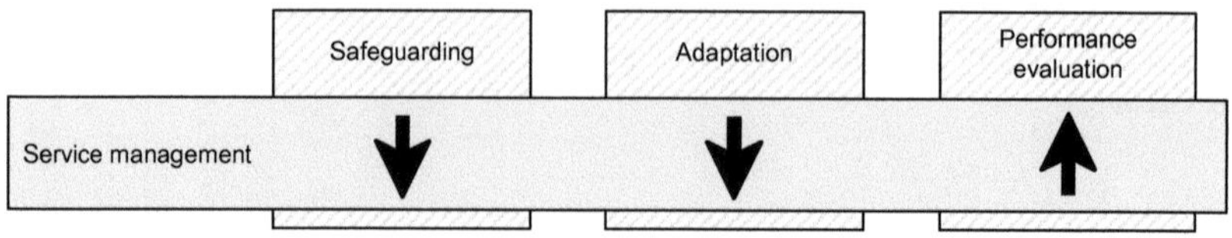

Figure 2.9 Explanatory power of SM for managing CMRs

2.6.4 Management of Strategic Alliances

The definitions of SA in the literature are broad but can be narrowed down to specific criteria that constitute an SA: Companies enter into an SA to improve their competitive position through the complementary capabilities of the partner (Isidor et al., 2014). The scope of the agreement is, in principle, flexible and can include the development, manufacturing, and distribution of products and services (Cooper & Gardner, 1993). SAs are characterized by relation-specific assets, exchange of knowledge, and complementary resources jointly leveraged to create value (Dyer & Singh, 1998). Consequently, the literature on SAs covers collaborative relationships' formation, governance, and performance (Aggarwal, Siggelkow, & Singh, 2011).

Therefore, many scholars assume that CMRs fall between supplier relationships and SAs and that the literature on SAs offers valuable insights into managing CMRs (Sanders et al., 2007). As task division among partners to leverage complementary resources is challenging, coordination of collaboration, systematic knowledge sharing, and alignment of interests are essential for managing SAs (Agarwal et al., 2015). The ambiguity of results and restrictions on measuring knowledge-intensive processes lead to management practices in SA focusing on the motivation of partner goodwill, collaborative work, and self-governance instead of operative performance control (Kang et al., 2012). Moreover, the ambiguity of outcomes and intangible quality criteria have led to SA being viewed as inherently unstable and dynamic in the eyes of researchers, as performance is often subjectively evaluated based on the partner's expectations (Isidor et al., 2014). Therefore, organizational learning and long-term relationship development have been discussed in the management of SAs (Doz, 1996).

The management of SAs overlaps significantly with frequent challenges of managing, especially capability-driven, CMRs. Since it involves partnering for competitive advantage, it sufficiently covers the *safeguarding governance problem*. Nevertheless, SAs are based on the assumption that both partners can gain competitive advantages from each other's capabilities (Isidor et al., 2014). However, in CMRs, due to the service character, this objective may be only one-sided. Consequently, a CMO may provide complementary knowledge for a client but can substitute for the client's order volume, giving him a position of power. In addition, the perception of eye-level collaboration limits the ability to holistically address the *performance evaluation problem* since alliance performance focuses on competitive advantage and joint value creation instead of a single partner's duties and operations performance. No clear answer can be given regarding the *adaptation problem* even though SAs promote mutual adaptation. Still, their integration object is complementary resources, and the further problem description remains abstract. The management of tangible entanglement of processes, systems, and structures is hardly addressed in SA literature. These insights are summed up in Figure 2.10.

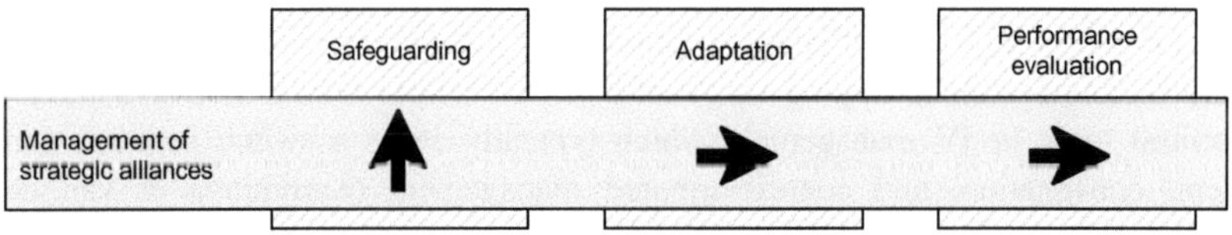

Figure 2.10 Explanatory power of SAs for managing CMRs

2.6.5 Management of Joint Ventures

JVs are companies where at least two independent partners participate financially as investors and in management (Rumer, 1994). Comparable to SAs, partners strive to profit from each other's capabilities by combining (intellectual) property, equipment, know-how, and financial capabilities within one new legal entity (Kang et al., 2014; Rumer, 1994). CMRs can be considered quasi-firms, making them comparable to JVs in the governance structure (Häkkinen, 2008). In addition, companies are expanding CMRs into JVs to mitigate risks at offshore locations or on challenging or strategic co-development projects (Nassimbeni, 1998; Rumer, 1994).

According to Kamminga and van der Meer-Kooistra (2007), the relationship management of JVs considers two primary relations: the hierarchical relationship between JV and parental companies and between parents. However, shared management over the JV lies at the core of the JV management literature (Kamminga & van der Meer-Kooistra, 2007). In this capacity, JV management literature borrows heavily from organizational control since management challenges typically arise within the JV (Kang et al., 2014). Based on the complexity of the JV literature distinguishes content, consultation, and context-oriented management approaches of JVs with gradually less direct control in favor of trust-based self-governance and strategic alignment (Kamminga & van der Meer-Kooistra, 2007). Complementary to established practices in IOR research, such as formal control and communication, personnel decision and financial practices play a significant role in JVs. Personnel decisions across hierarchies are considered the most effective practices for operative JV management since they influence decision-making, knowledge transfer, communication, and trust-building (Kamminga & van der Meer-Kooistra, 2007). On the other hand, financial contributions are either used as incentives for strategic alignment or to increase equity share and bargaining power to influence personnel decisions (Kamminga & van der Meer-Kooistra, 2007).

Furthermore, the longterm-orientation of JVs, significant lock-in effects, trust-based control, and changing bargaining power render relationship dynamics a central topic in JV management which typically cause a switch between content, consultation, and context-oriented management (Kamminga & van der Meer-Kooistra, 2007).

Similar to SAs, the management of JVs has resemblances to that of knowledge-driven CMRs. However, sharing one legal entity for collaboration results in significant differences in how the challenges can be overcome. For example, due to interorganizational restraints, JV practices such as personnel decisions are difficult to apply in CMRs. Nevertheless, the strategic, long-term orientation and high exit barriers require management approaches to solve the *safeguarding problem* for investment objects and intellectual property. In addition, JVs with close strategic and operational linkages are subject to high dynamics, making the *adaptation problem central* to their management. Finally, JV management focuses little on the *performance evaluation problem* because both partners have a stake in the success of the JV and few individual tasks are delineated and evaluated. Figure 2.11 illustrates the considerations.

Finally, impulses from the management of joint ventures can be integrated with the assessments of the other overlapping IORs to provide positioning for managing CMRs. Reviewing the literature, an inevitable overlap between CMRs,

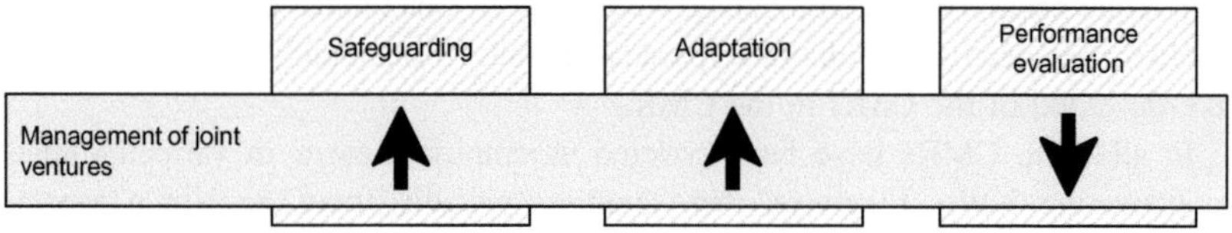

Figure 2.11 Explanatory power of JVs for managing CMRs

SRM, CRM, SM, SA, and JV from a management perspective is evident. Consequently, scholars can draw valuable impulses from these intersecting research streams for CMR management. However, none of the presented research streams captures the challenges of CMRs comprehensively. Thus, the partially one-sided heavy dependence and relevance on the CMO combined with close operational interdependence remain a differentiating factor for CMRs among IORs. The following chapter will elaborate on the concrete need for research on managing CMRs.

2.7 Specification of the Research Gaps

The previous chapters showed a significant interest in CMRs in various fields of literature. However, regarding the management of CMRs, many questions remain unanswered. The antecedents and outcomes of CM on network and actor levels of the supply chain are well-frequented in research (Kang et al., 2012). Scholars have been aware of the growth and transformation of the CM business model since the 1990 s and have addressed this phenomenon in various publications (Denicolai et al., 2015; Essig et al., 2013; Lüthje, 2002). However, the management of CMRs on the supply chain relationship level has mainly been neglected by scholars. Given the intensive network and actor-level investigation and the valuation of CMRs as a *'further development stage of relational procurement,'* this is somewhat remarkable (Essig et al., 2013, p. 112). However, most research focuses on typologies to capture the substantial heterogeneity of CMRs, as they hamper the generation of generalizable findings (Dekker, 2004; Häkkinen, 2008).

Even in dedicated research on operational management of CMRs, most studies focus on individual aspects of the relationship, such as contract management (Wiengarten et al., 2013), opportunism (Skowronski, Benton, & Hill, 2020), or quality management (Handley & Gray, 2013, 2015). For example, Webster et al. (1997) and Kang et al. (2012; 2014) follow the sub-stream of control mechanisms against the backdrop of contingency, while only Noonan and Wallace (2006) take a holistic perspective on relationship management. Noonan and Wallace, however, take the stand of the CMO in the CMR.

In addition, CMRs have been covered as empirical cases in various studies on managing IORs. Likewise, these studies typically focus on single aspects of relationship management, exploring or evaluating them through CMR case studies. Section 2.6 analyzed the similarities and differences between managing CMRs and other IORs described by literature, expressing that the corresponding research streams do not comprehensively cover the constituent aspects of CMR management. While many scholars such as Chan and Chung (2002), Dekker (2004), and Häkkinen (2008) share this perception, comprehensive studies on CMR management are still lacking.

Furthermore, from a theoretical perspective, Busi and McIvor (2008) and Dekker (2004) observe that most studies on CMR management either rely on no explicitly mentioned theory or a grounded theory or adopt a *'control perspective.'* A *'control perspective'* relates to, e.g., the frequent use of principal-agent or transaction cost problems, due to which CMOs need to be controlled. Therefore, the emerging collaborative perspective of CMRs based on trust and complementary capabilities in practice is insufficiently reflected in the choice of theory in literature.

As a result, researchers have called upon dedicated research into the operational management of CMRs and the development of systematic and operational management frameworks for managing CMR (Busi & McIvor, 2008). Busi and McIvor conclude *'that science is lagging behind practice'* in CMRs and *'that the generation of knowledge related to outsourcing is dominated by specialized publications, blogs, and outsourcing suppliers' so-called whitepapers'* (2008, p. 186). Likewise, as a result of their study, Boulaksil and Fransoo find *'that nothing has been documented in the literature on outsourcing at the operational planning level'* (2010, p. 1059). Therefore, they propose further research into the connection between strategic, operational, and ex-ante and ex-post activities in managing CMRs (Boulaksil & Fransoo, 2010). Mandjack et al. (2021) confirm that the interconnection of knowledge exchange to leverage complementary capabilities in CMRs extends across management layers and requires holistic management. Furthermore, in their investigation of parallel production in CMRs, Nordigården et al. (2014) attest that despite strategic typologies, there is little knowledge of the different manifestations of CMRs on the operational level.

Although new dedicated research has been published since some of these assessments, the core pattern remains. First, a dedicated management approach to managing CMRs has not been researched despite the dynamically growing relevance of CMRs in practice (Tsay et al., 2018). Second, the prospect of strengthening their competitive position leads many companies to enter into CMRs despite the often unsatisfactory results of these arrangements (Kaiser & Obermaier, 2020). Effective governance of CMR, therefore, remains a practical pressure point to achieve desired competitive advantages from collaboration (Dekker, 2004). Third, heterogeneity across CMRs plays a significant role in the difficulty of managing CMRs in practice, as the decisive elements to select reasonable management practices for a specific relationship are unknown, creating a *'black box'* character of CMR management in research and practice. Fourth, CMRs are highly dynamic, reversing initially relevant management requirements throughout the relationship due to changing strategies, personnel, and market developments. Finally, the literature's management philosophy towards CMOs focusing on control still outweighs the partnership perspective for collaborative value creation.

Consequently, as elaborated throughout Chapter 2, the relationship management of CMRs constitutes a research gap (RG) in the supply chain and IOR management fields. It is composed of:

- *RG_1 Management practices in CMRs:* Despite unsatisfactory results of CMRs, the recognition of changing business and collaboration models in external manufacturing have not led to a reassessment of the management of such arrangements. A mature knowledge base on managing IORs suggests an 'execution gap' in implementing established concepts from literature. Still, CMRs differ significantly from various types of IORs, indicating that established management practices may not be seamlessly transferable. Consequently, the main challenges of managing CMRs and the current management practices companies employ to address them are unknown. Therefore, an exploratory analysis of actual CMR management practices and their specific applications is necessary to understand the drivers of mixed results of CMRs and develop meaningful management recommendations.
- *RG_2 Assessment of management needs:* Precise characterization of distinctive types of IORs is an ongoing research topic for developing tailor-made management recommendations for various relationship forms. Amid the robust heterogeneity across CMRs, matching the proper management practices with individual CMRs is crucial to enable successful collaboration. However, despite numerous developed frameworks, the effect on the practice has dwindled since Krajic's (1983) influential supply framework. Consequently, it is critical to understand how and by what criteria client companies assign

management practices to each CMR to identify key complexity drivers and appropriate management practices.

- *RG_3 Adaptability of management:* Due to the long-term nature of CMRs, potentially covering the entire or multiple product life cycles, management requirements are changing significantly over time. End-to-end collaboration in value creation leads to close integration and requires continuous alignment of the chosen management practices with the CMR characteristics. Robust operational entanglement makes continuous adjustments of interfaces costly, calling for the right balance between trusted autonomy and control. Considering the increasingly dynamic environment, it is unknown which changes will cause companies to change CMR management and how a tailored selection of management practices can be achieved.

The presented research gaps complement each other as a holistic perspective of relationship management practices in CMRs along their life cycle. Hence, this dissertation project aims to fill these research gaps by providing insights for practitioners and progressing research on the management of CMRs.

The envisaged findings should guide practitioners in managing CMRs by providing the right *'construction plans'* (guidelines for assessing and adapting management practices) and *'tools'* (management practices) for customizing their management approaches to CMRs. Through an exploratory research approach, the dissertation aims to close the gap between established IOR management literature and CMRs. In this capacity, it integrates exploratory results with the mature knowledge base on the management of adjacent relationship types following a pragmatic research philosophy (see Section 3.2).

2.8 Research Questions

The previous chapters have highlighted the theoretical shortcomings of literature regarding the management of CMRs and carved out particular research gaps. This chapter formulates the research question guiding the dissertation project to close these research gaps. Addressing the overall research gap in the management of CMRs, the guiding research question of the dissertation is:

- *RQ_0: How can dynamic contract manufacturing relationships be managed from the client companies' perspective?*

To reflect the challenges of client companies in practice and contribute to research on relationship management on the supply side of the supply chain, RQ_0 defines the client company's perspective as the lens for the dissertation project. RQ_0 be further broken down into subsidiary research questions to structure the research process. The secondary research questions align with the research objectives presented in Section 1.3 and the previously identified research gaps. They are the foundation for the research design and empirical data collection in the remainder of the dissertation.

Intending to address the first research gap (RG_1) specifically and examine the status quo of the management of CMRs in practice, the current management practices of CMRs and their utilization need to be uncovered. RQ_1 addresses this research demand:

- *RQ_1: How can management practices be used in CMRs to support the management of the relationship?*

In addition, practitioners must select reasonable management practices which support overcoming particular management challenges in CMRs. However, the concept of CMR encompasses heterogeneous relationship characteristics with highly individualized challenges. Therefore, in alignment with RG_2, RQ_2 covers this issue:

- *RQ_2: How can the need for management practices for individual CMRs be assessed?*

CMRs are inherently dynamic, causing the relationship characteristics to change as time progresses. However, since the relationship and the environment constantly evolve, adjustments are practical only in particular cases. Therefore, partially addressing RG_3, RQ_3 captures this research need:

- *RQ_3: What relationship dynamics are relevant triggers for the adjustment of management practices in CMRs?*

Finally, a strategic framework must guide an ongoing operational task to assess management needs, apply management practices, and monitor and adjust relationships along the relationship life cycle. RQ_4 covers this gap in research to answer RG_3:

- *RQ_4: How can client companies adjust CMRs management practices to respond to changing management needs?*

In culmination, these research questions should answer the thesis' guiding research question RQ_0 and contribute to an integrated process for using management practices in dynamic CMRs. In this capacity, the dissertation aims to close the research gap and derive recommendations for practitioners regarding the managerial challenges of CMRs.

3 Research Access to Management of Contract Manufacturing Relationships

This chapter presents the research access to the dissertation topic. First, Section 3.1 introduces the relevant theoretical perspective of the research problem and the theory selection approach. Secondly, the selected theories and their constructs are applied in detail to the research problem to derive a research design for the dissertation in Section 3.2. Next, Section 3.3 presents a comprehensive research framework, and Section 3.4 contains the chosen research methodology for the dissertation project.

3.1 Scientific Theoretical Positioning

A theory aims to explain and predict phenomena to expand the scientific knowledge base (Hunt, 2014). Theoretical foundations can be instrumental in shaping a study's research design in several ways, first by understanding the investigated phenomenon through an initial explanatory framework and second by guiding the data collection and analysis based on previous knowledge (Walsham, 1995). Consequently, the use of theories is driven by the objective to create scientific rigor through a systemized and testable structure to explain and predict phenomena (Gregor, 2006).

The following section gives insights into frequently applied theoretic lenses in research on CMRs. Following the presentation of these theories, Section 3.1.2 deals with selecting suitable theories through a robust procedure.

T. Brandl, *Managing Contract Manufacturing Relationships*, Supply Chain Management, https://doi.org/10.1007/978-3-658-41359-0_3

3.1.1 Overview of Theories Relevant to the Research Questions

SCM is a comparatively young research field that draws mainly on intersecting research disciplines' theories (Defee et al., 2010; Essig et al., 2013). For example, Defee et al. show that relationship-related topics in SCM are mainly associated with *competitive, microeconomic, marketing, and social psychology theories* (2010, p. 417). Busi and McIvor list *transaction cost economics (TCE), the resource-based view (RBV), agency theory (AT),* and *the relational view (RV)* as the most frequently applied theories in research on outsourcing in supply chains (2008, p. 187). Furthermore, *dynamic capabilities (DC)* and *social exchange theory (SET)* have often been used in studies on dynamic supply chain settings (Defee et al., 2010). In addition, new theories have emerged that might provide insights into the dynamics and management practices of CMRs: Originating from marketing research, Palmatier et al. (2013) introduce the *relationship velocity perspective (RVP)* as an approach to relationship dynamics. As a complementary lens to the resource-based view, a *practice-based view (PBV)* has been proposed by Bromiley and Rau (2014) to focus on the contribution of imitable practices to a firm's performance. The following paragraphs briefly review the prospective theories and how they relate to the management of CMRs:

Competitive theories: According to Wang (2014), competitive theories position organizations in their respective environment and explain how they can outperform their contestants through specific attributes or actions. Penrose (1959) and Barney (1991) shaped the RBV in management research, which is now frequently found in connection with the contribution of suppliers to client firms' efforts to attain competitive advantage (Miles & Snow, 2007). The RV of Dyer and Singh (1998) extends this view beyond a firm's boundaries and argues that relational rents can be generated from IORs if governed effectively. DC offers a dynamic view of organizations' need to continuously attain new capabilities and resources, potentially providing a frame for managing relationship dynamics (Teece, Pisano, & Shuen, 1997). Lastly, Bromiley and Rau's (2014) PBV recognizes management practices as transferable constructs between companies and emphasizes the contribution of reasonable practices to firm performance.

Microeconomic theories: Following Defee et al. (2010), microeconomic theories have been building blocks of SCM and explain firm-level behavior by rationalizing activities and decisions taken by actors in microeconomic relationships. TCE decomposes business activities into transactions between actors and organizations and has been applied in SCM for reasoning their governance structures (Grover & Malhotra, 2003). In the supply chain context, AT sheds light on the self-interest of principals and agents in business relationships and recommends limiting covert actions and concealed information from agents to ensure relationship performance (Fayezi, O'Loughlin, & Zutshi, 2012).

Marketing theories: Marketing theories attempt to explain, predict, and understand how relationships between customers and suppliers function and why they excel or fail (Hunt, 2014). RVP builds on relationship commitment and focuses on relationship dynamics, providing explanations of the suitability and effectiveness of management practices at different stages and times of CMRs (Palmatier et al., 2013).

Social psychology theories: Social psychology theories are rooted in human behavior and applied to organizational behavior in management research. According to Defee et al. (2010), they are frequently found in the SCM literature to explain behavior in supplier relationships. For example, SET contributes to scholars' understanding of business-to-business transactions' governance through non-contractual controls (Lambe et al., 2001).

Based on their connection to the research topic and their proven utilization in supply chain literature, the eight theories presented above are considered for the research design of this dissertation. Figure 3.1 gives a graphic overview of the pre-selected theories. The following chapter will thoroughly examine the theories and their contribution to the research project through an adequate procedure.

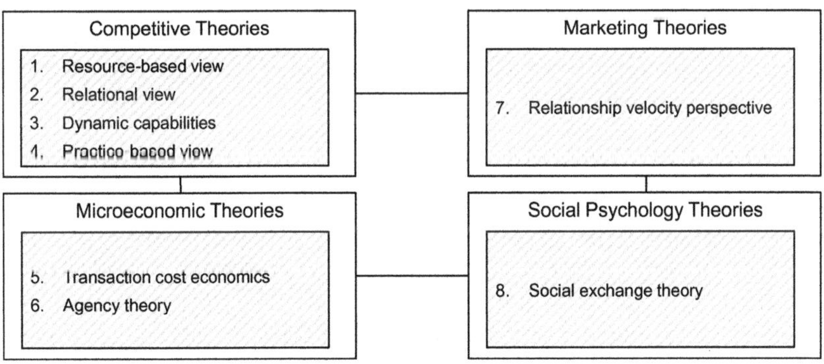

Figure 3.1 Pre-selected theories for the research design

3.1.2 Selection of Theories for the Research Questions

Theories support the research process on CMR management by explaining and predicting core aspects of the research problem through their constructs. Therefore, *context-specific criteria* for the theory selection can proceed from the state of knowledge presented in Chapter 2 and the research questions. These *context-specific criteria* are:

1. Potential to structure management needs of CMRs and systematize deployment options of management practices (RQ_1, RQ_2, RQ_4)
2. Insights into the dynamics of CMRs and their impact on management activities and decisions of the actors involved (RQ_3, RQ_4)
3. Acknowledgement of the potentially divergent perspective of brand-leading companies and CMOs in managing the CMR dyad (RQ_1, RQ_2, RQ_4)

Adding to the context-specific criteria of this dissertation, Stölzle (1999) names *general criteria* to guide the theory selection process:

- *Theoretical attractiveness:* The first criterion concerns the existence of a research paradigm and an orientation towards critical rationalism. The research paradigm relates to the explanatory power of a theory, its precision potential, and generalizability. The direction toward critical realism implies the explanatory contribution of a theory and its potential to generate hypotheses.
- *Design orientation:* From the content side, design orientation evaluates the inclusion of design variables, determinants, and efficiency criteria of a theory, which are crucial for operationalizing theoretical constructs. From the formal side, it considers informativeness, application potential, and empirical relevance and is thus significant for the transfer between theory and practice.
- *Integrative power:* The integrative power of a theory refers to its ability to synthesize different explanatory patterns through its learning, systematizing, and interfacing potential. The learning potential enables the expansion of explanatory patterns, while the potential for systematization results from the ability to structure theoretical constructs. Finally, the interface potential describes the ability to integrate theories.
- *Adaptability:* Adaptability relates to the applicability to the specific research context. The criterion is met if a theory satisfies one or more of the *context-specific criteria* and thus provides an explanatory approach to the research problem.

The integrative power of the theories examined is vital in this dissertation since it can be assumed that one theory alone cannot cover all *context-specific criteria*. Hence, not only the suitability of a single theory must be confirmed, but also its mutual compatibility. In the following, the pre-selected theories are evaluated against the seven criteria of the theory selection process. First, the *context-specific criteria* are examined.

Resource-based view: RBV explains how organizations can achieve competitive advantage through non-substitutable and imperfectly imitable resources (Barney, 1991). Despite the frequent application of RBV to strategic SCM issues, scholars point out its limited applicability to operations management because the competitive advantage is measured at the firm level and cannot be operationalized (Bromiley & Rau, 2016). Consequently, its applicability to management practices in dynamic CMRs is constrained. Moreover, RBV focuses on a firm's resource-based competitive advantage without making substantive claims about divergent perspectives. Consequently, RBV is discarded as it does not meet any context-specific dissertation criterion.

Relational view: RV argues that competitive advantage originates from relationship rents at the network level (Dyer & Singh, 1998). Through its dynamic refinement, the RV attempts to explain the relationship dynamics and interdependencies with the relationship environment and the capabilities and activities of the actors (Dyer, Singh, & Hesterly, 2018). As a limitation to RV, competitive advantage, similar to the RBV, is not measurable operationally. In addition, RV does not provide insights into the perspectives of the relationship partners. Nevertheless, because of its potential contribution to the second criterion, RV is further examined.

Dynamic capabilities: According to Teece et al. (1997), DC defines a firm's ability to transform internal and external competencies to achieve competitive advantages in dynamic environments. While the dynamic aspect is relevant to the research problem, it concerns an organization's capabilities and is not connected with activities or relationship dynamics. Furthermore, the orientation to competitive advantage makes statements on management practices difficult. Finally, DC centers around one investigated organization and does not recognize different actor perspectives. Overall, DC is not further examined in the following steps.

Practice-based view: Bromiley & Rau (2014) propose PBV to provide a practice orientation for strategy research. PBV is designed to show why firms apply specific practices and how practices contribute to a firm's performance under explanatory variables (Bromiley & Rau, 2016). However, PBV makes no statements on either relationship dynamics or partner asymmetries in business relationships. Consequently, since PBV might give insights into the first criterion, it is selected for further examination.

Transaction cost economics: Williamson (1979) extended TCE's application to governance issues of economic transactions. Since then, TCE has been interpreted as explicatory access to governance issues in many studies on supply chain collaboration (Stölzle, 1999). However, TCE does not recognize relationship dynamics (Cuypers, Hennart, Silverman, & Ertug, 2021). Still, TCE incorporates divergent perspectives of transaction stakeholders based on its basic assumptions of bounded rationality and opportunism (Grover & Malhotra, 2003; Hobbs, 1996). Consequently, TCE is considered a potential fit for this dissertation due to its contribution to the first and third criteria.

Agency theory: Jensen and Meckling (1976) introduce agency problems as relationships, where a principal needs to moderate conflicts of interest with an agent who performs tasks on the principal's behalf. AT is consulted to avoid adverse effects of information asymmetries in agency relationships (Eisenhardt, 1989). However, despite extensive analysis of divergent perspectives, AT suffers from limited operationalizability due to constrained assumptions about relationship management and actor behavior (Stölzle, 1999). Furthermore, AT acknowledges the influence of relationship dynamics on contract decisions and actor behavior but does not provide explanations (Fayezi et al., 2012). Nevertheless, based on potential insights into conflicts of interest in CMRs, AT is considered in the next phase of theory selection.

Relationship velocity perspective: Palmatier et al. (2013) reason that RVP builds on relationship constructs proven on human and organization levels and explains their behavior under the influence of different relationship dynamics. In this context, RVP links relationship dynamics to specific governance mechanisms considering a bilateral relationship view (Palmatier et al., 2013). Consequently, RVP might provide insight into the three context-specific criteria and is further examined.

Social exchange theory: SET builds on various social sciences to define organizational relationships as continuous *'exchanges of goods, material and non-material'* (Homans, 1958, p. 597). In an economic context, SET argues that outcomes of relationships need to meet the costs of relationship management and provide further benefits (Lambe et al., 2001). Exchanges in relationships follow one stakeholder's actions and the target's response, covering both perspectives of exchanges (Cropanzano, Anthony, Daniels, & Hall, 2017). Single beneficial exchanges set the basis for further exchanges creating a dynamic relationship based on trust and commitment (Cropanzano & Mitchell, 2005). Consequently,

SET might contribute to the *context-specific criteria* and is considered for the dissertation.

Table 3.1 Adaptability of pre-selected theories to the research problem

Theory	Potential to structure management needs and practices	Insights into the CMR dynamics	Recognition of divergent perspectives	Adaptability (Stölzle, 1999)
Resource-based view	No	No	No	Insufficient
Relational view	No	Yes	No	Sufficient
Dynamic capabilities	No	No	No	Insufficient
Practices-based view	Yes	No	No	Sufficient
Transaction cost economics	Yes	No	Yes	Sufficient
Agency theory	No	No	Yes	Sufficient
Relationship velocity perspective	Yes	Yes	Yes	Sufficient
Social exchange theory	Yes	Yes	Yes	Sufficient

Thus, according to the first stage of the theory selection process, only RV, PBV, TCE, AT, RVP, and SET meet the dissertation's *context-specific criteria* and remain for the second stage of the analysis. Table 3.1 illustrates the pre-selected theories' fit to the dissertation's context.

The analysis of the context-specific suitability of the theories aligns with Stölzle's (1999) criterion of adaptability. Finally, Table 3.2 presents the evaluation results using Stölzle's (1999) *general criteria, theoretical attractiveness, design orientation,* and *integrative power* for theory selection.

Consequently, as a result of theory selection, RVP and TCE are employed to form the theoretical foundation of the dissertation. As a single theory, both lenses meet the criteria established by Stölzle (1999) and collectively cover all the context-specific criteria of the research project: TCE allows the structurization of management needs and practices based on transaction efficiency. RVP connects

Table 3.2 Conclusive evaluation of the pre-selected theories

Theory	Theoretical attractiveness	Design orientation	Integrative power	Applicability
Relational view	Frequently used in SCM research (Wieland & Wallenburg, 2013), mainly in strategic relational contexts (Tescari & Brito, 2018)	Explains relationship success through the interplay of governing structures and relationship dynamics (Dyer et al., 2018); however, empirical support is not uncontested (Tescari & Brito, 2018)	Integrated with PBV (Carter, Kosmol, & Kaufmann, 2017), TCE (Johnson, Klassen, Leenders, & Awaysheh, 2007), and SET (Kembro, Selviaridis, & Näslund, 2014). Allows for integration with RVP (Palmatier et al., 2013)	**Medium**
	++	++	+++	
Practice-based view	Extended for application to the supply chain field (Carter et al., 2017; Shaw, Grant, & Mangan, 2021)	Proposes that management practices explain the success of CMRs (Bromiley & Rau, 2014). PBV validity is contested (Jarzabkowski, Kaplan, Seidl, & Whittington, 2016)	Previously integrated with RV (Carter et al., 2017)	**Low**
	+++	+	+	

(continued)

Table 3.2 (continued)

Theory	Theoretical attractiveness	Design orientation	Integrative power	Applicability
Transaction cost economics	One of the most influential theories in SCM research (Defee et al., 2010) and outsourcing (Busi & McIvor, 2008)	Contains variables to explain CMR governance choices based on transaction cost under the influence of bounded rationality of contract partners (Grover & Malhotra, 2003)	Frequently combined with AT (Kroes & Ghosh, 2010), RV (P. F. Johnson et al., 2007), SET (Khalid & Ali, 2017) and advocated to be integrated with RVP (Seggie, Griffith, & Jap, 2013)	**High**
	+++	+++	+++	
Agency theory	Widely used in SCM (Beal Partyka, 2021) and CMRs, respectively (Handley & Gray, 2013),	AT explains the role of CMO behavior in relationship performance (Handley & Gray, 2013). Difficult to operationalize due to the restrictive assumptions (Eisenhardt, 1989)	Frequently combined with TCE (Beal Partyka, 2021), SET (He, Yang, & He, 2018), and suggested for integration with RVP (Chmielewski-Raimondo, Shamsollahi, Bell, & Heide, 2022)	**Medium**
	+++	++	++	

(continued)

Table 3.2 (continued)

Theory	Theoretical attractiveness	Design orientation	Integrative power	Applicability
Relationship Velocity perspective	Applied to research on dynamic inter-firm buyer-supplier relationships (Kauffman & Pointer, 2021; Palmatier et al., 2013)	Captures CMR dynamics and makes claims about the time-dependent fit of practices. Considered promising approach to relationship dynamics despite early-stage of theory (Hussain, Jing, Junaid, Shi, & Baig, 2020)	Compatible with TCE (Chmielewski-Raimondo et al., 2022; Seggie et al., 2013) and AT (Chmielewski-Raimondo et al., 2022), previously integrated with SET (Kao, Pai, & Tsai, 2020). Connected to RV (Palmatier et al., 2013).	**High**
	+++	++	+++	
Social exchange theory	Used frequently in research on IOR management (Isidor et al., 2014; Khalid & Ali, 2017),	Provides explanations for CMR objectives, CMO behavior, and governance (Lambe et al., 2001). Operationalizability is under debate (Cropanzano et al., 2017)	Previously integrated with TCE (Young-Ybarra & Wiersema, 1999), AT (He et al., 2018), and RVP (Kao et al., 2020). Allows for integration with RV (Kembro et al., 2014)	**High**
	+++	++	+++	

management practices and relationship dynamics. Furthermore, TCE also covers divergent perspectives of client companies and CMOs.

Finally, both theoretical lenses are of great theoretical appeal concerning the governance of CMR and the dynamics of business relationships. TCE has proven strong design orientation and integrative power through a rich body of literature in related studies as a more mature theory. At the same time, RVP has attracted considerable interest as a novel lens capable of explaining and shaping dynamic relationships and has been proposed to complement the reasonably static TCE (Seggie et al., 2013). Despite its equally high suitability, RVP is preferred to SET because of its stronger dynamic orientation, which complements the weakness of TCE in this area.

As confirmed by the theory selection process, this dissertation will rely on more than one theoretical perspective. Consequently, this dissertation takes an eclectic approach, which means that different theoretical perspectives will be used to describe, explain, and synthesize the various phenomena of the dissertation (Friedli, 2006). An eclectic approach aims to achieve a more comprehensive perception of the research object and utilize multi-paradigm theoretical knowledge as effectively as possible (Friedli, 2006). Along with Walsham's (1995) perception of applying theory in the research process, TCE and RVP are deployed to build a theoretical explanatory framework that addresses the *context-specific criteria* of the dissertation. Section 3.2 outlines the research design and assigns the constructs of the theoretical framework to the research questions. TCE and RVP also guide the data collection process to integrate client companies' and CMO perspectives on management needs, practices, and dynamics in CMRs.

3.2 Research Design

According to Denscombe, a research design is a *'carefully constructed plan of action'* (2010, p. 3) to execute the research process. Likewise, Saunders, Lewis, and Thornhill (2020) emphasize that the research design draws on underlying beliefs and assumptions and lays the foundation for interpreting results and the methodological choice for data collection. Therefore, the author's research philosophy describing these underlying beliefs and assumptions should be disclosed to critically evaluate the research process and results. As shown in section 2.6, the management of CMRs as a dedicated research topic is only scarcely investigated. At the same time, there is substantive research on CMR management cases from the perspective of IORs.

Consequently, there is room for both inductive and deductive reasoning, for which an abductive approach is chosen for the dissertation (Saunders et al., 2020). Considering both the abductive logic and the aim to understand and guide practitioners' management of CMR as represented by the research questions derived in section 2.8, a pragmatic research philosophy fits the research design (Gregor, 2006). Kelly and Cordeiro state pragmatism centers around *'practical understandings of concrete real-world issues'* (2020, p. 1) instead of metaphysical debates about truth. A pragmatic research philosophy guides the research process emphasizing knowledge transfer between theory and practice through an adequate methodology (Kelly & Cordeiro, 2020). Concerning the complex reality of CMRs, a qualitative research approach is chosen in line with the pragmatic stance to analyze CMR management in practice and guide practitioners (Saunders et al., 2020).

The pragmatic research philosophy enables the systematic application of induction and deduction in the research design of the dissertation (Casula, Rangarajan, & Shields, 2020). The lack of dedicated research on managing CMRs calls for an exploratory empirical design covering the aspects of inductive reasoning (Busi & McIvor, 2008). In social science, exploratory research entails *'maximizing the discovery of generalizations leading to the description and understanding of an area'* (Stebbins, 2001, p. 3) and stays in sharp contrast to confirmatory research. Furthermore, the broad nature of the emerging results in exploratory research complements well with a qualitative research approach (Casula et al., 2020). The application of the exploratory research ideals through an appropriate methodology is presented in Section 3.4.

On the other hand, the management of IORs, where CMRs are frequently encountered as cases, is an extensively researched field that has produced rich findings over the past decades, which can serve as a framework for this research project (Walsham, 1995). Thus, the deductive thought process of the dissertation relies on the knowledge of the selected theoretical lenses, whose constructs are derived below to structure the research design (Saunders et al., 2020).

Transaction cost economics

TCE can be applied in research to explain companies' choices in managing interfirm business transactions (Häkkinen, 2008). In the context of CMRs, there is a continuous exchange of information, goods, and services, due to which long-term relationships are considered an ongoing series of transactions (Schmidt & Wagner, 2019). Therefore, the premise of TCE is to achieve efficiency by choosing appropriate forms of governance that minimize transaction costs (Bowen & Jones, 1986).

According to Rao, transaction costs are *'comparative costs of planning, adapting, and monitoring task completion under alternative governance structures'* (2003, p. 7), which include tangible costs from the execution of transactions and opportunity costs resulting from more advantageous governance structures. Häkkinen interprets them as the managerial costs of *'adaptation of organizational features, costs of operating an organizational entity, including information gathering and processing and alternative modes of resource deployment'* (2008, p. 47). Furthermore, TCE operates under the basic assumptions of bounded rationality and opportunism of the involved parties, which creates the need for control and safeguarding (Stölzle, 1999). In addition, TCE distinguishes between transaction costs that arise before (ex-ante) and after (ex-post) the signing of the contract (Stölzle, 1999). Even though ex-ante and ex-post transaction costs are interdependent, the research object is CMR management after signing the contract, which is why the ex-post transaction costs are the primary focus of this dissertation (Rao, 2003).

TCE recognizes two pure forms of governance to minimize transaction costs, hierarchy and market, with hybrid forms in between (Grover & Malhotra, 2003; Stölzle, 1999). Considering the two extremes, a trade-off must be made to find the ideal form of governance: While the hierarchy exchanges solid control for high bureaucratic costs, the market assumes low direct governance costs but high uncertainty due to loss of control (Bowen & Jones, 1986).

When applying TCE to CMRs, the three levels within a supply chain must be considered: Network, relationship, and actor. (Essig et al., 2013). At the network level, CM can be seen as hybrid transaction governance between vertical integration and the free market (Ketokivi & Mahoney, 2020). However, CMRs can be managed at the relationship level by either a hierarchy, hybrid, or market-based form of governance based on the degree of control asserted by one dyad partner (Grover & Malhotra, 2003, p. 460). The necessary degree of control a client company should enact on the CMR depends on the relationship's characteristics, which drive the exchange's transaction costs. Williamson (1979) identified asset specificity, transaction frequency, and uncertainty as the three decisive characteristics of transactions. Later scholars have further segmented uncertainty into environmental and behavioral uncertainty based on the possibility of partners influencing this characteristic (Schmidt & Wagner, 2019). Consequently, the four transaction characteristics can support this dissertation's investigation of the need for management practices in CMRs (RQ_2).

➢ The four transaction characteristics of *asset specificity*, *transaction frequency*, *environmental uncertainty*, and *behavioral uncertainty* are applied to the research project. A detailed elaboration is provided in sub-section 3.2.2

Based on the principal transaction characteristics, Rindfleisch and Heide (1997) introduce three TCE governance problems in dyads: Safeguarding, adaptation, and performance evaluation. Each governance problem is associated with different transaction characteristics and requires specific responses to balance transaction costs (Schmidt & Wagner, 2019). Solving the governance problems is the motivation for using management practices in CMRs. Therefore the presented constructs are the theoretical basis for analyzing the application of management practices in CMRs (RQ_1).

➢ The three governance problems of *safeguarding*, *adaptation*, and *performance evaluation* are applied to the research project. A detailed framing is provided in sub-section 3.2.1.

While TCE can provide valuable explanations for CMR management, its contribution has limitations that restrict its applicability to all identified research questions. For example, it has been remarked by multiple scholars that TCE overemphasizes costs as the driving factor of relationship management and neglects social aspects of the exchange (Dekker, 2004; Emerson, 1976). Thus, TCE fails the reciprocal interaction between partners, open collaboration, and the continuous development of the relationship (Marshall, McIvor, & Lamming, 2007; Meira et al., 2010). Lastly, the constructs of TCE do not explain the influence of relationship dynamics on the governance choices or outcome of inter-firm transactions (Cuypers et al., 2021). Therefore, TCE is supplemented in the research design through RVP to cover these shortcomings.

Relationship velocity perspective

RVP gives theoretical access to how companies should manage long-term business relationships and adapt governance over time (Palmatier et al., 2013). It draws on findings from various mature research fields, such as relationship marketing, SET, DC, and the RV, to provide a theory of relationship dynamics (Morgan & Hunt, 1994; Palmatier et al., 2013). RVP builds on the perception of relationships as a series of linked transactions based on one party's reaction to the other's action (Cropanzano & Mitchell, 2005). Consequently, the outcome or performance of a relationship is not determined at the outset but influenced by both the relationship formation and the development of actor interplay over time (Cropanzano et al., 2017; Lambe et al., 2001). This rationale has already demonstrated its viability in industrial relationships and strategic alliances and provides a promising framework for CMRs (Doz, 1996; Palmatier et al., 2013).

Because there is a cost to maintaining inter-firm relationships, successful relationships must ensure that each partner's returns exceed their investments into the relationship to create commitment (Cropanzano et al., 2017; Lambe et al., 2001). In addition, since the actions of a relationship partner influence expectations of success, the relationship must be actively stimulated on an ongoing basis through deliberate management (Palmatier et al., 2013). Thus, commitment is well established as an indicator of relationship stability and success in research on organizational behavior (Lambe et al., 2001; Morgan & Hunt, 1994). Commitment expresses a partner's perception to benefit from the relationship and, as a result, willingness to maintain the relationship (Morgan & Hunt, 1994, p. 23). RVP builds on the static construct of relationship commitment and offers a dynamic perspective by investigating the rate and direction of commitment changes under the influence of relationship dynamics (Palmatier et al., 2013). Palmatier et al. (2013) argue that the expectation of future benefits from the relationship has a more decisive influence on the decision to invest and engage in the relationship than the perception of the current usefulness of the connection.

This rationale has two consequences applied to CMR management: First, client companies are more likely to invest in the relationship and engage in more costly management practices when they deem the CMR to generate significant benefits in the future. Likewise, when the expectations of future success are low, they will likely cut back on investment and reduce engagement. Second, client companies must actively support CMOs' commitment to the relationship through deliberate management practices to avoid opportunism and create stable CMRs.

As a means to influence the commitment of a relationship partner, RVP proposes three drivers of commitment trust, communication capabilities, and investment capabilities (Palmatier et al., 2013). Since client companies need to address these drivers to enhance the CMO's commitment to the relationship for a successful long-term relationship, the commitment driver constructs are the foundation for answering RQ4.

➢ The three commitment drivers of *trust*, *communication capabilities*, and *investment capabilities* are used in the research project. A detailed explanation is provided in sub-section 3.2.4

The effectiveness of the introduced commitment drivers in RVP depends on the present relationship dynamics. RVP offers three perspectives on relationship dynamics that have different implications for the commitment drivers companies should address at specific points to strengthen relationship commitment: Relationship age, relationship stage, and industry turbulence (Palmatier et al., 2013). Relationship age and relationship stage assume that commitment in a relationship grows incrementally over time along a typical trajectory and, therefore, can be predicted to a certain extent (Palmatier et al., 2013). On the other hand, industry turbulence captures the volatility of the relationship environment and represents the hardly predictable dynamics the business partners face (Palmatier et al., 2013). These perspectives on relationship dynamics can contribute to the research project by structuring events based on which CMR management must adapt management practices proactively or reactively (RQ_3).

➢ The two types of relationship dynamic components of *relationship age and stage* and *industry turbulence* are applied in the research project. A detailed description of their use is provided in sub-section 3.2.3

Motivation for joint application of TCE and RVP

Similar to TCE, there are limitations to RVP that suggest it should be used in conjunction with another theory. Although it draws on established constructs, RVP is a comparatively young theory, and few empirical studies have been conducted to validate its findings (Palmatier et al., 2013). Scholars advocate integrating established grand theories with innovative theories to adapt them to the research field of SCM and provide a stronger theoretical foundation for the field (Spina, Caniato, Luzzini, & Ronchi, 2016). In this context, various studies have recently attempted and encouraged the complementary use of TCE and RVP ideas at the example of relationship velocity (Seggie et al., 2013), relationship commitment (Shahzad, Ali, Takala, Helo, & Zaefarian, 2018) and relationship dynamic components (Chmielewski-Raimondo et al., 2022).

Jointly TCE and RVP can overcome the dilemma of overemphasizing purely economic or social aspects in the governance of CMRs (Isidor et al., 2014). The combination of both theories echos the developments in practice where the focus of CMRs is shifting from cost optimization to collaboration (Denicolai et al., 2015). A joint application provides insights into management practice's costs and application, different possible relationship development paths and recognizes motivations and limits of engagement (Isidor et al., 2014, p. 14; Lambe et al., 2001).

Both theories exhibit compatibility of basic assumptions, as both TCE and RVP assume economically measurable self-interest as the motivation for their behavior in CMRs (Bowen & Jones, 1986; Hobbs, 1996). Referring back to the supply chain levels, the consistency of the goals of TCE and RVP also becomes apparent: At the relationship level, the RVP proposes investments in management practices to achieve the supplier commitment necessary for a stable CMR. TCE minimizes the residual transaction costs of the management practices required to complete a transaction with a specified degree of commitment at the actor level (Ketokivi & Mahoney, 2020).

Table 3.3 gives an overview of the relevant constructs of the applied theoretical lenses. The framing of the constructs to the specific research questions is provided in the following sub-sections.

Table 3.3 Applied theoretical constructs in the research design

Research question	Applied theory	Relevant constructs
RQ_1: How can management practices be used in CMRs to support the management of the relationship?	TCE	Governance problems
RQ_2: How can the need for management practices for individual CMRs be assessed?	TCE	Transaction characteristics
RQ_3: What relationship dynamics are relevant triggers for the adjustment of management practices in CMRs?	RVP	Relationship age and stage, industry turbulences
RQ_4: How can client companies adjust CMRs management practices to respond to changing management needs?	TCE & RVP	Commitment drivers

3.2.1 The Relationship between Management Practices and Governance Problems

Bromiley and Rau define a practice as a bundled set of activities performed for a specific aim (2014). Management practices originated to meet particular needs for organizing the execution of business processes (Aggarwal et al., 2011). These needs can encompass *'collecting information, deciding, and disseminating information to resolve conflicts and guide interdependent actions'* (Aggarwal et al., 2011, p. 707). Another aim of management practices in interorganizational contexts includes dividing rewards between parties (Bowen & Jones, 1986). Silva,

Fritz, and El-Garaihy (2022) broaden the purpose of practices and state they aim to achieve performance improvement Drawing on TCE performance in the management of CMRs can be understood as *'a function of the appropriate alignment of governance mechanism(s) with transaction characteristics given the mico and macro contexts'* (Cuypers et al., 2021, p. 128). The deployment of management practices generates transaction costs depending on the specific practice, making it essential for client companies to estimate the benefit of practices against specific governance problems (Schmidt & Wagner, 2019). However, the failure to use practices for governance is usually associated with more substantive costs (Argyres, Mahoney, & Nickerson, 2019).

Consequently, to answer $RQ_{1,}$ it is necessary to investigate the management practices used in CMRs and the government problems they address. As elaborated in the previous chapter, TCE distinguishes three main governance problems, *safeguarding*, *adaptation,* and *performance evaluation* which arise from the characteristics of the transaction.

Safeguarding

The safeguarding problem in CMRs arises from investment in relation-specific assets with limited value outside the relationship, binding the client company to the CMR due to the risk of sunk costs (Rindfleisch & Heide, 1997). Moreover, the difficulty of switching the CMO shifts the balance of power in the CMR and allows the CMO to exploit the situation through opportunistic behavior (Schmidt & Wagner, 2019). Opportunistic behavior may manifest in poor delivery or quality performance, the CMO's demand for various concessions, or the outright improper use of the assets in play (Rindfleisch & Heide, 1997; Stump & Heide, 1996). Therefore, a key to safeguarding is balancing power asymmetry by aligning the CMO's interests through incentives or risk-sharing practices with little direct control (Schmidt & Wagner, 2019). Another option is to meticulously control the behavior and performance output of CMOs through appropriate management practices (Rindfleisch & Heide, 1997). Consequently, management practices can address the safeguarding problem of CMRs if they either reward the CMO for appropriate behavior, penalize the CMO for opportunistic behavior, or track the CMO's behavior for proper action (Stump & Heide, 1996).

Adaptation

The adaptation problem in CMRs occurs when partners need to adapt their transactions due to volatility in the relationship environment, causing adjustment costs (Rindfleisch & Heide, 1997). Adjustment costs can originate from the need to redeploy capital, renegotiate contracts, change or modify products, equipment, or assets, or adapt processes, procedures, routines, and training (Argyres et al., 2019). Since the reassessment and adjustment of interfaces, assets, and activities are more time-consuming when there is a high degree of interdependence, adjustment problems are more costly in the case of asset specificity (Dyer et al., 2018; Rindfleisch & Heide, 1997). In the case of environmental disruptions, CMRs either adapt the relationship by paying adjustment costs or leave the ties unaltered and suffer maladaptation costs due to lost efficiency or effectiveness (Rindfleisch & Heide, 1997). However, the costs of adjustment and maladaptation can be mitigated by investing in transparency, such as sharing forecasts, or flexible structures, such as spreading operations across different geographic sites (Geyskens, Steenkamp, & Kumar, 2006; Schmidt & Wagner, 2019). Moreover, while the primary source of adaptation problems often lies in the CMR environment, practices such as increasing transparency can also be directed at the partner's internal organizations (Rindfleisch & Heide, 1997; Schmidt & Wagner, 2019). Thus, management practices can counter adaptation problems by reducing environmental uncertainty or contributing to flexible structures which allow cost-efficient adjustment.

Performance evaluation

Due to behavioral uncertainty, client companies face performance evaluation problems when managing CMRs (Rindfleisch & Heide, 1997). For example, under opportunism, CMOs can exploit an information asymmetry that stems from the client company's restricted transparency and possibly limited knowledge of the CMO's business model and internal processes (Schmidt & Wagner, 2019). In such a case it may be more advantageous for a CMO to reduce quality control in the manufacturing process because of the associated costs or prioritize resources for other customers' orders (Rindfleisch & Heide, 1997). Hence, client companies need to constantly evaluate the compliance of CMOs regarding agreed behavior and performance (Geyskens et al., 2006). A performance evaluation may be associated with increased transaction costs for monitoring but mitigates the risk of performance losses (Rindfleisch & Heide, 1997). Depending on CMR's subcontracted tasks, performance may not be measured easily. Thus, the management practices for performance evaluation may relate to the outcome of a transaction carried out by the CMO or to the CMO's behavior under specified guidelines (Stump & Heide, 1996).

In summary, management practices can contribute to the management of CMRs from the client company's perspective if they address the relationship's governance issues while considering the transaction costs they generate. Figure 3.2 visualizes the research design for RQ_1.

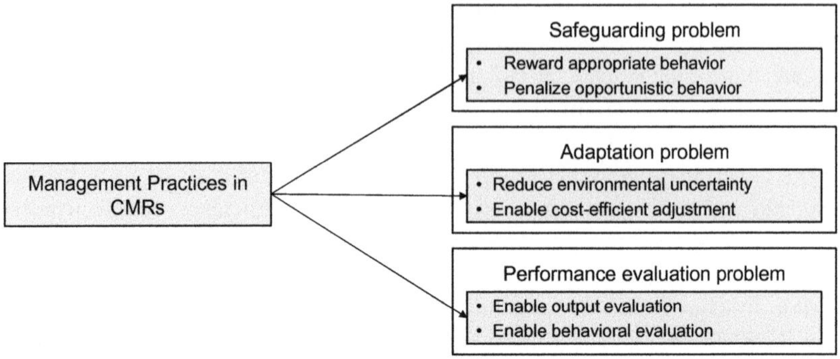

Figure 3.2 Research design for RQ_1

3.2.2 The Relationship between Management Practices and Transaction Characteristics

Since governance incurs transaction costs, the need and justification for specific management practices are rooted in the CMR's governance problems (Rindfleisch & Heide, 1997). According to Hobbs (1996), the specific transaction characteristics determine governance problems and choices when combined with the underlying assumptions of bounded rationality and opportunism. TCE names four transaction characteristics that influence the governance style of companies in interorganizational exchanges: asset-specific investments, environmental uncertainty, behavioral uncertainty, and transaction frequency and volume (Schmidt & Wagner, 2019).

Hence, according to TCE, a procedure needs to be established to analyze given CMR's transaction characteristics of *asset specificity*, *environmental uncertainty*, *behavioral uncertainty*, and *transaction frequency* to answer RQ_2. Therefore, a description and framing of the named constructs are provided below.

Asset specificity

Asset specificity describes the degree of non-transferable relation-specific investments in the CMR that raise significant exit barriers for the client company (Geyskens et al., 2006). As such, asset specificity drives the safeguarding problem of CMRs and affects the need for management practices to govern the relationship (Rindfleisch & Heide, 1997). For example, asset specificity might restrict organizational flexibility due to contractual and financial constraints on repositioning. Furthermore, it might drive performance-weakening organizational inertia (Argyres et al., 2019).

Scholars have identified multiple types of asset specificity in IORs, which drive the need for managing the safeguarding problem: Lohtia, Brooks, and Krapfe (1994) name investments in sites, human, physical, dedicated, brand name capital, and temporal assets: First, site-specificity aims at the geographic positioning of plants to leverage synergies. Second, physical asset specificity refers to investment made into relation-specific equipment to manufacture particular products. Third, human asset specificity describes dedicated training or hiring of personnel for the relationship. Fourth, dedicated asset specificity recognizes investments not entirely specific to the relationship but only profitable under the transaction's expected volumes (warehouse facilities or stock are examples). Fifth, brand name capital specificity relates to an investment where the CMO's misconduct can damage the OEM's brand name. Lastly, temporal asset specificity refers to investments into the time-critical delivery of the subcontracted activities, such as the ability to provide just-in-time deliveries in the automotive industry. In addition, the dimension of procedural asset specificity emerged in later years: Procedural asset specificity expresses the investment in standards, procedures, workflows, and routines that cannot be transferred to another CMR (Vita, Tekaya, & Wang, 2011). However, the impact of different asset specificity types on a specific CMR might differ. Analyzing the specificity of assets in a given CMR provides insight into the types of safeguarding problems and the management practices needed to control them. Therefore, asset specificity must be included in assessing the need for management practices.

Environmental uncertainty

Environmental uncertainty captures the volatility and ambiguity around the CMR, which continuously influences the change in management requirements, thus creating the adaptation problem (Rindfleisch & Heide, 1997). Schmidt and Wagner (2019) name the changes in supply, demand, technology, regulations, and economic shifts as sources of environmental uncertainty. Volatility can be understood as the *'unpredictable rate of change'* in supply and demand (Gregory, 2011, p. 73). It leads to volume uncertainty in CMRs. Volume uncertainty affects the ability and costs to forecast volume requirements such as finished products, raw materials, staff, warehousing, and capacities (Geyskens et al., 2006). As a result, client companies might face stock-outs or excess inventory due to significant volume uncertainty (Geyskens et al., 2006).

In contrast, CMOs must deal with demand spikes or excess capacity, requiring closely aligned communication structures and flexible capacity use. However, ambiguity includes a lack of specific information, proper assessment of data, uncertainty about interdependencies, and a lack of understanding of appropriate countermeasures (Gregory, 2011). Furthermore, ambiguity is less tangible than volatility, making it more costly to reduce uncertainty. In TCE, ambiguity is often expressed as technological uncertainty, referring to whether the client company's product or the CMO's technical capabilities will meet future consumer requirements (Geyskens et al., 2006). Technological uncertainty about future technology requirements can render transactions useless due to significantly different costs, leading to a setting where both parties might instead prefer lower exit barriers to closer integration (Gregory, 2011).

Consequently, environmental uncertainty influences the need to collect and analyze information and reveals the operational and strategic dynamics causing the adaptation problem (Rindfleisch & Heide, 1997). Thus, it offers a lens to evaluate CMRs for the need for specific management practices.

Behavioral uncertainty

Behavioral uncertainty offers an internal lens on uncertainty (complimentary to environmental uncertainty), fueled by the behavior of the involved CMR parties (Ketokivi & Mahoney, 2020). It expresses the degree of difficulty a company has in assessing a business partner's contractual compliance and performance, causing the performance evaluation problem (Rindfleisch & Heide, 1997). In this context, the two underlying assumptions of TCE: bounded rationality, which causes information asymmetry in CMR's governance, and opportunism, are the main catalysts for behavioral uncertainty (Ketokivi & Mahoney, 2020; Rindfleisch & Heide, 1997).

Given the information asymmetry, measuring compliance and performance becomes more complex, as results can be implicit and difficult to interpret for the client company due to knowledge gaps (Schmidt & Wagner, 2019). Furthermore, information asymmetry can be either explicit through limited access to production sites and processes, patented knowledge, or implicit through experience, and cultural and linguistic distance, making partner behavior more difficult to interpret and predict (Cuypers et al., 2021). As a result, information asymmetry in behavioral uncertainty drives the need for information gathering and interpretation practices (Rindfleisch & Heide, 1997).

The second perspective of behavioral uncertainty is the presence or latitude for opportunism. Cuypers et al. (2021) recognize that opportunism goes beyond mere self-interest, limiting objective judgment and including the intention to harm the business partner for personal gain. Appropriability is a vital indicator of the risk of opportunistic behavior in CMRs (Cuypers et al., 2021). Appropriability of knowledge is the degree to which intellectual property can be protected from leakage to other parties, which is essential in coopetitive CMRs (Cuypers et al., 2021; Han et al., 2012). Relating to asset specificity, the appropriability of specific assets, such as equipment, can be an indicator of estimating risk from opportunism. Consequently, opportunism requires behavioral control in CMRs, which drives the performance evaluation problem (Geyskens et al., 2006). Behavioral uncertainty supports the research process to RQ_2 since it provides indicators for management practices to gather and analyze information and control CMO behavior.

Transaction frequency

Transaction frequency follows the rationale that high volume and frequency transactions are more likely to amortize the overhead cost of internal production (Cuypers et al., 2021; Schmidt & Wagner, 2019). However, so far, transaction frequency could neither be linked to a governance problem of TCE nor shown to affect the governance of transactions (Gregory, 2011). Therefore, transaction frequency is not supported in the literature, and its effects on vertical integration have not been proven or disproven (Rindfleisch & Heide, 1997; Williamson, 1979).

Acknowledging that transaction frequency, in contrast to the other three transaction characteristics, is not an indicator of the need for management practices, Williamson's (1979) thoughts on it nevertheless reveal relevant aspects for managing CMRs. The deployment of management practice for governance is associated with transaction costs depending on the specific method and setting (Schmidt & Wagner, 2019). In TCE, the incurred transaction cost for governance is balanced with the opportunity costs for inadequate management. A high transaction volume and frequency allow the amortization of more costly management practices (Cuypers et al., 2021). Since transaction frequency does not describe the need for management practices but somewhat limits the justifiable costs of management, the author proposes its use as a mediating variable for the assignment of management practices.

A fictitious example illustrates the application of transaction frequency: A client company may finance a CMO abroad equipment for manufacturing a proprietary product. Since the client company does not fully utilize this equipment, the CMO may opportunistically use it for other customers' orders, promoting wear and tear on the equipment. The result is that delivery performance and quality to the OEM may be affected. However, measured by transaction volume and frequency, the brand-leading company is not willing to invest in a physical presence near the CMO to monitor the utilization of the equipment since the monitoring costs exceed any potential opportunity costs.

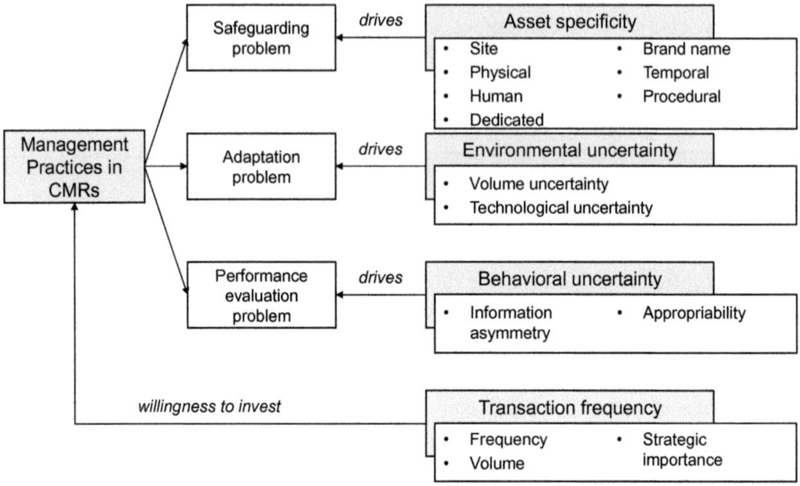

Figure 3.3 Research design for RQ_2

The implications of such novel use of transaction frequency might require an expansion of the volume and frequency aspects. The transaction characteristics of *asset specificity* and *environmental* and *behavioral uncertainty* provide insight into management practices. They might serve as indicators in a guided assessment. Complimentary *transaction frequency* can be used as a lens as to which degree companies are willing to invest in the respective management practices to design the most efficient form of governance in alignment with TCE. Figure 3.3 visualizes the application of the presented constructs in the research design for RQ_2.

3.2.3 The Relationship between Management Practices and Relationship Dynamics

Relationship dynamics pose a challenge for the management of CMRs since they change the transaction setting in which specific management practices are recommendable (Denicolai et al., 2015; Pernot & Roodhooft, 2014). Furthermore, CMRs are influenced by many discrete and continuous dynamic changes over time (Hussain et al., 2020). However, since changing the management approach is associated with adjustment costs (see Section 3.2.1), not every dynamic within the relationship and its environment will trigger management adjustment. Thus, from the management-centric perspective of this dissertation, it is essential to identify the relevant relationship dynamics that organizations recognize impact management and incorporate them into the solution design. RVP distinguishes three perspectives on relationship dynamics: relationship age, relationship stage, and industry turbulence, which offer a comprehensive theoretical view of relationship dynamics (Hussain et al., 2020).

Relationship age (RA) assumes that relationship dynamics affect relationships incrementally, implying that CMRs evolve continuously over time (Huang & Wilkinson, 2013; Hussain et al., 2020). A practical example is building trust through interpersonal exchanges, leading client companies to reduce active control of the CMR (Palmatier et al., 2013). Consequently, RA uses time as an indicator to estimate the development of a relationship. However, relying on time as a relationship development indicator, RA proposes that all CMRs develop at the same pace and reach the same level of commitment at a given point (Palmatier et al., 2013).

On the other hand, the relationship life cycle (RLC) classifies CMR by predesigned life-cycle stages that a relationship passes from initiation to dissolution (Doz, 1996; Huang & Wilkinson, 2013). While relationships within the same life cycle stage are subject to similar relationship dynamics, they differ significantly from those at other stages (Palmatier et al., 2013). For example, communication routines and mutual investments vary vastly across the early and mature stages of CMRs (Palmatier et al., 2013). Although this rationale acknowledges the varying pace of CMR development, a precise classification of CMRs into certain developmental stages of the relationship may prove challenging and ultimately not reflect reality (Palmatier et al., 2013).

Both perspectives agree that there exists an underlying and typical growth trajectory that is similar across relationships. Palmatier et al. name this the course by which a relationship *'matures'* (2013, p. 20), indicating a natural and inevitable dynamic. These relationship dynamics are inherent to a CMR and likely affect management decisions at variable times. However, adaptation due to the relationship age and stage dynamics is not always necessary, as maturation is generally perceived as positive because it can promote the stability and performance of the relationship without costly adjustment (Palmatier et al., 2013). Conversely, in a mature CMR, control practices could be scaled back to reduce transaction costs associated with governance for both parties.

The dynamics captured by relationship age and stage include incremental changes, such as building trust and routine, and discrete choices, such as contract renewals or investment decisions (Hussain et al., 2020). As a result, the outcomes of these dynamics are, to some extent, predictable for managers, allow active preparation, and are comparable to other CMRs, which allows for benchmarking. Consequently, the relationship age and stage perspectives allow the structuring of the dynamics into high-probability events that can be monitored to initiate appropriate management actions.

Complimentary to the structured relationship age and stage perspectives, RVP recognizes industry turbulence as an external source of dynamics affecting relationships (Palmatier et al., 2013). Industry turbulence covers the effects of dynamics, such as shocks to supply, demand, competition, or regulation in the market, causing potentially high adjustment costs (Argyres et al., 2019). In addition, shocks induced by industry turbulence are characterized by the rapid change they produce and the limited control and transparency companies have over their drivers (Argyres et al., 2019). While industry turbulence can create new opportunities to expand CMRs or reduce transaction costs, turbulence is mainly associated with harmful disruptions (Argyres et al., 2019). After an industry-induced shock, decision-makers are forced to reevaluate the CMR and decide whether to adjust the deployed management practices (Argyres et al., 2019). Since accurately predicting disruptions is costly, literature on supply chain risk management advocates classifying impact risks by relevance and developing responses for the most relevant scenarios of industry turbulence (Heckmann, Comes, & Nickel, 2015). Furthermore, client companies must establish procedures to react to shocks quickly, reassess the management practice fit and align with the CMO. Therefore, the industry turbulence perspective is appropriate for identifying dynamics that trigger management reassessment.

In summary, the perspectives of *relationship age and stage* on inherent dynamics of CMRs and *industry turbulence's* view on external influences and shocks provide a frame for analyzing the relevant dynamics in managing CMRs. Hence, they are applied in the research design for RQ_3, as depicted in Figure 3.4.

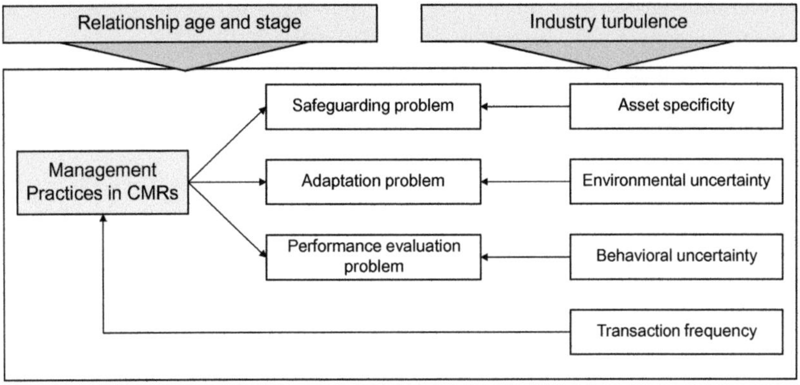

Figure 3.4 Research design for RQ_3

3.2.4 The Relationship between Contract Manufacturing Relationships and Commitment Drivers

To achieve efficient CMR governance, client companies need to fit their choice of management practices to the changing requirements of the relationship (Rindfleisch & Heide, 1997). However, since relationship dynamics also affect the CMO side of CMRs, client companies should be mindful that partners do not drift apart in their attempts for efficient relationship management (Morgan & Hunt, 1994). For example, a CMR might develop over time with the internal and external circumstances changing vastly compared to the beginning of the relationship (Palmatier et al., 2013). As a result, the strategic aims of the CMO might not be met anymore, which gives room for opportunistic behavior (Rindfleisch & Heide, 1997).

In this context, commitment is regarded as the essential social variable that promotes stability, longevity, and the generation of valuable outcomes of business relationships (Palmatier et al., 2013). That is because commitment expresses the will of both partners to sustain the relationship and reduce potential threats such as uncertainty and opportunism, leading to more productive relationships. (Morgan & Hunt, 1994). Conversely, the lacing or diminished commitment often shrinks relationships to more short-term-oriented transactions (Morgan & Hunt, 1994). In SCM, the stabilizing effect of commitment to supplier relationships is acknowledged and often actively fostered through specific future-oriented investments (Essig et al., 2013). These practices connect with the findings that commitment grows with relationship age and stages but needs to be assisted through supportive behavior and practices (Palmatier et al., 2013).

RVP distinguishes three approaches to drive commitment, investment capabilities, communication capabilities, and trust, to be addressed in relationship management (Palmatier et al., 2013).

Investment capabilities

Specific investments can increase commitment because they signal that a party will not leave the relationship in the near future and has a strong self-interest in a successful collaboration (Essig et al., 2013). However, it is more effective to replicate the investment effect over time by strengthening partners' capabilities, including CMOs, through joint financing, project support, or contract guarantees, than through one-time investments (Doz, 1996; Palmatier et al., 2013). Regarding TCE, strengthening investment capabilities relates to the governance problem of safeguarding, which increases with the number of specific investments. However, with increasing commitment, the risk of opportunistic behavior by the CMO can be lowered (Stump & Heide, 1996). Essig et al. point out that reciprocity is the decisive aspect of investing in SRM (2013). When both parties are involved in the investment or its benefits, neither partner is likely to mistrust the other over misuse of specific assets or the other partner's plans to reduce dependence. Therefore, investment capabilities address the safeguarding problem of TCE and drive commitment in RVP.

Communication capabilities

Communication capabilities are critical to creating commitment because they enable both parties to align and coordinate their efforts to optimize relationship management while reducing the relationship's risk of diverging interests (Palmatier et al., 2013). The availability of formal and informal information through communication makes the trajectory of a CMR more predictable for either partner, deters conflicts, risks, and uncertainties, and thus raises confidence in future relationship development (Shahzad et al., 2018). Among the commitment drivers, communication capabilities set the pace for developing commitment through continuous interaction as a practice with little self-obligation and serve as a mediator in turbulent times (Doz, 1996; Palmatier et al., 2013). In addition, communication capabilities can address the adaptation problem in CMR governance. Communication is the key to quick responses to changing requirements and efficient adjustment and coordination (Palmatier et al., 2013). Hence, communication capabilities are commitment drivers and practices that address the adaptation governance problem in CMRs.

Trust

The positive effect of trust on commitment in supply-side relationships is well documented (Doz, 1996; Lambe et al., 2001). In contrast to formal governance mechanisms, trust expresses the partners' belief that extraordinary efforts invested in a single transaction within a business relationship will be repaid over time across all transactions (Cropanzano & Mitchell, 2005). Consequently, trust is built based on previous successful transactions but can easily be destroyed by opportunistic behavior (Essig et al., 2013; Khalid & Ali, 2017). Trust functions as a catalyst because mistrust leads to even more mistrust, which weakens the commitment of both parties and fosters opportunistic behavior (Morgan & Hunt, 1994). Therefore, trust as a governance mechanism in supply chains is a double-edged sword, as it is fragile and requires reciprocity to be effective (Essig et al., 2013, p. 296; Lambe et al., 2001, p. 11).

Nevertheless, trust is regarded as a decisive variable for the long-term success of CMRs since it is the requirement for collaborative problem-solving outside of contractual obligations (Morgan & Hunt, 1994). Furthermore, trust decreases transaction costs because it enables quicker negotiation and decision-making and reduces conflict, formal safeguards, opportunistic behavior, and behavioral uncertainty (Dyer & Singh, 1998; Shahzad et al., 2018). Thus, it can be concluded that trust addresses the governance problems of TCE and is a driver of commitment to the CMR.

Application of commitment drivers through management practices

The previous paragraphs show that the commitment drivers of business relationships are among the countermeasures against the governance problems in CMRs. Transparent decision-making and mutual benefit of activities are suggested as an indicator for management practices that drive commitment across the three drivers. However, without reciprocity of investments, communication and trust relationship stability is expected to soar. Therefore, these management practices and their impact on TCE governance problems and commitment must be considered when managing CMR under dynamically changing requirements. Furthermore, the different commitment drivers interact differently with the two types of relationship dynamics and directly influence the deployment of the related management practices (Palmatier et al., 2013). For example, while communication and trust show similar effects, investments' substantial obligations and future orientation become more potent as relationships mature. Consequently, the management practices that offer the traits of commitment drivers should be deployed at different maturity levels of the relationship and in case of industry turbulence.

Thus, the research design for RQ_4 utilizes the *commitment drivers* of *investment capabilities, communication capabilities,* and *trust* to connect management needs and practices with relationship dynamics to develop a comprehensive management approach to dynamic CMRs. Figure 3.5 visualizes the applied constructs in the research design.

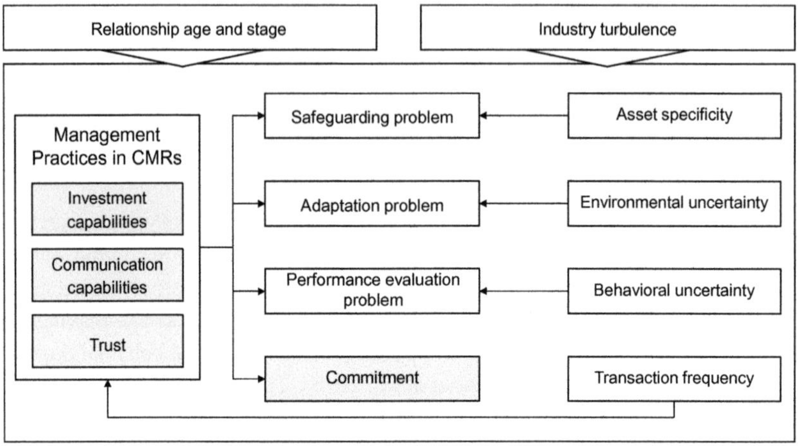

Figure 3.5 Research design for RQ_4

3.3 Research Framework

The developed research designs for the RQ_1 to RQ_4 elaborated in the sections above represent the theoretical perspective on the research problem of the dissertation project. However, the theoretical perspective accounts for only a fraction of the overall research topic. Therefore, this chapter introduces a comprehensive research framework to integrate the theoretical and practical perspectives on the research setting. The framework links the relevant influences from the managerial relevance in Chapters 1 and 2 with the applied theories and constructs from this section.

The applied theories of TCE and RVP form an eclectic approach because a single-theory approach is considered insufficient to answer the research questions holistically. TCE serves as a theoretical frame to explain the behavior and aims of client companies and CMOs in CMRs, which management practices address. RVP compliments TCE by explaining the forms and effects of relationship dynamics on behavior and the aims of the related parties from social perspectives. Thus, the RVP provides insights into the CMR's triggers and direction for changing deployed management practices.

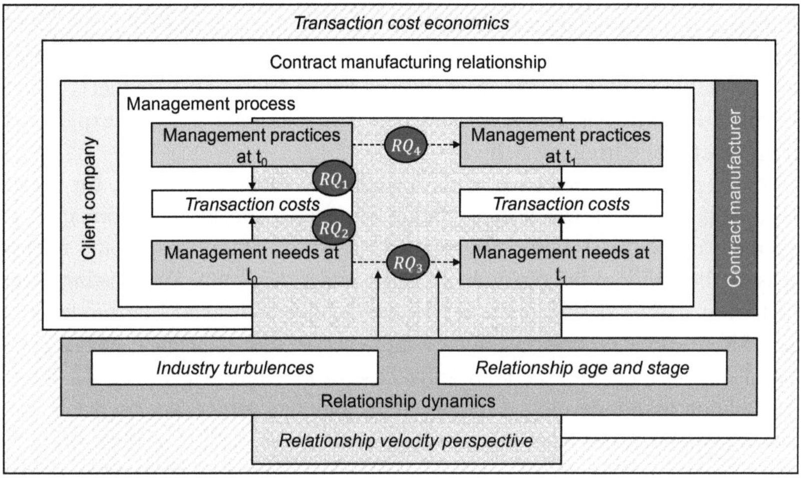

Figure 3.6 Research framework of the dissertation

The research framework also covers the perspective, unit of analysis, and unit of observation of the dissertation project graphically: The dissertation takes the client company's perspective. The unit of analysis encompasses relationship management of CMRs, particularly the management practices and their selection. Lastly, CMRs across different industries are examined as the unit of observation. In the research framework shown, the research questions are mapped to the elements of the research topic to which they relate. Figure 3.6 visualizes the research framework. The solid arrows represent impact effects, while the dashed arrows represent change over time.

3.4 Methodology

This chapter lays out the chosen methodology to structure data collection and analysis to answer the research questions according to the presented research framework. Following the considerations from Section 3.2, the research methodology needs to fit a pragmatic philosophy and support a qualitative approach for exploratory research. Thus, the *design science research* (DSR) methodology is applied in the dissertation.

Introduction to Design Science Research

DSR takes its place in business research as a design-oriented methodology, which allows for *'evidence-based'* improvement of business practices (Winter & Aier, 2016, p. 478). In addition, as a participatory methodology, DSR connects with a pragmatic research philosophy (Saunders et al., 2020) and fits with exploratory research settings (Briggs & Schwabe, 2011).

DSR's paramount objective is the creation of valuable artifacts, for which purpose its design allows the integration of various streams of information to generate knowledge (Hevner, March, Park, & Ram, 2004). Despite the intense focus on the utility of the research outcomes rather than truth, DSR distinguishes itself from routine design processes by the duality of results: The products of the DSR research process encompass artifacts for use in practice and generation of new insights into the knowledge base of literature (Hevner et al., 2004). The solution design developed through DSR may be context-specific but is centered around an artifact that is transferable and can be applied to other problem contexts (Papas, O'Keefe, & Seltsikas, 2012). For example, collaborative design science research with practitioners may create an IT system for a specific context. However, the artifact is not the operating system but the innovative and validated models and procedures, which are transferable to other contexts. Consequently, artifacts of DSR are rarely fully grown systems but designs (Hevner et al., 2004). March and Smith (1995) distinguish between four types of artifacts:

- *Constructs*: Constructs are formalized language and knowledge to identify and describe elements of the problem or solution.
- *Models*: Models are sets of constructs with specified relationships among each other that can represent design problems and solutions.
- *Methods*: Methods enable the operationalization of models through a defined series of steps (e.g., an algorithm) based on the underlying constructs.
- *Instantiations*: Instantiations operationalize constructs, models, and methods in the application environment. They can be fully functional or used for testing purposes in the development cycle.

The application of DSR to create the described types of artifacts follows an iterative cycle that utilizes feedback for further improvement of the solution design

(Winter & Aier, 2016). In addition to the design cycle, the iterative process contains two other elements: an inductive relevance cycle and a deductive rigor cycle. DSR can incorporate abductive logic and various streams of knowledge through these three interdependent cycles. Hevner (2007) elaborates on the three cycles as follows:

- *Design cycle:* The design cycle substantiates the core of the DSR process, bringing together the knowledge from the relevance and rigor cycles to construct, test, evaluate and refine the projected artifacts. Since the design cycle assembles the research process's output, it sets the pace of the research process. Hence, it controls the number of iterations of each cycle in the research project until the designed artifact fits both the relevance and rigor requirements.
- *Relevance cycle:* The relevance cycle embeds the research project in its application domain and users of the projected artifacts. The main objective of DSR is to address problems in the application domain through valuable artifacts. Therefore, the relevance cycle identifies the relevant issues and seeks validation from practitioners throughout the artifact development.
- *Rigor cycle:* The rigor cycle distinguishes the DSR process from routine design projects. It considers the existing knowledge base inputs to drive and shape the DSR process to deliver theoretical grounding. Consequently, it positions the designed artifact in literature to ensure academic rigor and scientific contribution to the knowledge base.

The three-cycle design of DSR can be considered a strength of the methodology since it allows a mixed-methods approach across the iterations of the design, relevance, and rigor cycles (Winter & Aier, 2016). First, the inductive reasoning of the relevance cycle can be facilitated by qualitative methods such as case studies, semi-structured interviews or focus groups, and quantitative methods, including surveys and experiments. Next, a literature review on the knowledge base enables analysis and framing of the first results and provides frameworks for artifact development in the design cycle. Finally, depending on the research question and preliminary results, the DSR process can draw on each cycle multiple times before producing a rigorous and relevant artifact. Figure 3.7 visualizes the DSR three-cycle framework.

Van Aken and Romme point out that the close collaboration with practitioners in the relevance cycle involves the researcher in the research process from a *'participant observer perspective'* (2012, p. 45).

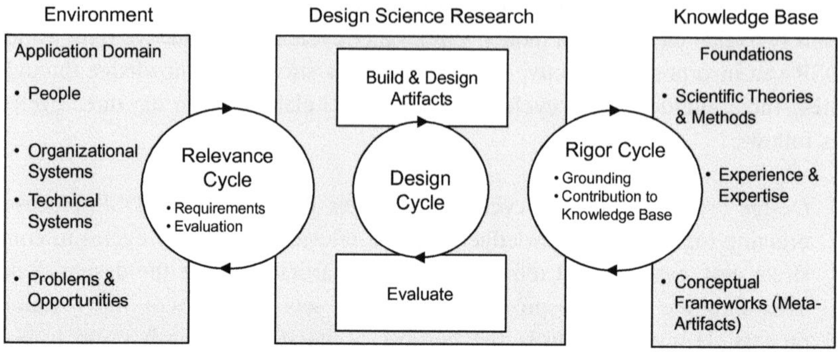

Figure 3.7 The design science research approach[1]

However, besides the advantages mentioned above, the central position of the researcher in DSR is accompanied by limitations. In contrast to the relevance and rigor cycles backed by established research methods, the design cycle is primarily based on the intuition and experience of the researcher, which can produce bias (Hevner et al., 2004). The dissertation project recognizes and addresses these limitations in its application of DSR through comprehensive artifact evaluation.

Utilization of the methodology in this dissertation project

DSR was applied as an umbrella for this research project's overarching research process and artifact design. First, the problem statement of the dissertation was shaped through semi-structured data from exploratory interviews, practice reports, and grey literature in the relevance cycle. During this phase, the primary problem of the management of CMRs was segmented into sub-problems, namely the use of *management practices*, the *assessment of management needs*, and the *adaptability of management*. Secondly, a first iteration of the rigor cycle compared the sub-problems with the existing knowledge base through a systematic literature review described in Section 2.1 to identify research gaps. Finally, it resulted in research questions presented in Section 2.8., which were screened against suitable theoretic lenses in Section 3.1.

From this point forward, dedicated iterations were conducted to address each research question's need for information separately. In this second phase, semi-structured interviews were conducted in the relevance cycle to gather data on specific practices and challenges of CMRs. Complementary, exploratory literature

[1] Adapted from Hevner (2007, p. 88)

reviews accessed the broad knowledge base of managing IORs in subsequent rigor cycles to build the artifacts on a sound theoretical grounding. Finally, the developed artifacts were evaluated through expert focus groups to assess their validity and improve their design.

The empirical design of the DSR cycles, including the order and conducted iterations, is laid out in Chapter 4. The applied methods for data collection and analysis are outlined in the following paragraphs.

Data collection and analysis

DSR structures the research process and integrates various sources of information as a '*multimethodological approach*' (Prat, Comyn-Wattiau, & Akoka, 2015, p. 230) but lacks specific methods for evaluating the artifacts, data collection, and analysis. Data evaluation, in particular, needs methodological enforcement in DSR research, according to Winter (2008). Therefore, following Venable, Pries-Heje, and Baskerville's (2016) recommendations, formative and summative evaluations were part of the research process. Venable et al. (2016) further distinguish between natural and artificial evaluation, of which the latter is incorporated into the dissertation. In this case, the review followed a '*Technical Risk & Efficacy Strategy*' (Venable et al., 2016, p. 82) due to the difficulty of testing the artifacts in the application domain. The formative evaluation took place through continuous exchanges with practitioners, followed by a summative evaluation at the end of the research process.

Data triangulation was ensured by employing a multi-method approach in artifact evaluation and data collection, sampling interviewed experts across industries, including client companies and CMOs, and analyzing academic and practice-related literature. Miles and Huberman's (1994) approach to data analysis guided data processing to increase validity by systematically reducing, classifying, and interpreting the collected data. Integration of data from different sources was facilitated by a two-layered approach to data analysis, according to Gioia, Corley, & Hamilton (2013). The procedure included a first-order analysis built on informant-centric (e.g., company and industry-specific) labeling. It was followed up by a second-order analysis based on consistent labeling with the research design. The developed research designs (see Sections 3.2.1 to 3.2.4) served as frameworks for data display. In sync with the iterative character of qualitative analysis proposed by Mayring (2010), the process steps were re-evaluated based on practitioner feedback and dissent between statements, consequently systematically reducing bias.

Following these premises, the applied formal research methods across the three cycles of DSR were *semi-structured interviews*, *focus groups*, and *literature reviews.*

- *Semi-structured interviews* are the most prevalent method for data collection in qualitative research, allowing for in-depth insights from the interviewee's perspective (King, 2004). This feature is beneficial in the context of CMRs because their management covers social aspects and possibly conflicting parties' interests. Saunders, Lewis & Thornhill (2007) suggest using semi-structured interviews in exploratory research settings since the researcher is free to deviate from prepared questions and themes to explore new aspects of the topic if they arise from the conversation. However, flexibility may come at the cost of rigor since openness requires dedicated efforts to ensure the completeness of covered topics and the limitation of subjective interpretation in data analysis. Adams (2010) furthermore emphasizes the need for time management in semi-structured interviews. These aspects were addressed by following the recommendations of Adams (2010), Saunders et al. (2007), and King (2004). The application of semi-structured interviews took place in the relevance cycle to generate qualitative data on the management of CMRs.
- *Focus groups* find their use in data collection for exploratory research settings and formative and summative evaluation strategies (Krueger & Casey, 2010; Morgan, 1996). For example, in DSR, exploratory focus groups can be applied in the relevance cycle to evaluate and refine the artifacts (Tremblay, Hevner, & Berndt, 2010). Concerning CMR management, focus groups are recommendable since they allow interaction between participants, highlighting different opinions and motivations of client companies and CMOs (Morgan, 1996). However, due to the interaction between participants, focus groups require appropriate, unbiased moderation not to marginalize standpoints or diverge from the topic (Krueger & Casey, 2010). In addition, since several people are interviewed simultaneously in focus groups, sufficient time must be allowed. Regular focus groups last around two hours (Tremblay et al., 2010). The ideal group size and composition vary between research topics, but a number between five and ten is generally recommended (Krueger & Casey, 2010). Furthermore, group composition can impact the willingness of participants to talk about particular topics openly (Morgan, 1996). Due to its challenging implementation, focus groups are frequently combined with other research methods for a rigorous approach (Tremblay et al., 2010). The potentially heterogeneous data gathered in a focus group requires a thorough group-level analysis to avoid missing individual dissents (Onwuegbuzie, Dickinson,

Leech, & Zoran, 2009). To this aim, Onwuegbuzie et al. (2009) provide frameworks for consensus analysis and sub-group responses to track dissent, e.g., between client companies and CMOs. In addition, the guidelines of Morgan (1996) and Krueger and Casey (2010) for using focus groups were followed. This dissertation applied focus groups in the relevance cycle to evaluate the designed artifacts formatively and summatively. All focus groups were conducted with the same group of client companies and CMOs to build a shared understanding of the issue before evaluating the artifacts.

- *Literature reviews* are part of most research projects to assess the knowledge base and identify gaps for potential contribution by designing innovative artifacts (vom Brocke et al., 2015). Complimentary to the conducted systematic literature review, described in Section 2.1, narrative literature reviews were performed in the rigor cycles. However, narrative literature reviews do not follow scientific quality criteria for finding evidence (Collins & Fauser, 2005). Therefore, their application for identifying research gaps and answering research questions on their own is limited (vom Brocke et al., 2015). Instead, narrative literature reviews are conducted in management research to provide a *'comprehensive narrative synthesis of previously published information'* (Juntunen & Lehenkari, 2021, p. 330). In this capacity, they were employed in a complementary manner to flexibly consult the knowledge base in response to issues in the design phase or to deepen empirically obtained data.

Empirical Findings on the Management of Contract Manufacturing Relationships

4

Empirical research is *'the systematic process of deriving and analyzing data from direct or indirect observation'* (Roth, 2007, p. 354). Hence, this chapter presents the approach to data collection and the empirical findings. The data collection process is embedded into the DSR methodology and the methods elaborated in Section 3.4, building on iterative relevance and rigor cycles that provide a foundation for artifact design. Figure 4.1 illustrates the approach. The following empirical design presents the data sample, collection procedure, and preparation before sharing the empirical findings of RQ_1 to RQ_4. Lastly, further exploratory insights beyond the defined research question are summarized in Section 4.6.

4.1 Empirical Design

The empirical design structures the data collection process, which can be divided into the sample, the observation procedure, and data preparation. The author's approach to data collection is elaborated in the following paragraphs.

Sample

Seawright and Gerring (2008) emphasize the necessity for systematically sampling cases to avoid bias in empirical results. The literature recognizes various case selection strategies that fit different research strategies (Gerring, 2017). A diverse sample was sought in alignment with the explorative nature of the dissertation (Seawright & Gerring, 2008). The sampling strategy was composed of

---

Supplementary Information The online version contains supplementary material available at https://doi.org/10.1007/978-3-658-41359-0_4.

T. Brandl, *Managing Contract Manufacturing Relationships*, Supply Chain Management, https://doi.org/10.1007/978-3-658-41359-0_4

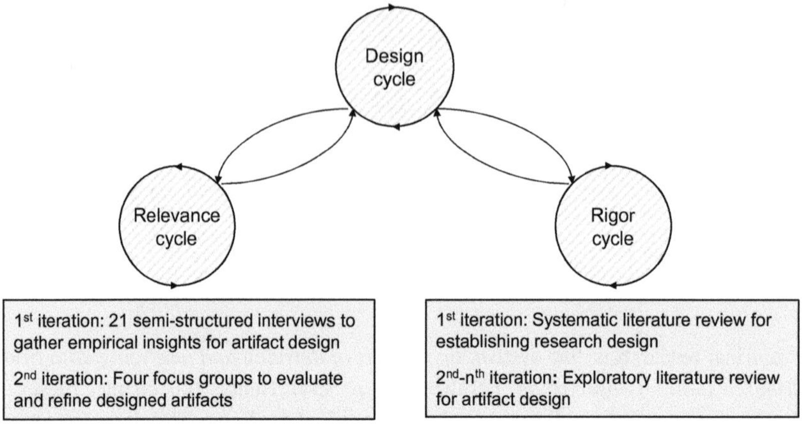

Figure 4.1 DSR-based iterative process for empirical data collection[1]

a two-step approach following the recommendations by Saunders et al. (2007). First, due to the perceived impact of industry regulation and product characteristics on the management of CMRs, which emerged from informal conversations with practitioners, various industries were targeted purposively. However, the sensitivity of CM made companies reluctant to participate in the interviews. Therefore, in a second step within the industry, self-selection and snowball strategies were applied in the sampling process in a complimentary manner. Out of 50 addressed companies, 21 companies across four industry sectors were open to interviews. This resulted in an illustrative and exploratory sample concerning the industry, product characteristics, and company size without claiming completeness. The explorative interviews were conducted in three content phases, each with customized interview guides.

Phase I served to identify appropriate artifacts to contribute to the practical relevance and the research gaps concerning *management practices*, the *assessment of management needs*, and the *adaptability of management*.

Phase II focused on incorporating the CMOs' perspective in refining the previously identified artifact requirements and preparing for the exploratory focus groups by capturing the positions of participating companies.

[1] Loosely based on Hevner (2007, p. 88).

Phase III was dedicated to developing and refining the prepared artifacts based on the theoretical research design, including insights and requirements across various industries.

The prominent empirical share of the pharmaceutical industry in interview phases I and II is firstly based on the research interest due to the high maturity of CM in pharma. Secondly, it reflects the willingness to discuss the research topic and advance it through participation by sharing and recommending contacts and participating in focus groups. As outlined in Section 1.1, the pharmaceutical sector is one of the primary industries to employ contract manufacturers. High regulatory requirements, knowledge-intensive processes, increased investment risk, and significant market dynamics characterize the management of pharmaceutical CMR and render it an illustrative example of the development of CMRs (Zhang et al., 2013). Consequently, the pharmaceutical industry represents high requirements for CMR management and is a suitable case to explore the management challenges as a foundation for artifact development. Table 4.1 depicts the empirical sample including the associated research phases.

Table 4.1 Overview of conducted semi-structured interviews

Phase	No.	Industry	Perspective	Company representative
I	1	Pharma	Client	Head of Global Supply Chain Head of Contract Manufacturing Head of International Procurement
I	2	Pharma	CMO	Global Head IT & Procurement
I	3	Pharma	Client	Head of Technical Operations
I	4	Pharma	Client	Head of External Manufacturing Platform
I	5	Pharma	Client	Head Direct Procurement Technical Operations
I	6	Pharma	Client	Head of Global External Manufacturing
II	7	Pharma	CMO	Chief Executive Officer
II	8	Pharma	Client	Head Technical Operations & Quality
II	9	Pharma	Client	Head Global Alliance Management
II	10	Pharma	Client	Vice President External Manufacturing
II	11	Pharma	CMO	Senior Vice President KAM / SCM / Marketing

(continued)

Table 4.1 (continued)

Phase	No.	Industry	Perspective	Company representative
II	12	Pharma	CMO	Chief Executive Officer
III	13	Pharma	Client	Director Supply Chain Optimization
III	14	Food	Client / CMO	Head of Procurement / Contract Manufacturing
III	15	Engineering	Client	Chief Purchasing Officer
III	16	Food	Client / CMO	Team Leader Purchasing
III	17	Food	Client / CMO	Head of Supply Chain Management Europe
III	18	Clothing	Client	Manager Sourcing Strategy & Projects
III	19	Engineering	Client	Head of Supply Chain
III	20	Food	Client / CMO	Director of Co-Manufacturing
III	21	Pharma	Client	Head of Contract Manufacturing Digitalization

In the case of the focus groups, the method was applied four times throughout the research process with recurring participants. The composition of the focus groups encompassed four client companies and three CMOs, from the pharmaceutical industry, which allowed for a bilateral evaluation of relationship dynamics and the impact of management practices on commitment (see Section 3.2.4). In addition, one client company and CMO within the focus group were engaged in a CMR with each other. All seven participating companies had been interviewed before during interview phase I or II. This approach allowed the focus group participants to get familiar with the topic beforehand. In addition, the participant companies were allowed to bring one additional senior staff member to ensure all participating companies' presence throughout the focus groups. Furthermore, companies that could not attend individual meetings despite this arrangement gave their feedback in bilateral discussions. Table 4.2 provides an overview of the focus groups conducted.

Hence, the participants were familiar with the topic, covered the perspective of both partners, and represented an industry with high demands on CMR management and, thus, qualified for rich feedback. Furthermore, following the recommendations of Tremblay et al. (2010), a senior researcher was present during the focus groups to monitor and mitigate moderation bias by the author. Additionally, consistent with Gibson and Arnott (2007), an assistant joined as a second observer to take notes of participant responses and reactions.

Table 4.2 Conducted focus groups

No.	Date	Participants		Duration	Form	Focus topic
		Client	CMO			
1	April 2022	4	3	Two hours	Videocall	CMR management practices
2	June 2022	4	3	Four hours	Workshop in person	CMR management assessment
3	July 2022	4	2	Two hours	Videocall	CMR relationship dynamics
4	August 2022	2	2	Three hours	Workshop in person	Integrated CMR management

Procedure

Following Lillis's (1999) suggestions, the semi-structured interviews were prepared and conducted using a structured interview guide. Each research phase's interviews were supported by corresponding interview guides, which were thematically aligned with the research objectives and sent to the interviewees in advance for preparation. The interviews were conducted through video calls online, using a complete auto transcription, extensive personal notes taken by the interviewer, and a complete image and sound recording. Depending on the flow of the conversation, the order of the questions deviated from the interview guide, and subsequent questions were asked to allow interviewees to give detailed insights without interruption. Furthermore, the interview guide was continuously refined based on the participant's feedback and explorative objectives (King, 2004). In addition, two focus groups took place through video calls, while two were conducted in person in St. Gallen. The evaluative focus groups addressed the qualitative criteria for DSR artifacts proposed by Sonnenberg and vom Brocke (2012). Copies of the interview guides are attached in the ESM. Two digital focus groups lasted two hours, and the in-person workshops encompassed four and three hours (including breaks).

Preparation

The interview recordings and auto-transcripts were evaluated and compared to the personal notes to create a joint database in preparation for analysis. The data was then visualized descriptively through the developed research designs (see Sections 3.2.1 to 3.2.4) to avoid personal bias before interpretation. In addition, visualization was used to identify missing data and unclear terminology in the responses, which required deeper understanding through further consultation of practice or the knowledge base. Finally, consistent with Gioia et al. (2013), the data visualization allowed different perspectives (e.g., industry-specific). The following sections contain empirical insights into the research questions from the prepared data. The artifacts developed from the prepared data to answer the research questions are presented in Chapter 5.

4.2 Empirical Findings on Management Practices

This chapter presents empirical insights into client companies' management practices in CMRs from which requirements for designing the DSR artifacts emerge. In essence, the results convey two kinds of information necessary for developing a management toolbox archetype in Section 5.1: First, the types of activities and methods used, and second, the objective the observed practices aim to achieve. In addition, including CMO perspectives in the interviews and focus groups allowed for a critical evaluation of the reception of client companies' practices by their business partners.

Overview of management practices applied in CMRs

Figure 4.2 gives an overview of the assessed CMR management practices using the research design developed in Section 3.2.1. The empirical design captured thirty management practices following the understanding given in Section 2.2. Within the identified practices, however, there are sometimes divergent forms of application so that the recognized practices can be understood as an overarching term for variants contained therein. Still, given CMR's dynamic growth and diversity, the use of additional practices not captured in this dissertation is likely. Furthermore, management practices have a lifecycle themselves. For example, an interviewee from the food industry stated that *the third man* practice is becoming more popular while *co-investments* and *locked recipes* are declining.

At first glance, it is evident that CM draws inspiration from IOR management, as elaborated in Section 2.6. Many practices, such as *key performance indicators (KPIs)* or *business reviews,* are standard across IORs and can be considered universal. For example, the influence of SRM on CMR management can be seen through the application of *purchase guarantees* and supplier development through dedicated *qualification programs.* Furthermore, the key account

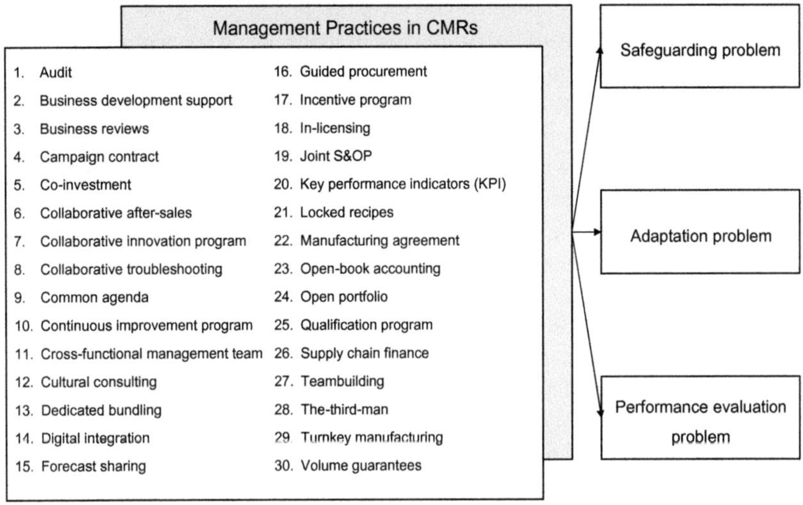

Figure 4.2 Empirical insights into CMR management practices

management concept, originally from CRM, is also widely spread in the form of cross-functional management teams led by an account manager, often referred to as a *'virtual plant manager.'* Finally, *co-investment, cultural consulting,* and *common agendas* highlight the evolving strategic nature of CMRs as, similar to SAs and JVs, increasingly investment-intensive, long-term, and highly integrated collaborations emerge. The influx of commitment-oriented management can be seen as safeguards becoming increasingly intangible. For example, with growing co-dependency CMRs rely on proofs of trust through access to sensitive data such as partner portfolios, product portfolios, and IT systems, replacing explicit rewards or sanctions.

Moreover, intraorganizational management practices from operations management are adapted for collaborative use across companies in CMRs. For example, *continuous improvement programs* encompassing lean, six sigma, and operational excellence principles with robust dissemination in internal manufacturing are opened to CMOs for knowledge transfer or extended to their manufacturing sites. Another example is *joint sales & operations planning (S&OP).* The client's and CMO's S&OP are limited in a CMR since the client only oversees sales, and the CMO only conducts operations planning. Therefore, both parties must coordinate on value chain planning, from sharing forecasts to integrated S&OP with joint resource planning. Finally, several identified practices have no apparent connection to existing fields of literature. For example, *the third man* is a decision support and legitimization practice in the food industry, involving a neutral third party for pricing, quality, and investment decisions to safeguard goodwill in the CMR. *Locked recipes* to protect unpatented recipes from analysis and *dedicated bundling* to ensure CMO margins are other specific CMR management practices. A more detailed description of the individual management practices and their application in CMRs is given as part of the artifact design and presentation in Section 5.1. The first empirical insight, therefore, is that CMRs share management practices with other relationship types, as hypothesized. Moreover, CMRs develop their concept-specific practices or adapt methods primarily used in vertically integrated manufacturing for cross-company applications. Consequently, a detailed description of the identified management practices in CMRs is required for a transparent *'management practice toolbox'* artifact.

The dissemination of the identified practices varies significantly across industries and implementing companies. For example, some practices, such as *KPI*s and *business review*s, can be considered universal due to their widespread use. On the other hand, *locked recipes* and *supply chain finance* exemplify findings that have only been observed in single companies and industries. Figure 4.3 provides an overview of the dissemination of the identified management practices based on the number of mentions and industries. The industry mentions are plotted on the upper secondary axis and the total mentions on the lower primary axis.

First, *KPIs* and *business reviews* are the most common practices across industries, building a foundation for CMR management. They are followed by *audits, forecast sharing, cross-functional teams, collaborative troubleshooting, incentive programs, guided procurement*, and *turnkey manufacturing* which are either not found in all sampled industries or less disseminated. The next cluster, including *collaborative innovation programs, team building, open portfolio*s, and *dedicated bundling*, represents practices often limited to specific industries or less shared across industries. Lastly, about a quarter of the identified practices are used in individual industries or companies.

The substantial variation in practice dissemination despite the significant representation of the pharmaceutical industry in the exploratory sample is indicative of the vast heterogeneity of CMR across sectors and companies. Furthermore, practice diffusion results from practice complementarity; for example, *business reviews* and *KPIs* support each other, while *guided procurement* and *turnkey manufacturing* are opposing practices on the same topic. Moreover, while half of the practices are used in three or more different industries, only three were applied

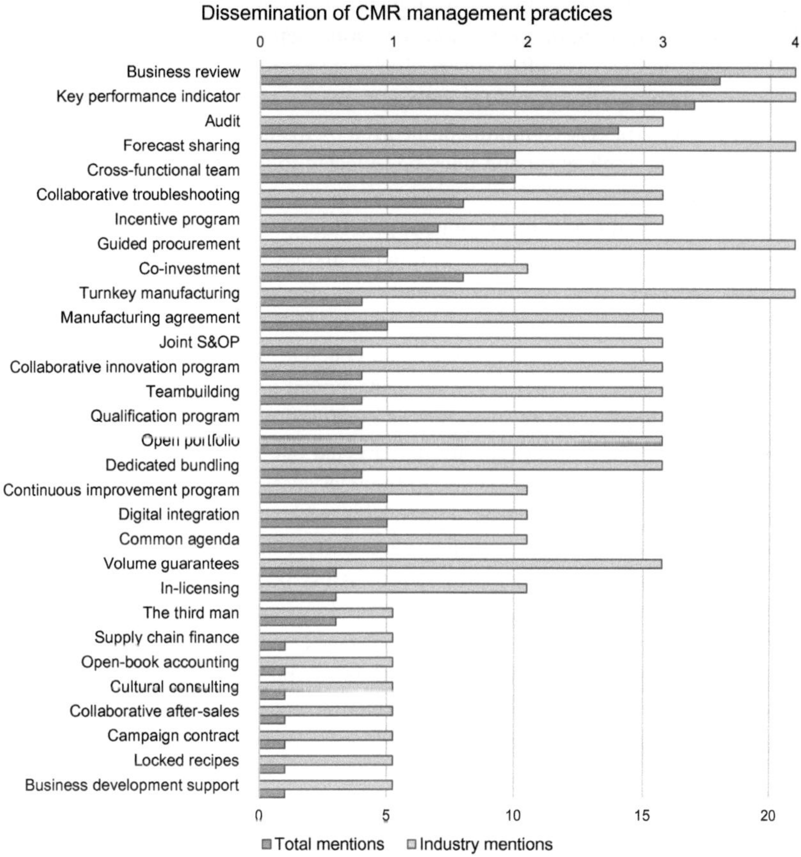

Figure 4.3 Dissemination of the assessed CMR management practices

by more than half of the companies, indicating a lack of CMR management standards or recognized *'best practices.'* Section 4.3 deals with the selection process of management practices by client companies and provides deeper insights into this issue.

Furthermore, since management practices incur managerial costs and might carry substantial risk, client companies try to limit sophisticated practices such as *team building* and *digital integration* to certain distinguished CMRs. These practices are limited because they require dedicated investments, tie up capital, allow only limited performance measurement, or increase dependency and IP risk. The holistic application of *qualification programs* across CMRs, for example, was discontinued in one case after supervision costs rose sharply. Therefore, the use in practice is weighed against the relevance of the respective CMR. Hence, the level of financial or risk commitment incurred by management practice is a viable concern in their application and must be reflected in the artifact design.

Implementation of CMR management practices

The second important aspect of answering the first research question lies in understanding the objectives of applying particular management practices to enable matching use with management requirements. However, the second empirical insight is that practitioners frequently lack concrete awareness of the suitability of specific practices for solving certain management problems as a foundation for the systematic application of management practices. As a result, despite the drive to apply best practices, practices are not targeted but spread wholesale across all existing CMRs or specific segments. In frequent cases, this results in implementing identical practices within an organization with different CMOs to different ends. For example, client companies often collect operational KPIs by default for all CMO partners but only use them to assess performance for non-strategic partners. In contrast, strategic partners are rarely measured against operative performance, using the metrics to monitor changes and identify the potential for improvement. In addition, penalties in incentive programs are frequently handled the same way, consequently re-interpreting predetermined practices to suit the individual purpose. Likewise, in some cases, consignment can be driven by the motivation to hedge against delivery failures, inflated prices, and quality issues through greater control. In other cases, it is pursued collaboratively to take advantage of better purchasing terms from the client. Hence, tailoring management practices remains a significant issue and interest of practitioners in CMRs. Thus, the accurate description of addressed governance problems of the identified management practices is one prerequisite for their targeted use.

In addition, as a third insight, there is sometimes a significant divergence between clients and CMOs in their assessment of the appropriateness of management practices, posing a risk in the collaborative management of CMRs. *Dedicated bundling*, for example, is seen by clients as a means to offer substantial manufacturing volume to the CMO and increase their leverage. CMOs, on the other hand, often benefit from the bundling effect to a lesser extent than the client itself due to the cross-product effort. In addition, *open-book accounting* is viewed by clients as a transparent method for fair pricing but is rejected by CMOs as interference with entrepreneurial liberty. These practices are examples of an overarching conflict between control and self-governance witnessed in the application and design of management practices which will be investigated in the next chapter. However, concerning the effective use of management practices, their perception by the CMO and their effect on the CMR are essential for stable relationships. Therefore, artifact design must recognize the impact of potentially contradicting perceptions of management practices.

Thus, three significant insights can be drawn from the empirical sample, which leads to four requirements a DSR artifact addressing RQ_1 needs to follow:

- *Insight 1:* CMR management borrows practices from established research streams concerning IOR management. However, it also actively adapts intraorganizational methods from operations management, refines practices for use in CMRs, and develops propriety management practices.
- *Insight 2:* Despite understanding management practices as *'targeted sets of activities,'* management objectives are not broken down into individual management practices. Management practices are often applied in defined sets, with ambiguous individual contribution and performance evaluation. The lack of transparent motivation for individual practices leads to occasional opportunistic reinterpretation by client companies after deployment.
- *Insight 3:* The appropriateness of specific practices for CMRs is judged very differently by client companies and CMOs. Since CMO control and detailed performance evaluation become challenging with progressing integration, trust-based collaboration is essential. However, using practices not accepted by the CMO can strain the trust environment and affect the CMR's long-term performance.

Concerning the design of an artifact that supports practitioners in selecting reasonable management practices, four requirements emerge:

- *Requirement 1:* The concept and the different forms of CMR management practices must be clarified to evaluate the usefulness of an adaptation for individual CMRs.
- *Requirement 2:* The ability of management practices to address particular problems in managing CMRs must be presented for targeted application.
- *Requirement 3:* The costs associated with using management practices must be transparent to assess their use's proportionality for specific CMRs.
- *Requirement 4:* The impact of practices on the relationship quality of CMRs must be considered to ensure the long-term stability and performance of CMRs.

These requirements are represented in the design of a *'CMR management practice toolbox'* artifact introduced in Section 5.1.

4.3 Empirical Findings on Management Needs Assessment

This chapter presents the empirical results on client companies' procedures to assess the need for management practices in CMRs. The findings lay the groundwork for answering RQ_2 by containing design requirements for the DSR artifact developed in Section 5.2. Through evaluating current management practice assignment procedures by practitioners, the data illuminate the most critical action points for improving CMR management.

Management needs assessment procedures by client companies

The approach to selecting management practices varies widely and depends on the total number of CMRs the client maintains simultaneously. The procedures observed differ primarily in their granularity, the degree of standardization, and the frequency with which they are updated. Regarding granularity, client companies that engage in many CMRs simultaneously seek to reduce complexity by segmenting CMOs into groups and assigning CMR management practices accordingly. A smaller number of CMRs is usually associated with a partner-driven selection of management practices. However, partner-driven attribution of management practices to CMRs is usually guided by experience and evolved standards that are not systematically implemented, challenged, and refined. More sophisticated approaches are found primarily in companies that tailor CMR management to segments. These companies use deliberate assessment processes based on questionnaires with predefined criteria filled out by the client company and CMO to assign the CMR to a specific segment with defined practices. In some instances, reassessment and adjustment of segments are conducted systematically and regularly.

Segmentation is a significant concern for client companies in structuring CMR management and is preferred over the individual assignment of management practices to specific CMRs. The goal is to bundle competencies and reduce the costs of CMR's complex assessment and management amid differences in covered products, services, and partner profiles through standardization. Although various company-specific segmentation concepts with different granularity and terminology are in circulation, a pattern of three primary segments can be identified.

First, a strategic segment includes CMRs with strong business relevance and close, self-governed collaboration under aligned objectives. Strategic CMRs evolve from primarily existing CMRs by formally expanding the partnership. Second, a tactical segment includes CMRs in which the client is notably dependent on specific capabilities of the CMO, such as expertise, technologies, or market access. At the same time, tactical CMRs lack the foundation for strategic cooperation, such as related strategic interests, commercial growth opportunities, and cultural fit. The assessment of CMR at the interface between the tactical and strategic segments poses particular challenges for clients, as it often involves only one-sided efforts to deepen cooperation. Finally, in the third segment, the remaining CMRs are managed as opportunistic relationships on an arm's length basis with standardized control practices focused on operational results.

Essential and mandatory operational control practices such as KPIs audits and business reviews are considered a basic requirement across all segments. Furthermore, additional practices are employed depending on individual needs. For example, in tactical CMRs, turnkey manufacturing is used if the CMO has superior material or sourcing expertise. Finally, the strategic segment often represents a paradigm shift, as operational control practices, e.g., KPIs and penalties, remain nominally in place but are eased in favor of trust-based autonomy. In addition, CMR management in the strategic segment is complemented by collaborative practices designed to deepen the relationship. In addition, the reactive assessment of emergency practices such as troubleshooting or additional reviews and audits can be mentioned, which are used temporarily for specific triggers independent of the segment, as outlined in Section 4.4.

Although client companies gained substantial transparency and scaling effects, setting up their CMR management by standardizing operational control practices, e.g., through dedicated audit teams, clients and CMOs recognize the tendency of excessive control due to lack of individual assessment. On the client side, this leads to high administrative costs, while CMOs often complain about a lack of freedom to enable the agility and innovation demanded by the customer. As a result, client companies often fail to assess development opportunities and systematically support the growth of partnership relationships, even though they intend to do so. On the one hand, strategic alignment can prevent opportunism on the part of the CMO, thereby reducing operational costs in favor of more efficient CMO self-management. On the other hand, however, strategic alignment is essential for trusting long-term collaboration and exploiting business opportunities. Consequently, the relationship-building aspect of the management needs assessment holds significant potential for CMRs, as they are associated with high opportunity costs for future business opportunities, overhead costs for control, and a lack of long-term stability.

As relationship building involves consideration of social fit and intangible partner expectations, established assessment methods based on business criteria, questionnaires, and intuition reach their limits, neglecting social factors required for collaborative partnerships. Hence, gaps in expectations and perceptions not addressed in management assessment frequently hamper CMR performance beyond contractually fixed targets and in volatile environments. For example, mismatched expectations on order development can affect CMOs' willingness to extend contracts and remain in the CMR amid more lucrative business options. Moreover, clients are seldom aware of the CMO's perception of their management approach, which can damage agreement on goals and trust building. For example, clients often value comprehensive oversight of external manufacturing as an *'extension of internal manufacturing'* but are perceived by CMOs as overarching and intrusive to their business model. In addition, clients often misjudge the CMO's benefits of practices intended to benefit both partners. As a result, they design, for example, dedicated bundling, questionnaires, or open book accounting, in a way that causes significant additional effort for the CMO and is not endorsed.

As a result, a relationship gap can quickly emerge in which one partner unconsciously alienates the other, hampering the desired relationship progress due to a lack of shared understanding. Practitioners find that relationship gaps between written agreements and expectations are frequently bridged by personal relationships at the interfaces making up for institutional inadequacies. However, growth opportunities and relationship gaps must be assessed and managed systematically for targeted CMR development.

Consequently, measuring the management needs of CMRs can be divided into two main stages. First, CMOs are evaluated based on primary business criteria and segmented to assign control-oriented practices in a standardized procedure. Second, individualized assessment and planning of CMR development paths based on the CMR's growth potential and relationship quality are intended by client companies but are not currently pursued systematically. Figure 4.4 summarizes the empirical findings on how client companies assess management needs in CMRs.

Criteria used in management assessment by client companies

In addition to the process, the criteria for selecting appropriate practices play a substantial role in management assessment. However, client companies still struggle with meaningful segmentation of the CMO portfolio amid numerous

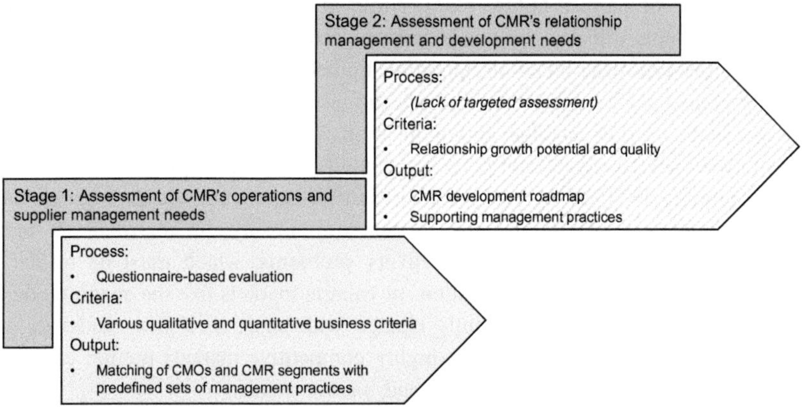

Figure 4.4 Current status and fields of action in management assessment of CMRs

applied criteria. Moreover, although some criteria could not be captured due to the number of experience-based procedures, two fundamental challenges can be noted. First, client companies frequently apply descriptive criteria which are easily measurable but have limited explanatory power for management requirements. For example, CMO company size represents an ambiguous criterion potentially associated with financial stability, investment power, the balance of power, and the maturity of quality standards without providing clear guidance for management practices. Second, other criteria, such as the balance of power, are considered extremely important but are not reflected in the selection of management practices due to poor measurability.

Therefore, the criteria gathered from the client companies and used in the management evaluation procedures were evaluated with practice experts in the focus groups and reduced to a meaningful set. For structurization TCE's transaction characteristics were applied. However, since TCE's transaction criteria did not cover all captured criteria seamlessly, a fifth category was added to structure the findings.

- *Asset specificity* encompasses criteria that indicate the CMR's safeguarding needs. For example, shared investments relate to the need to protect against asset misuse. In addition, a high level of integration, the partner's contribution to the CMR, and the client's business strategy raise exit barriers for client companies, requiring efforts to retain CMOs in the relationship. Next, the likelihood of partner failure plays a role in establishing backup systems to ensure supply. Finally, the power balance determines the extent to which the customer can resist potential opportunistic behavior by the CMO.

- *Environmental uncertainty* comprises the criteria by which client companies assess the need to establish communication routines, adjustable interfaces, and transparency to offset environmental volatility. For example, due to varying uncertainty, the product life cycle phases differ significantly regarding required coordination and communication. Technology novelty can contribute to start-up difficulties and quality and delivery problems, which must be resolved through transparent communication. In volatile markets like the apparel industry, product portfolios frequently change with short shelf lives and varying production requirements. Lastly, highly competitive markets require constant monitoring of third-party behavior and market trends.
- *Behavioral uncertainty* concerns criteria that make statements about recommended performance evaluation practices. Significant performance risk requires appropriate monitoring and mitigation measures. Performance complexity, in turn, addresses the difficulty of adequately interpreting a CMO's performance. Evaluation complexity is concerned with the measurability of the CMO's performance. Opportunism risk refers to the likelihood that CMOs will not act in the CMR's best interest due to external incentives. Finally, appropriation risk addresses the likelihood of involuntary disclosure of proprietary information, which must be mitigated.
- *Transaction frequency* defines the customer's willingness to invest based on the value of the CMR to its business. First, the strategic transaction value includes the intangible value that the CMR contributes to the customer company's business strategy or competitive position. Second, transaction volume refers to the CMR's commercial contribution to the customer's revenue. Third, transaction scope scales the relationship by referring to the number and type of subcontracted activities.
- *Further criteria* were not initially included in the framework but can refine the selection of management practices based on the four types of criteria presented. For example, certain management practices, such as audits, may be mandated by industry standards. In addition, the relationship quality and growth opportunity criteria reference the goal of identifying CMOs for close partnerships and selecting appropriate practices for targeted relationship development.

The described assessment criteria are summarized in Figure 4.5, applying the theoretical framework developed in Section 3.2.2.

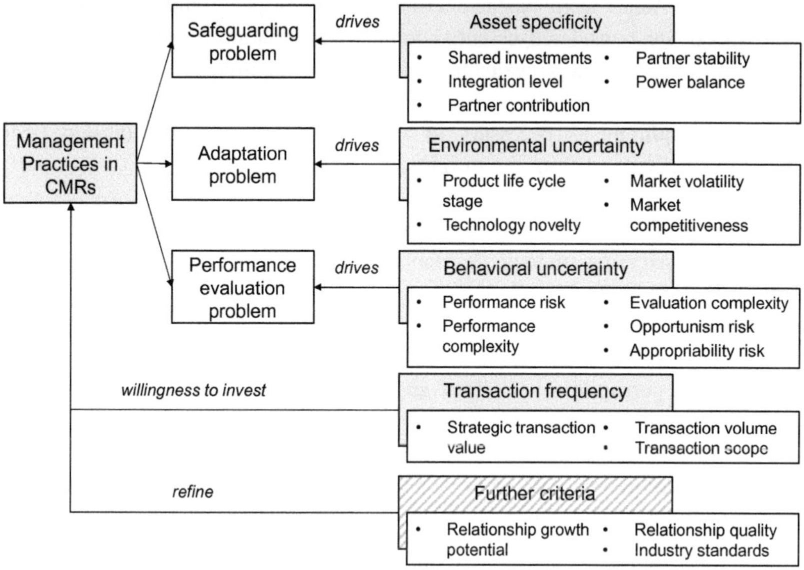

Figure 4.5 Empirical insights into CMR management needs criteria

The criteria identified were considered by the focus group participants to provide a comprehensive overview. Nevertheless, their definition is intentionally broad, as the exact metrics and thresholds for assessing the criteria presented may vary significantly across companies and industries. Moreover, the empirical results show that the observed evolution of CMOs from service providers to strategic partners in CM is reflected in the CMR portfolios of client companies. The purposeful transition of CMRs from arm's length relationships to strategic partnerships presents an obstacle for clients and CMOs that can be addressed through improved management needs assessment and relationship planning. Consequently, the following main insights can be summarized:

- *Insight 1:* Maturity of systematical management needs assessment varies significantly across companies without universal practice standards. However, in the most systematic approaches, the primary management practices for operational control are standardized via segments into which CMOs are grouped.

- *Insight 2:* Aside from business criteria, social aspects and future business prospects are considered essential for targeted relationship development but are underrepresented in evaluating management requirements.

The three requirements necessary to answer RQ_2 through a dedicated DSR artifact can be derived from the insights.

- *Requirement 1:* The artifact must support selecting operational control practices and analyzing strategic development opportunities.
- *Requirement 2:* The applied evaluation criteria must have a demonstrable influence on the selection of specific management methods.
- *Requirement 3:* The procedure must include and compare both parties' expectations and perceptions to evaluate social fit and future prospects for proactive relationship planning.

The derived requirements are incorporated in the artifact design for a management assessment procedure outlined in Section 5.2.

4.4 Empirical Findings on Relationship Dynamics

This chapter provides empirical insight into the relationship dynamics relevant to adjusting CMR management practices. The findings establish the requirements for designing the DSR artifact proposed in Section 5.3. to map management-relevant dynamics for decision support. The empirical results convey continuous and disruptive changes within the CMR and external shocks that need to be covered by CMR management. In addition, the open discussion of the results in the focus groups allowed for an assessment of the relevance of inherent and external relationship dynamics from a management perspective.

Figure 4.6 provides an overview and categorization of the assessed relationship dynamics according to the theoretical framework developed in Section 3.2.3. However, the identified dynamics do not have to be mutually exclusive and can coincide or influence each other in chain reactions. The synthesis of relationship dynamics aims to highlight direct management impacts instead of classifying disruptive events.

Industry turbulences

External relationship dynamics named by the interviewees encompass shocks to *prices*, *supply and demand*, *industry*, and *market structure*.

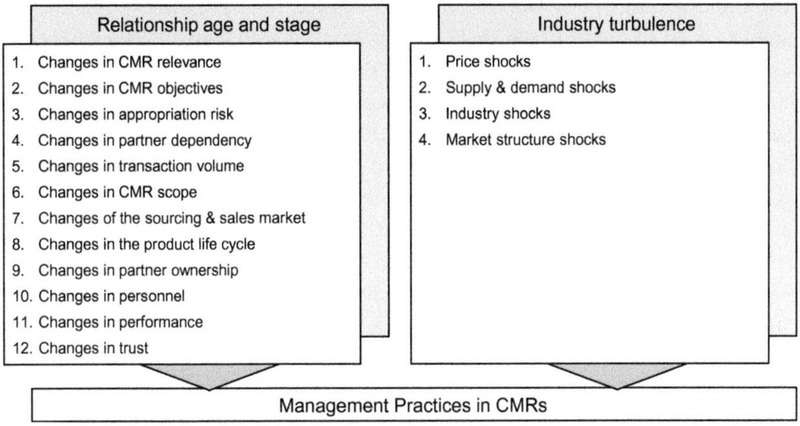

Figure 4.6 Empirical insights into CMR dynamics

- *Price shocks* are particularly relevant for CMRs when the CMO purchases materials at fluctuating market prices. When a price shock occurs, changes to management practices for compensation or procurement may be required.
- *Supply and demand shocks* can appear when supply chains are disrupted or consumer demand suddenly fails to materialize. In recent years, the number of supply and demand shocks due to natural disasters and geopolitical changes has increased, forcing clients and CMOs to evaluate management practices concerning production volumes, inventory levels, and supply chain financing.
- *Industry shocks* can be triggered by innovation or regulation and change fundamental industry standards and practices. As a result, shocks to the industry require a reassessment of established procedures and practices, for instance, in quality assurance, data processing, environmental friendliness, and possibly adjusted compliance monitoring.
- *Market structure shocks* occur when third-party actions such as acquisitions, bankruptcies, or alliances reshape the competitive landscape and affect CMR's competitive position by increasing or decreasing its freedom to operate.

Although these industry turbulences have a massive impact on CMR operations, interviewees consider their relevance to the management of CMR relationship dynamics to be modest. CMR agreements contain predefined emergency procedures and crisis management guidelines that can be activated accordingly. Practitioners agree, however, that these procedures are only guardrails and that trust and commitment to working together outside regular business routines are paramount. In addition, in the event of temporary disruptions, management practices return to their original state after the shock ends. On the other hand, shocks with long-lasting effects, such as regulatory, technology, or market shifts, usually require far-reaching adjustments that must be thoroughly analyzed and coordinated, manifesting themselves with a delay in a changed CMR strategy.

More significant to practitioners than individual shock events is their accumulation in recent years, which has sparked new discussions about supply chain resilience and business continuity. Due to the diversity of shock events, clients are pushing for increasing integration and partnership with CMOs on a solid foundation of trust. However, shock-induced adjustment of management practices is considered impractical; instead, trust-based suspension of control mechanisms and needs-based support are sought. Finally, interviewees consider managing CMRs' internal relationship dynamics a priority, as ongoing management adaptation promotes a robust and resilient relationship when a shock occurs.

Relationship age and stage

The dynamics associated with the relationship's age and the stage manifest themselves in several ways. In contrast to the term *'shock'* in industrial turbulence, internal dynamics are often continuous and proceed slowly or result from deliberate actions. Therefore, they are referred to as *'changes'* in the following paragraphs.

- *Changes in CMR relevance* for either partner can be caused by shifts in the CMR's product portfolio, corporate strategy, or covered products and influence management attention. Subconsciously declining management attention is identified by CMOs, in particular, as a reason for deteriorating collaboration over time.
- *Changes in CMR objectives* can deliberately change the performance goals of CMRs. For example, CMRs are often temporary test beds for a lean and rapid product launch. Then, if the market response is positive, they can be transitioned into permanent relationships focused on quality and efficiency.
- *Changes in appropriation risk* are driven by the CMO's behavior and therefore require dynamic adaptation of safeguarding practices. As part of their business dealings, CMOs engage with other companies in direct competition with the client or launch original design products on the market, entering direct competition with the client.

- *Changes in partner dependence* are driven by the progressive specialization of the product or partner and the deepening of the partnership, which underscores the need to raise exit barriers for the CMO. Conversely, acquiring knowledge, technologies, or production facilities can reduce partner dependence and lessen the need for protective measures.
- *Changes in transaction volume* directly relate to the management's attention and willingness to invest in the relationship. Transaction volume is affected by the development of supply and demand but also assigned manufacturing volume considering second sources, bundling, and seasonal demand spikes.
- *Changes in CMR scope* are triggered by the CMO's forward or backward integration in the joint supply chain, for example, when taking over engineering activities in turnkey manufacturing. Consequently, the adaptation of task profiles affects the design of performance management and coordination of interfaces accordingly.
- *Changes of the selected sourcing or sales market* are typical in expansion phases. They may require adaptation due to new interfaces with other CMO sites or representatives, new regulatory requirements, different market dynamics, and consumer expectations, affecting multiple management practices.
- *Changes in the product life cycle* can significantly impact the manufacturing requirements of individual products in terms of production volumes, target weighting, and coordination requirements. In CMRs with single or dominant products, the product life cycle radiates directly to the relationship management practices applied.
- *Changes in the ownership structure* of the CMR partner are interpreted as precursors of future shifts in partner commitment triggering reevaluation of the strategic fit between client and CMO and adaptation of operational routines.
- *Changes in personnel* are critical to performance management, as employees in critical positions of responsibility such as customer service, operations, or quality management have a decisive influence on collaboration and product manufacturing. Consequently, new personnel must be inducted, and trust and commitment must be built beyond standard processes.
- *Changes in performance* are frequent triggers for action with a high degree of standardization in management practice response. Performance shortfalls and deviations from the expected service are met with tighter control, communication, and operational support.
- *Changes in trust* in the CMO's goodwill or capabilities affect the degree of control clients exert on the CMR. Trust is often used as a substitute for

control practices allowing self-governance, which is less costly and fosters commitment, so control must be recovered when trust is lost.

Additionally, interviewees state that CMRs react to predetermined changes, which are agreed upon in the contract or set by regulations, such as the number of audits or business reviews. Given that the occurrence and contents of these changes are determined, they are not considered relationship dynamics.

Internal dynamics arising from the relationship's age and stage are of primary concern to practitioners because their occurrence is anticipated, and their impact is significant. The longevity of CMRs, multiple and changing products, and high switching barriers lead to regular strategic realignments along the CMR lifecycle that influence the willingness and perceived need to invest in and adapt CMR management practices. CMR relationship managers are most concerned with finding the right time for active realignment to better fit CMR development and management practices. However, internal dynamics are challenging to manage because many are reminiscent of the boiling frog apologia: several metrics relevant to CMR management design, such as trust, performance, or transaction volume, change gradually over time so that a single change does not warrant a management reassessment. Still, over time, all these gradual changes add up to more significant shifts in the course of relationships that require adjustments in management practices. Moreover, the progression of internal dynamics is gradual but not linear, as the activities of the customer and CMO can affect the CMR even in the short term. For example, transaction volume can rise or fall quickly due to the client company's orders, trust can be lost immediately due to the exposure of opportunistic behavior, and performance can plummet in a short time due to operational changes.

- *Insight 1*: CMR management is sensitive to industry turbulence and dynamics arising from the age and stage of the relationship. Practitioners consider internal dynamics more relevant to CMR management because they occur frequently, have traceable impacts, and allow for appropriate mitigation.
- *Insight 2*: Developing management responses for relationship dynamics is challenging because they occur gradually and disruptively and influence each other, making them difficult to monitor, isolate, and analyze.

Consequently, empirical findings underline the relevance of controlling relational dynamics to achieve stable CMRs. Therefore, to answer RQ_3, the following requirement for artifact design can be noted:

- *Requirement 1*: The artifact must enable comprehensive visualization of the relationship dynamics of CMRs and their impact on the need for management practices.

The artifact *'CMR strategy cycles'* developed in 5.3 incorporates this requirement.

4.5 Empirical Findings on Adjustment of Management Practices

This chapter outlines CMR management's success factors and requirements to maintain the relationship amidst dynamically changing requirements successfully. The empirical results are analyzed using the theoretical framework developed in Section 3.2.4 and form the basis for answering RO_4 by developing the artifact presented in Section 5.4. Clients and CMOs value commitment to the relationship as a critical aspect of enabling lasting CMR and overcoming relationship dynamics that arise. In an increasingly dynamic supply chain environment, relationship changes are inevitable and often only dealt with reactively due to their diversity. In CMRs, contracts cannot regulate all processes due to the intensity of the collaboration and do not reflect the latest state of knowledge shortly after signing. Escalation levels and crisis management are largely standardized but primarily support the resolution process through appropriate communication, while solutions must be found individually.

Client companies and CMOs, therefore, emphasize a high level of commitment as a requirement to work together flexibly and efficiently outside agreed standards. Consequently, relationship dynamics originating from partner behavior within the CMR are seen as a critical factor in successful long-term CMR since they directly affect and indicate the partner's commitment. According to the interviewees, the partners' behavior in terms of investment, communication, and trust level influence the successful establishment and maintenance of the relationship commitment.

Investment capabilities

Investment capabilities are an essential practice to offset power imbalances in the CMR, which are considered incredibly destabilizing in the long run. Therefore, in addition to operational improvements, shared investments and integration of systems and processes aim to create exit barriers and divert management attention to the CMR. The basis for companies to make CMR-specific investments is a reasonable return on capital, so development opportunities for both partners need to be explored. Furthermore, unilateral exclusive investments are becoming scarcer due to the dynamics of CMRs and greater bargaining power on the part of CMOs. CMOs expect reciprocity of investments, substantial trust, or contractual guarantees before taking client-specific investments. Thus, client companies often must abandon opportunistic mindsets to mirror CMO investment activities. Especially in the operational phase of the relationship, client companies often fail to pursue a precise relationship strategy, as a result of which the commitment of both partners slowly declines. Thus, practitioners emphasize the need for regular evaluation of the relationship to consider opportunities for new investments for both parties and a reliable outlook.

Communication capabilities

Coordinating manufacturing across client companies and CMOs requires effective communication channels, routines, and tools. However, building and maintaining relationship commitment in CMRs goes beyond fulfilling contractual obligations and is achieved by transparently communicating business interests, personal expectations, and values. One industry expert called this the *'irrational side'* of the business relationship because, for all their professionalism and operating standards, CMRs are run by people and interpreted through their perceptions. Since mismatched expectations are a significant reason for CMR failure, it is necessary to create a platform for business partners to share their expectations and possible dissatisfaction. Here, the personal goals of the responsible parties and exit criteria must be outlined, even if the business partner is not contractually obligated to comply with them or can influence them. Mutual understanding of the partners' business interests and expectations is considered a success factor, as CMR must remain profitable for the customer and CMO alike amidst the relationship dynamics.

Furthermore, communicating those interests and expectations allows partners to consider the factors in their management and relationship monitoring. However, because social aspects are challenging to measure, they are vastly underrepresented in partner communication. For example, verbal recognition of partner performance is often underestimated and missed, while explicit business incentives are generally avoided due to performance measurement issues. As a result, mainly negative topics, which are not supportive of commitment, dominate communication. Hence, social aspects must be regularly discussed or made visible to effectively monitor deviations in expectations and perceptions and uncover potentially hidden dissent.

In addition, standardized crisis management procedures, including clearly defined hierarchical levels and even symbolic punishments, are well accepted as nonverbal communication and serve as reference points during difficult and potentially tense phases of collaboration. Nevertheless, CMOs, in particular, are critical of their customers' desire for extensive standardization of communications to ensure strategic alignment, as routine provides a sense of security that reduces management attention and increasingly deteriorates the relationship in the long run. As a result, they advocate for specific communication practices to firmly embed sincere, personal, and semi-structured exchanges into relationship management.

Trust

Trust is the conviction that the partner will fulfill or implement the expressed expectations and perceptions to the best of his or her knowledge and belief. Consequently, explicit non-opportunistic behavior signals trust and may generate more trust. However, since trust is intangible, there are different views on using trust in CMRs. In addition, willingness to trust is considered part of the corporate culture, leading to significant discrepancies between partners in CMRs. As a result, client companies and CMOs are increasingly looking beyond the strategic fit for partners with a suitable cultural fit and binding them by building up joint new business opportunities. Therefore, when alternatives are available in partner selection, trust in collaboration is preferred to explicit business metrics as a strategy for minimizing risk. Furthermore, strategic CMRs evolve from existing relationships over time when enough trust has been built for further integration of activities without extensive control despite prevalent strategic fit.

An imbalance in the willingness to trust directly impacts CMR management practice and can impede commitment. For example, some practitioners believe frequent renegotiation of contracts from a position of strength is fair to adjust the relationship to changing regulations, transaction volumes, prices, or performance, while others oppose it altogether. In addition, the ambiguity between the communicated CMR strategy and operational implementation can significantly affect partner commitment. While individual development paths and trusting cooperation are strived for at the strategic level, these goals are often not sufficiently anchored at the operational level. As a result, the operational management of CMRs is often dominated by risk minimization, local target optimization, and short-term target achievement, which undermines trust. While firm partner specialization can increase the CMR's value creation potential, practitioners find that clients who provide CM services can more easily build trust with CMOs since they deeply understand the business model. Likewise, CMOs, that produce proprietary brands align more effectively with client companies' expectations and perceptions.

Consequently, trust can be purposefully fostered by building shared understanding and interpersonal relationships. Team building is generally well received but rarely implemented due to a lack of measurable return on investment. Furthermore, for compliance reasons, the personification of business relationships is viewed critically. Therefore, institutionalizing interpersonal trust systematically across all relationship interfaces is necessary. As a sign of institutionalized trust, the partners expect each other to act as ambassadors representing the CMR's aligned interests within their respective companies. Non-uniform communication at interfaces or inappropriate communication from organizational functions not involved in the relationship's operating core is seen as a lack of sincerity and trust. For example, legal, finance, and IT departments are often involved in CMR operations or process design but are not usually included in relationship management. As a result, departments at the interfaces of the CMR could pursue their agendas in terms of contract clauses, billing procedures, or technical support without considering the relationships' alignment.

As a result, trust in CMRs is partly predetermined, requiring a thorough assessment of partner preferences. However, it can also be actively built up and damaged by targeted management measures or lack thereof. Figure 4.7 summarizes the drivers for commitment as a central metric to understand CMR stability amidst relationship dynamics.

Concerning answering RQ_4, the empirical findings provide several key insights on how to adapt CMR management practices to the dynamically changing relationship.

- *Insight 1:* Commitment is a crucial variable for managing dynamics because it leads partners to act in the best interest of CMR, even when established management routines do not seamlessly address management needs.
- *Insight 2:* Relationship dynamics must be proactively managed by controlling CMO commitment to avoid or minimize CMR performance losses due to partner behavior or external dynamics.
- *Insight 3:* Measured by their importance, commitment, and social aspects are severely underrepresented in monitoring and management practices due to a lack of ability to measure them and their return on investment.
- *Insight 4:* The role of their behavior in CMO commitment is not well understood by clients, which is why sincere feedback by the CMO and transparency about the impact of applied management practices are required.

Thus, the following requirements for the design of a valuable artifact to assist with CMR management in dynamic settings can be derived:

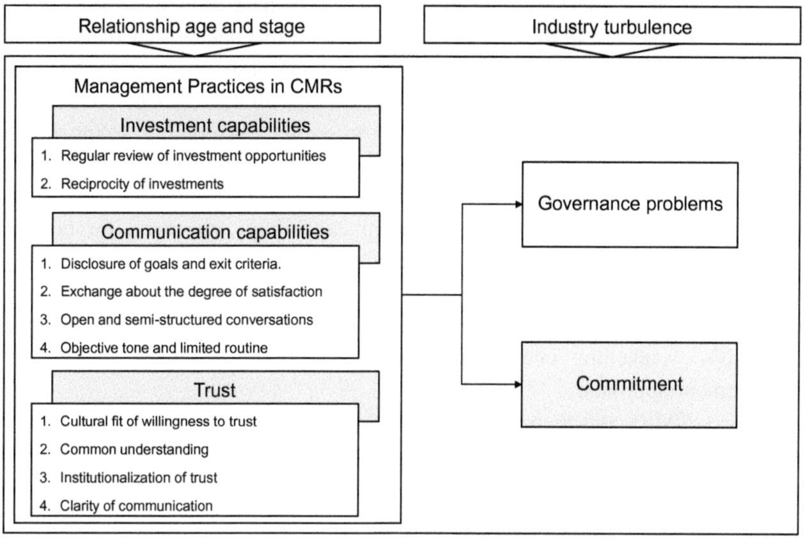

Figure 4.7 Empirical insights into the drivers of commitment to CMRs

- *Requirement 1:* Commitment must be made visible as a metric of relationship quality to signify the need for action to safeguard against opportunistic behavior by timely adjustment of management practices.
- *Requirement 2:* The CMR's relationship quality and prospects need to be assessed regularly to allow for proactive adjustment of management practices.
- *Requirement 3:* The client needs to gain awareness within their organization of their own active and passive opportunities to influence the CMO's commitment through a transparent review of the impact of management practices.

The artifact presented in 5.4 considers these requirements to provide a comprehensive framework for applying management practices in dynamic CMRs.

4.6 Empirical Findings on Industry Characteristics

The exploratory research design of the dissertation allowed semi-structured discussions with practitioners across industries, as a result of which further insights beyond the defined research questions could be captured. These insights shed additional light on the development of the CM business model, the maturity of CMR management, and the industry's influence on management challenges.

Practitioners confirm the growth of CM and the shift to an integrated business partner with complementary skills consistent with authors Chan and Chung (2002) and Han et al. (2012). In contrast to earlier outsourcing arrangements, CMOs have grown to not only support but enable client companies' business models. Due to the ongoing customer orientation of client companies enhancing their marketing, sales, and product design capabilities, the need for complementary manufacturing, material, and logistics know-how provided by CMOs is rising. Consequently, customer orientation of brand-owning companies drives the contact manufacturing business model. It creates a stronger dependency on CMOs, weakening clients' negotiation power and requiring an eye-level management approach.

Hence, CMRs and their management gain interest within the polled companies as the concept grows in relevance. However, relationship management adapts slowly to the evolving objectives and requirements of CMRs. So far, CMR management remains very transactional, with few exceptions, despite the recognized need to develop sophisticated and fitted management approaches. Many companies polled are reorganizing their responsible management organizations and management practices. An interview partner from the clothing industry described his company's management practice toward CMOs as *'chaotic'* and *'not from the book.'* Another interviewee from the food industry stated that his company's management approach *'is grown over many years and not actively decided on.'*

Initially rooted in the procurement organization, practitioners question the ability to manage CMRs by SRM. Practitioners on the client and CMO side in the pharmaceutical industry emphasized that including procurement and sales staff in meetings often leads to discussions about pricing and additional service offers, dividing participants into opposing groups. A senior food industry expert finds from his experience that CMRs are more successful when managed through the supply chain or manufacturing organization than through procurement or sales. In his estimation, this is because there is a common process-related understanding between these organizations and CMOs, which facilitates strategic alignment. Correspondingly, CMR management is often located in the operations organization.

In addition, observations suggest that despite the asserted goal of strategic partnerships, the client's CMR management practices lean towards opportunism and fail when the power balance is not in their favor. In this context, a representative from a pharmaceutical CMO suggested that the vital aspect of managing CMRs successfully is understanding the partners' business model, which puts

CMOs at an advantage due to a customer-oriented business focus. Consequently, CMR management is particularly challenging for client companies, as their dependence on the CMO cannot be mitigated by their client status in the relationship and needs to be addressed actively.

However, apart from these general similarities, different conditions and practices for CMR management play a role in the industries examined, which are presented below.

Pharmaceutical industry

Pharmaceuticals are technically complex, highly regulated, investment-intensive products whose development and approval take decades. Patents shape commercial phases of the pharmaceutical product life cycle, protecting brand owners from competition for a certain period and allowing them to charge high prices to recover development costs. However, after patent expiration, competitors can offer product copies as generics, driving competition and shifting manufacturing focus to cost efficiency.

The strong foundation of CM in the pharmaceutical industry derives from the need to mitigate the risk of high capital commitment for development and manufacturing over long approval periods with substantial uncertainty. Hence, the considerable complexity of pharmaceutical manufacturing favors an increasingly fragmented market with co-specialized client companies and CMOs focusing on particular technological, regulatory, or life-cycle phase niches. As a result, formerly vertical-integrated companies shift to dynamic licensing and subcontracting products or acquiring innovative companies for a strong product portfolio, systematically reducing capital committed to in-house manufacturing. Furthermore, since pharmaceutical manufacturing capacities are expensive, they offer excess capacities through CM services to one another, creating opportunistic CMRs with strong coopetition.

Thus, CMRs address the industry's demand for capital-intensive state-of-the art production facilities, including manufacturing licenses, technologies, and know-how. Consequently, CMOs are deeply embedded in the pharmaceutical value chain enabling fast commercial product launch in the vital patent-protected life-cycle phases and cost-efficient manufacturing in the mature stages. Due to the heavy reliance on CM, clients in the pharmaceutical industry usually simultaneously engage in high numbers of CMRs, relying on segments to tailor CMR management. Based on the segment, client companies experience significant lock-ins due to high regulatory and technological switching barriers despite the advantages in company sizes and pursue highly integrated or opportunistic management approaches.

Amid the dynamic development of the CM business model in the pharmaceutical industry, CMR management goes through a learning phase, balancing cost-efficiency and effective collaboration across management segments. In the pursuit of *'best practices,'* clients increasingly turn to automotive industry supplier practices and personnel experiencing mixed results. Limited by the fact that many clients lack the focal supply chain position to implement automotive practices, successful cooperation becomes imperative. However, interview partners remarked that the industries' *'operative mindset'* focused on quality and cost, neglects long-term CMR objectives and strategic alignment.

Concluding, CMRs in the pharmaceutical industry are driven and characterized by the strongly regulated and investment-intensive production of medicines. As a result, manufacturing decisions cannot be overturned easily, creating high asset specificity and strong lock-in effects. The industries' most widely spread CMR management practices reflect these challenges: Most audits are mandatory by regulation, with additional audits functioning as further safeguards. Co-investments into dedicated equipment are a standard to enable exclusive access to investment-intensive machinery, and cross-functional management teams with a strong quality core reflect the technical complexity and operative management focus.

Food industry

CM in the food industry shares strong product quality regulations with the pharmaceutical industry but differs profoundly concerning the consumer market. First, groceries, especially staple foods, represent necessities of daily life and must therefore be provided to society at an affordable cost. Second, while food quality is heavily regulated, the intellectual property of recipes cannot be patented, leading to strong competitive pressure between brands, driving down margins, and fostering a consumer-centered market. As a result, the substantial cost pressure has sparked a downsizing of formerly integrated brand owners with simultaneous strong growth of CM. Like the pharma industry, brand-leading companies focus their resources on product development and marketing while limiting their manufacturing investments to core technologies.

Due to the cost focus and high risk of intellectual property appropriation, food CMRs remain opportunistic with frequent changes in CMOs. In contrast to the pharmaceutical industry, however, the share of CM services provided by specialized CMOs is comparably low, as low product margins have made this business model unattractive. At the same time, the fragmentation of production volumes across constantly growing product portfolios reduces the profitability of vertically integrated food companies. As a result, food industry CMRs comprise mainly brand-leading companies collaborating to utilize manufacturing capacities and co-develop products. Co-developing is the primary origin of food CMRs since the weak intellectual property protection poses a high risk of subcontracting the manufacturing of self-developed products to competitors. Thus, food CMRs provide access to external capabilities and manufacturing capacities to postpone investments amid uncertain customer demand for new products. Moreover, the food industry experiences an increasing specialization, in which some companies might, for example, focus on baked goods and others on dairy products.

Consequently, this causes a dynamic and unstable environment for CMRs due to constant coopetition between partners. According to the interviewees, the increasing trend toward co-development and coopetition has recently sparked a shift in the industry. Similar to the pharmaceutical and electronic industries, integrated and specialized CMO, such as Hearthside Food Solutions, are targeting the niche of scalable development partners, testbeds, and dedicated CM services without direct coopetition following the Foxconn or Flextronics business models.

However, their impact on the CM sector of the food industry is still evolving. As a result, CMRs are dominated by appropriation considerations, with dynamic shifts in product ownership and manufacturing responsibility. For example, successful co-developed recipes are often insourced or subcontracted to another CMO, with limited development capabilities to safeguard intellectual property. Other recipes may be sold to the co-developing company or other market participants and then sourced as a white-label product, outsourcing further recipe development.

The food industry's prevalent coopetition, dynamics, and quality regulation manifest themselves in firm control in CMR management. Clients tend to track and evaluate numerous KPIs depending on their bargaining power in the CMR. Furthermore, audits are widespread in the industry to assess compliance with quality standards and other KPIs. However, co-investments are diminishing due to weak legal protection of recipes and low margins that extend amortization periods past usual CMR lifecycles. The third map reflects the dynamics of CMRs in the food industry: On the one hand, client companies push for more control and transparency as safeguards in a coopetitive environment. On the other hand, brand-leading companies offering excess capacities for CM show little dependency on their clients, requiring client companies to foster goodwill and commitment in the relationship.

Clothing industry

CM in the clothing industry originated from the last century's manufacturing outsourcing and offshoring waves. Currently, most global clothing production is located in Asia and is run by local companies. In contrast to the pharmaceutical and food industry, clothing manufacturing is mainly subcontracted with insignificant internal production representing a clear separation of tasks in the supply chain. As a result, client companies and CMOs have developed complementary design, marketing, and manufacturing capabilities over the last decades.

However, brand recognition is essential in clothing and influences the expected product margin. Furthermore, solid CMO competition and short product life cycles provide clients with enough sourcing and switching options to avoid a lock-in effect. Thus, western client companies have maintained a powerful bargaining position in the supply chain, often multisourcing with many CMOs, despite the dependence on CMO know-how concerning materials and processes. In the activewear segment, dynamic technology development, such as sustainable fabrics, is a competitive factor. In addition, large segments of the apparel industry change their product portfolios throughout the year and assign products to CMOs per season. Seasonal strategy cycles require continuous adjustments to products, manufacturing processes, price calculations, and negotiations. At the same time, failure to quickly adapt CMRs is costly because supply chain delays can quickly render products obsolete. Finally, clothing CMRs typically encompass various products bundled to achieve economies of scale and ensure reasonable margins for the CMO since shoes, for example, generate higher margins than bodywear. Hence, the number of subcontracted products and manufacturing volume under the umbrella of the CMR changes constantly following the seasons, strategic decisions, and CMO performance.

The frequent geographical separation between western client companies and CMOs located in Asia poses a central challenge in managing the CMRs in the dynamic environment of the clothing industry. Compliance with agreed cost, quality, service level metrics, and social standards must be monitored over great distances amid cultural interfaces. Managing cultural differences in social norms is particularly relevant since end-consumer awareness concerning social issues has risen, and failure to meet them can damage the brand. Therefore, some client companies subcontracting to Asian CMOs, have established local branches dedicated to monitoring compliance and insourcing innovation. Since the clients have lost the know-how to manufacture a significant share of their products, CMRs often start from a client's design, which the CMOs implement by proposing suitable materials and prices. Joint developments or designs suggested by the CMO are sometimes used for niche or innovative products.

The central cornerstones of CMR management in the apparel industry are the advanced segregation of duties between specialized clients and CMOs, short seasonal product life cycles, and low switching barriers for both partners. The contracting companies thus use their bargaining power as customers and brand owners by enforcing strict controls or targeted development practices based on their CMR management philosophy. Audits, KPI, incentive, and penalty clauses build the backbone of CMR control in the apparel industry. Furthermore, CMO-developing approaches include management practices concerning supply chain finance, joint S&OP, and assisted business development.

Mechanical and plant engineering

CM in the mechanical and plant engineering sector has a long tradition of being an *'extended workbench'* for client companies ranging from tailor-made components to complete modules or systems. In contrast to the pharma and food industry, continuous improvement of products is not infringed by regulation, and brand relevance is comparably low, focusing primarily on product innovation and functionality. Therefore, it is noticeable that CM in mechanical and plant engineering is primarily used as a supplement following the traditional arrangements. Engineering industries' CMRs rarely commercialize core products. Instead, they function to secure the supply of relevant systems at an affordable cost. For example, it is common to in-license and subcontract specific modules when the OEM ceases to manufacture them.

Another typical use case is when an existing supplier's product is significantly improved and co-developed to fit the client's specific demands within its product portfolio. Such cases are widespread in the project business when client companies design and deliver comprehensive logistics or manufacturing systems and the CMO provides individual consumer-ready machinery within the portfolio. In such cases, dependencies comparable to pharma, food, and clothing CMRs can emerge when demand dynamics increase the product's strategic value in the client company's portfolio.

However, since client companies maintain a strong manufacturing core, preferring internal production of core products, the CM business model is a side business for CMOs comparable to the food industry. Likewise, specialized manufacturing service providers in the industry typically cover low value-added depth segments to achieve economies of scale and do not provide services for complex products and systems. Consequently, client companies have little leverage and experience substantial lock-in effects when a subcontracted product becomes strategically important. In line with the strong manufacturing core, strategic CMRs are avoided by client companies seeking in-licensing of the subcontracted products if internal production is economically feasible and technologically possible.

Thus, since CMRs only account for a comparably small share of the supply portfolio in the mechanical and plant engineering sectors, CMR management builds on the client company's SRM practices, including joint S&OP. Due to the vital relevance of product functionality, joint innovation programs encompassing innovation roadshows and roadmaps are prevalent in mechanical and plant engineering CMRs.

Industry specifics, therefore, shape the objectives of CMRs, firmly affecting the applied management practices. Table 4.3 summarizes the characteristics of CMRs in the pharmaceutical, food, clothing, and mechanical and plant engineering industries utilizing TCE transaction characteristics. While CMRs within industries may vary significantly, industry characteristics play an essential part in the heterogeneity of CMRs, making them challenging to manage and indicating the lack of dedicated management research. It is noteworthy that similar characteristics of CMRs across sectors are caused by different underlying factors, making generalizable management solutions for all CMRs cumbersome.

Table 4.3 Industry characteristics of contract manufacturing relationships

	Asset specificity	**Environmental uncertainty**	**Behavioral uncertainty**	**Transaction frequency**
Pharmaceutical industry	High asset specificity due to dedicated sites, physical assets, and procedures	High technology uncertainty of subcontracted products	Medium information asymmetry due to co-specialization	Medium transaction frequency due to partial external commercialization
Food industry	Medium asset specificity due to dedicated procedures	High volume uncertainty of subcontracted products	High appropriability of recipes	Medium transaction frequency due to partial external commercialization
Clothing industry	Low	High volume uncertainty due to short product life cycles and seasonality	High information asymmetry due to robust co-specialization	High transaction frequency due to full external commercialization

(continued)

Table 4.3 (continued)

	Asset specificity	Environmental uncertainty	Behavioral uncertainty	Transaction frequency
Mechanical and plant engineering industry	Low	High volume uncertainty due to prevalent project business	Medium appropriability of innovation	Low

For example, pharmaceutical CMRs are inherently strategic, placing their management closest to the SA and JV literature. Second, food CMRs represent the most dynamic arrangements due to strong coopetition, applying practices from all presented types of IORs. Third, clothing CMRs operate in markets with little asset specificity and robust CMO competition enabling client companies to use SRM and SM practices. Third, CMRs in mechanical and plant engineering are typically not designed for strategic products, primarily drawing on SRM and SM practices. However, all industries shape adapted management practices uniquely and develop propriety methods according to their needs. The clothing industry, for example, focuses on collaboration and CMO development, while the food industry invests mainly in safeguarding practice development.

Still, the central integrator of CMR management challenges across sectors is the need to apply tailored management practices amid firm heterogeneity of relationships. Moreover, due to the high degree of operational and strategic interdependence, goodwill and strategic alignment are essential for the client company to effectively leverage the CMO's capabilities, as the CMO's contractual obligations do not adequately guarantee them. Therefore, after assessing CMR's prevalence, management challenges, and practices based on empirical data from the dissertation, Chapter 5 presents artifacts that address these challenges.

Findings on the Management of Contract Manufacturing Relationships

5

Following the DSR methodology, this chapter presents the developed artifacts to respond to the managerial relevance and research needs of RQ_1 to RQ_4 in chronological order. First, Section 5.1 contains a *CMR management practice toolbox* in response to RQ_1. Second, Section 5.2 answers RQ_2 by introducing a *'CMR management needs assessment guide'* artifact. Third, for answering RQ_3, Section 5.3 presents the *'CMR strategy cycles.'* Finally, Section 5.4 lays out an *'Integrated CMR management process'* to integrate all findings for answering RQ_4.

5.1 Management Practice Toolbox for Contract Manufacturing Relationships

Practitioners in CMR management strive to identify and implement best practices for controlling the CMR's development. These practices should improve operative performance, facilitate collaboration and knowledge exchange, enable trusted self-governance, minimize operative and strategic risks, and maximize efficiency. However, since the objectives are manifold and CMR management is not a unified field of research, there is a movement toward adapting various management practices from different IORs or specific industries. Practitioners are the primary driving force behind this movement, refining existing practices and developing their propriety approaches with little support from literature or industry associations as guiding umbrellas. As a result, the practices used to manage CMRs are fragmented, and their contribution is ambiguous.

Supplementary Information The online version contains supplementary material available at https://doi.org/10.1007/978-3-658-41359-0_5.

T. Brandl, *Managing Contract Manufacturing Relationships*, Supply Chain Management, https://doi.org/10.1007/978-3-658-41359-0_5

Consequently, a frame of reference for practitioners for identifying, comparing, and evaluating management practice is lacking. Bromiley and Rau (2014) emphasize the need to define management practices and their purpose for application transfer. Without understanding practices' prerequisites, application areas, and effects on the partner, the transfer is prone to fail in achieving successful relationship management or harm the collaboration.

Therefore this chapter presents a management practice toolbox for CMRs contributing to the managerial need for *'best practices'* and a frame of reference in two ways. First, the toolbox contains the thirty identified management practices gathered from exploratory interviews and focus groups across four industry sectors. Although this selection is not exhaustive, it provides an exploratory and illustrative set of practices that companies can use as a guide. Second, through a TCE-based qualitative evaluation, the toolbox offers profiles of the contained practices that address practitioners' information needs for adoption to avoid frequent application problems. The profiles serve as a frame of reference for practitioners' evaluation of the appropriateness of a given practice in a specific CMR. Naturally, the profiles cannot make definitive statements of implementation costs and impact on the relationship quality. Still, they can guide the evaluation process by covering these aspects for an individual assessment in practice. Complementary to the empirical findings on management practices, the artifact equally draws on the knowledge base presented in Chapter 2 according to the pragmatic philosophy and the DSR methodology. These findings include the requirements of description, application cases, costs, and sensitivity from Section 4.2 within the management profile outlined in the following paragraphs. Practitioners are often explicitly interested in 'industry-specific' best practices to benchmark themselves against their competitors. Nevertheless, industry references are intentionally not included in the artifact to foster the transfer and evolution of practices and to not reinforce industry silos.

Sections of the CMR management practice profiles

- *Description:* A description of the practice in the profile is necessary to understand its implementation in a CMR. The identified practices include several variants for different use cases. Although there is a substantial overlap between CMR management practices and those of other IORs, the adopted practices' setup, procedure, and objectives might vary. Furthermore, the toolbox contains less disseminated practices which are not self-explicatory. Still, the description is not intended to serve as a step-by-step analysis and implementation guide. Substantial basic information, scientific literature, and regulation are available for most practices, but their interpretation of application in CMRs may vary significantly. Concerning their specific use in CMRs, the description aims to provide the key aspects for the successful transfer and adaptation for individual applications.

Consequently, the description responds to the first requirement derived in Section 4.2 but limits itself to the central *concept*, *customizing*, and *scope* of the practices in CMRs. The *concept* gives a short but comprehensive description of the practice's key elements and motivation. *Customizing* provides the main practice variations and levers for individual adoption and interpretation. Finally, the *scope* refers to the recommended CMR settings and implementation barriers.

- *Application case:* Many management practices serve ambiguous goals or are applied ambiguously without pursuing a systematic goal. In response to the second requirement, the application case section of the management profile clarifies the possible uses of the management practices presented. Based on the TCE governance problems, extensively described in Section 3.2.1, the application cases are tailored to CMRs. The management profile recognizes three application cases: safeguarding, operative alignment, and performance management. A management practice fits a safeguarding application when it serves the alignment of CMO interests explicitly through incentives and penalties or indirectly by increasing commitment and mitigating potential dissent. CMR management practices that help operative alignment within the CMR enable a more efficient flow of goods and information, reduce overhead and per-unit costs, or create greater transparency to offset relationship dynamics. Finally, practices that allow collecting and analyzing performance data of the CMO's behavior or output support the performance evaluation use case. In addition, practices intended to improve the CMO's performance explicitly are added to this category because they often substitute direct performance evaluation in CMRs due to the complexity of transparent decomposition of tasks and deliverables.
- *Application cost:* The application of management practices in CMRs is associated with their implementation or operation costs. These costs include training, hiring dedicated staff, IT tools and hardware, meeting expenses, and opportunity costs of time spent or capital tied up, the risk of performance degradation due to lack of control, and the risk of misuse of information access. Client companies aim to optimally allocate limited monetary budgets to existing CMRs and balance non-monetary costs with countervailing benefits in the best possible way. Because the cost of applying the practices affects their

viability for a given CMR, as a response to the third requirement, the management profile includes a cost estimate that considers the client company's monetary and opportunity costs. In addition, the CMO may be required to participate in or adjust its activities due to a particular practice, which will incur costs for the CMO. As these costs affect the CMO's business case and goodwill, their impact is also included. Furthermore, management practice variations may vary significantly in application costs. However, due to individual requirements, exact costs cannot be calculated. Therefore, the profile ranks the expected costs from low to high, considering scale and repetition, and shows an estimated medium cost level as guidance.

- *Application sensitivity:* The empirical results show significant dissent between clients and CMOs concerning individual practices. While conflicting opinions in CMRs are expected and not inherently harmful, CMR types that rely on trust, goodwill, and self-governance to lever CMO capabilities should apply sensitive practices consciously and in agreement with the CMO to limit the negative impact on commitment and performance. Client companies might implement practices with high application sensitivity with the best intentions for the CMO or a dominant power position. Nevertheless, low levels of trust and lack of understanding of the CMOs business culture, model, or processes can cause the approach to fail. While the profile description section points out levers for tailoring practices and including CMO interests, responding to the fourth requirement, the application sensitivity aims to signal practices that either manifest significant involvement in CMO's affairs or are prone to miscalculation of CMO benefits. Therefore, it is recommendable to thoroughly analyze prerequisites for CMR management practices with a high application sensitivity score jointly with the CMO. Application sensitivity complements the TCE safeguard use case by attributing the potential secondary effects of all management practices on CMO goodwill and commitment. Therefore, application sensitivity refers to the long-term stability of the CMR.

Application of the CMR management practice profiles

The following section employs the designed application profiles to the identified CMR management practices. However, due to the scope of the dissertation, not all practices can be presented in detail. Therefore, the following section focuses on exemplary practices for a comprehensive introduction. These practices are *dedicated bundling*, *the third man*, and *joint S&OP*. Dedicated bundling is a response to the challenge that CMRs can lead to CMOs having to manufacture unprofitable product volumes with no control over related business development. The third man is a practice developed in the food industry that serves as decision-making support and balances the interests of the client and the CMO through the involvement of a neutral third party. Lastly, joint S&OP constitutes a necessary alignment of manufacturing planning to the CMR environment, representing a primary challenge of their management. The remaining practices are presented through their management profiles in the ESM.

Dedicated bundling

Description: In CMRs, demand for a particular product is limited by a single customer, while contractual obligations prevent the CMO from discontinuing production in favor of more profitable alternatives. The lower the CMO manufacturing margin and the higher the product specialization, the less likely it gets that the relationship can provide a profitable outcome for the CMO based on economies of scale. Dedicated bundling entails pooling complementary or equivalent products to elevate a CMR to a financial volume attractive to the CMO. Therefore, in competition-intensive industries, CMRs often include multiple products or deliberately pair high and low-margin products to provide financial value to the CMO. In highly specialized CMRs, manufacturing volumes are more problematic than profit margins. Given the profitable returns for both partners, client companies seek to strengthen their bargaining position through dedicated bundling to offset strategic dependence on CMO capabilities and technologies. Since the expected development of manufacturing volume can be roughly derived from the product life cycle, bundling products of different maturity levels can emancipate CMR from individual products and enable long-term, partner-oriented cooperation. Consequently, the customization of dedicated bundles is determined by the extent to which the subcontracted bundle reflects either party's interests of low transaction costs, high margins, and strategic dependency. Target metrics and degree of CMO involvement in designing the bundle can thus be adapted to the intended practice utilization.

Application cases: Dedicated bundling aims at increasing CMR longevity and stability by binding the CMO through greater transaction volume. The objective of safeguarding by dedicated bundling can be pursued through two different design options. First, when designing the bundle of services, clients can aim to leverage bargaining power by subcontracting manufacturing volumes with low strategic relevance. Consequently, the CMO's dependence on the offered manufacturing volume should be greater than the respective clients' dependence, locking in the CMO and enabling the client to control the relationship more significantly. Second, dedicated bundling can be implemented in a CMO-centric manner to compensate for low CMO margins caused by client requirements to drive engagement and goodwill. Dedicated bundling finds widespread application in the CM of low margin or low volumes products, but also in high-tech industries with expensive manufacturing capacities hedging against diminishing demand in the declining product life cycle phases.

Application costs: Dedicated bundling costs comprise expenses for analyzing potential bundle options and opportunity costs for choosing a CMO-oriented bundle despite more financially attractive alternatives. Opportunity costs are negligible because dedicated bundling targets low-margin transactions, assuming little bargaining leverage and price differentials. The analysis of design options is also associated with low operational costs, resulting in an overall low application cost for dedicated bundles.

Application sensitivity: Since dedicated bundling can improve partners' margins in a win-win situation or change CMR's balance of power in its favor, ambiguous intentions lead to high application sensitivity. Actively limiting a partner's bargaining power by strengthening one's own can be seen as mistrust and detrimental to long-term cooperation prospects. However, even in a collaborative application case, a lack of understanding of the partner's business can negate the intended benefits of the product bundle if the CMO's manufacturing setup and complexity costs are disregarded. As a result, reciprocal bundling often overemphasizes the optimization of bundling on the client side over the interests of CMOs, which weakens the promotion of CMO commitment. In addition, targeted bundling in dynamic CMR environments is also considered an incentive mechanism. Additional production volume is added to the bundle to reward strong performance. Conversely, shrinking the dedicated bundle for no apparent reason can be misinterpreted as punitive behavior. Frequent dynamic shifts of the dedicated bundle may be interpreted as a sign of instability and opportunism, reducing CMO commitment. Thus, it is recommended to scan bundling opportunities thoroughly and discuss the underlying motivation and their implementation with the CMO beforehand.

The qualitative evaluation of the dedicated bundling practice is summarized in Table 5.1 below.

The third man

Description: The third man, 'critical friend' or 'invisible third,' is an emerging practice for decision support and control in the food industry. The name derives from the process of involving a neutral party in decision-making and implementation. The goal of the practice is to prevent opportunism and promote an unbiased agreement for a long-term commitment by the partners. Three variants of the practices have been observed:

Table 5.1 CMR management practice profile for 'Dedicated bundling'

<table>
<tr><td colspan="2">CMR management practice</td><td colspan="2">Dedicated bundling</td><td>No.</td><td>13</td></tr>
<tr><td>Section</td><td colspan="5">Qualitative evaluation</td></tr>
<tr><td rowspan="3">Description</td><td>Concept:</td><td colspan="4">Dedicated bundling describes a specifically composed set of products subcontracted to a CMO to increase the stability and scope of the CMR in both parties' businesses.</td></tr>
<tr><td>Customizing:</td><td colspan="4">Dedicated bundling can be designed based on financial metrics that target low transaction costs or high margins.
Hedging through dedicated bundling can be achieved through an arm's length approach (increasing bargaining power against the CMO) or a collaborative approach (ensuring mutual bundling benefits).</td></tr>
<tr><td>Scope:</td><td colspan="4">Dedicated bundling is recommendable for low margin or low manufacturing volume products in CMRs.
Because of its ambiguous nature, it is critical to align dedicated bundling adaptation with the CMR's management style.
Since client-centric transaction cost optimization through dedicated bundling is not inherently profitable for the CMO, two-way testing is recommended.</td></tr>
<tr><td>Application case</td><td colspan="2">Safeguarding</td><td>Operative alignment</td><td colspan="2">Performance management</td></tr>
<tr><td>Application cost</td><td colspan="2">Low</td><td>Medium</td><td colspan="2">High</td></tr>
<tr><td>Application sensitivity</td><td colspan="2">Low</td><td>Medium</td><td colspan="2">High</td></tr>
</table>

1. Determining fair prices is a central issue in food CMRs since market prices of raw materials and regulations influence final product prices heavily and are often intransparent to the client. In this instance, the third man-practice involves an external auditor conducting open-book accounting analyses or long-term consulting to determine fair and viable prices for both parties without disclosing their cost structures.
2. Quality requirements of client company's product designs and CMOs quality assurance procedures must be aligned at product launch. As a result, process adaptations and investments are usually necessary to achieve specific quality requirements. However, because of their detailed knowledge of manufacturing processes and materials, CMOs can analyze the customer's quality requirements and negotiate with them to make fewer adjustments. Therefore, neutral

quality assurance laboratories are often brought in to evaluate quality tolerances and mandatory adjustments as a basis for cost-sharing between the client and CMO.

3. The third variation can result from the second use case, which involves monitoring investment decisions. Dedicated adjustments to capacity, technology, or quality with shared investments might be necessary to manufacture the client's product in the desired quality and quantity. Clients use the third party practice to involve neutral third parties in reviewing or monitoring the investment project to prevent their funds from being diverted, for example, in the form of more expensive machinery that the CMO can use for different clients.

Application case: The practice emerges directly from client companies' need to ensure compliance in situations with conflicting interests and the limited ability to monitor, evaluate and analyze complex cross-company issues in CMRs. Therefore, it can be viewed as an extension of the widely distributed audit practice in the food industry, aiming at decisions instead of processes. The central theme of the practice is to create transparency in decisions and achieve a balancing of interests through a neutral expert. Consequently, the third man addresses the safeguarding problem of CMRs by limiting opportunistic use of funds, overpricing, and systematic undercutting of quality targets. Furthermore, it aims to increase CMO commitment through signaling sincere treatment by the client company and enabling co-determination rights.

Application cost: Depending on the use case, hiring external experts is associated with medium to high explicit costs. Furthermore, partners must provide the third man access to relevant data. However, since the third man is designed as a decision-support practice, there are no recurring costs, resulting in an overall medium application cost.

Application sensitivity: The application of the third man is susceptible because the third-party involvement requires disclosing sensitive data in the presence of conflicting interests. First, a professional inquiry into a business partner's stance on a decision is tantamount to questioning the available data or the partner's intentions and signals distrust. Therefore, this practice should only be used when there is significant mistrust in the CMR or open dissent regarding the data supporting the decision. Second, the third party's trustworthiness must be uncompromised, requiring proper and transparent selection procedures and financing. Table 5.2 summarizes the insights on the third man through its management practice profile.

Table 5.2 CMR management practice profile for 'The third man'

CMR management practice		The third man	**No.**	28
Section	**Qualitative evaluation**			
Description	Concept:	The third man involves a neutral third party who assists with CMR decision-making and implementation in an advisory capacity to support an equitable and transparent balance of interests.		
	Customizing:	The third man is applied for pricing decisions, quality assurance, and investment projects. There are variations in the third man's selection process, financing, and legal structure.		
	Scope:	Recommended in cases of distrust or open dissent		
Application case	**Safeguarding**		Operative alignment	Performance management
Application cost	Low		**Medium**	High
Application sensitivity	Low		Medium	**High**

Joint S&OP

Description: Joint S&OP is a collaborative CMR management practice that represents the transition from an arms-length relationship to an integrated CMR. Sales and production planning are separated in CMRs; thus, the client and CMO must work together to balance sales and supply-side fluctuations. Without a joint S&OP, the customer company must rely on safety stock to offset peak demand and CMO supply issues that tie up capital and cause products to age. Similarly, the CMO must invest heavily to predict demand accurately and remain flexible during volatile markets. Vendor-managed inventories, end-consumer market analysis, safety stocks, and reserve capacities are CMO practices encountered in disconnected S&OP. Predicting demand is especially difficult for CMOs in CMRs since they have little consumer market intelligence, given that the manufactured product is proprietary to the client.

Consequently, the greater the planning uncertainty for both parties due to the specificity of the product, the volatility of the market and the product life cycle, and the cost of reserve stock, capacity, and raw materials, the more advisable a joint S&OP is. Through direct and ongoing collaborative planning of supply and demand, risks can be shared and costs reduced. Customizing joint S&OP for specific CMRs can be conducted along the granularity and automation of the integrated planning process. Common activities jointly decided upon as part of S&OP are inventory levels, (seasonal) production campaigns, business continuity and order postponement, delivery windows, batch sizes, and staffing of flexible workers. Furthermore, joint S&OP often builds a platform for improving processes and products and extending cooperation through additional logistics services offered by the CMO. Second, the degree of process automation of joint S&OP can be adjusted according to the digital maturity and integration within the CMR. While sharing sales forecasts is a well-established supplier management practice, joint S&OP requires active decision-making and coordination. Therefore regular planning meetings are necessary to make joint decisions on the scope for action. Digitalization allows further mutual transparency on batch orders, live inventories, quality data, and capacities, enabling synchronized planning through management by exception. Potentially digital order releases established in internal manufacturing could be implemented in CMRs in the future, allowing remote-controlled CM.

Application cases: Joint S&OP fosters operative alignment allowing client companies and CMOs to adjust planning interfaces dynamically to share and minimize operational risk amid environmental uncertainty. In exchange for greater operational dependence, joint S&OP enables client companies to transfer operational control of demand management to the CMO, potentially reducing supply risk and costs according to the CMO's planning capabilities. On the other hand, the CMO can benefit massively from greater customer binding and planning security through targeted coordination with the client. In addition, joint S&OP can optimize service levels and transaction costs throughout the supply chain, resulting in higher financial profits for both parties.

Application costs: According to the chosen granularity and degree of automation of joint S&OP, application costs may vary significantly. First, personnel capacity needs to be freed to attend regular planning meetings. Second, automation requires variable investments in digital integration and operational costs. Finally, greater reliance on the CMO creates opportunity costs for customers that could pose a risk to the supply portfolio. Consequently, joint S&OP incurs recurring operative costs and variable investments depending on the degree of automation. Thus, overall medium application costs for implementation of joint S&OP are indicated, which need to amortize through mitigated supply risk and expenses.

Application sensitivity: The benefits of joint S&OP information sharing are transparent to both parties and potentially far outweigh the risks, such as CMO concerns about losing authority over operational planning. In addition, the increased integration is a sign of the customer's commitment and the future viability of the CMR. Hence, the application sensitivity ranks at a medium level. The qualitative assessment of joint S&OP is visualized in Table 5.3.

Table 5.3 CMR management practice profile for 'Joint S&OP'

CMR management practice		Joint S&OP		**No.**	19
Section	**Qualitative evaluation**				
Description	Concept:	Joint S&OP involves clients and CMOs in joint planning of volumes, batches, inventory, and staffing to optimize capacity use, manufacturing costs, and delivery service.			
	Customizing:	Variations in granularity of the joint S&OP and covered planning activities Degree of automation: Joint planning tool or meeting-based planning			
	Scope:	Recommendable in case of dedicated assets, volatile environment, high capacity or inventory expenses			
Application case	Safeguarding		**Operative alignment**	Performance management	
Application cost	Low		**Medium**	High	
Application sensitivity	Low		**Medium**	High	

Application of the toolbox in practice

In addition to the three presented practices, the artifact contains the practices discovered in this dissertation but does not claim to be exhaustive. Hence, the artifact needs to be understood as a frame for analyzing CMR management practices supporting their application, allowing for further extension in the future. Especially the practice of digital integration experiences dynamic growth, making later refinement of the respective management profile's contents likely. Table 5.4 provides an overview of the management practice toolbox's current practices. The artifact illustrates the need to safeguard against partner dependence and opportunism in CMRs by highlighting the number of practices applied for this exact purpose. Furthermore, the collected practices indicate the explanatory power of the artifact, as the nominal and ordinal distinguishing features show low redundancy even without the content description of the practice. Only two pairs of practices delineated by their complete profiles have the same application, cost, and sensitivity when viewed through the artifact lens, providing an informative overview for practice alignment.

The artifact can be used in CMRs as a reference for designing and evaluating relationship management. First, the user should be aware of the primary challenges the practice must address and compare them to the application cases of the included practices. Second, the particular relevance of the CMR to the client organization must be analyzed to assess the resources available to apply and sustain the practice. Third, the relationship's power balance and the dependence on the CMO's goodwill must be considered to ensure relationship stability. Finally, the complete profile description provides opportunities to tailor management practices to specific CMR types to determine appropriate applications in an open discussion.

The artifact does not include a sophisticated analytical procedure for selecting and evaluating practices for specific CMRs, as this would have a relationship-oriented nature that is not present in the context of the first research question. However, the outlined straightforward process allows for flexible application of the artifact in different CMRs in line with the intended goal of artifact usefulness in DSR.

Artifact evaluation and contribution to RQ_1

The three selected CMR practice profiles illustrate how the artifact addresses the four requirements derived in Section 4.2 for applying management practices in heterogeneous CMRs. First, it describes the management practice and its utilization in CMRs. Furthermore, it highlights application variations, recommended relationship settings, and customization levers for practice transfer. Second, following the understanding of management practices as targeted sets of activities, it provides the application objectives within the theoretical TCE framework of the dissertation. Third, it includes cost considerations in management practice applications based on the assumptions of TCE. Finally, it considers the reception of the practices by the CMO, which emerged as a primary challenge for practitioners in the empirical design. This previously represented a research gap in the literature, as management practices in inter-organizational collaboration have not been studied for application in CMRs. Therefore, the artifact reveals the specific design requirements of established management practices used for CMRs, which can support more successful CMR management. Customization, ambiguity, and reception of management practices by CMOs have been widely neglected in literature and practice-oriented grey literature, making their inclusion in the artifact helpful for adapting management practices.

Table 5.4 Artifact 'CMR management toolbox'

No.	CMR management practice	Application case			Application cost	Application sensitivity
		Safeguarding	Operative alignment	Performance management		
1	Audit	X			High	Medium
2	Business development support	X			Medium	High
3	Business review			X	Low	Low
4	Campaign contract	X		X	Medium	Medium
5	Co-investment	X	X	X	High	Medium
6	Collaborative after-sales			X	Low	Medium
7	Collaborative innovation program	X		X	Medium	Medium
8	Collaborative troubleshooting	X			Low	Low
9	Common agenda	X			Low	Medium
10	Continuous improvement program			X	Medium	High
11	Cross-functional team		X		Medium	Low
12	Cultural consulting	X			Medium	Low
13	Dedicated bundling	X			Low	High
14	Digital integration		X		Medium	Medium
15	Forecast sharing		X		Low	Low
16	Guided procurement	X		X	Low	High
17	Incentive program	X		X	Medium	Medium

(continued)

Table 5.4 (continued)

No.	CMR management practice	Application case			Application cost	Application sensitivity
		Safeguarding	Operative alignment	Performance management		
18	In-licensing	X			High	High
19	Joint S&OP		X		Medium	Medium
20	KPI	X		X	Low	Low
21	Locked recipes	X			Medium	Medium
22	Manufacturing agreement	X	X		Low	Low
23	Open-book accounting	X		X	Medium	High
24	Open portfolio	X			Low	High
25	Qualification program		X	X	High	Low
26	Supply chain finance	X			Medium	High
27	Teambuilding	X			Low	Low
28	The third man	X			Medium	High
29	Turnkey manufacturing			X	Low	Low
30	Volume guarantees		X	X	Medium	Low

Table 5.5 details the artifact development throughout the focus group evaluation cycles. As an introduction to the focus groups, the first implementation focused on management practices because of their tangibility. The first focus group confirmed the dimensions of application cases, description, scope, and customization. Furthermore, the integration of social practices was suggested. In focus groups two and three, the impact of management practices on the social relationship level was gradually refined and integrated. Finally, in the fourth focus group, the management practice profiles were evaluated and tested in a workshop setting to customize management to specific segments and lifecycle phases. The management practice profiles were well received in the evaluation. One participant noted that companies do not develop profiles of management practices on their own, although this would be helpful for focused discussion and improved transparency. Consequently, the management practice toolbox was found to be

an appropriate management tool for more effective adaptation of management practices to the CMR's individual needs by the participants.

Table 5.5 Focus group evaluation of 'CMR management practice toolbox'

Focus group (No.)	Utility evaluation	Participant feedback
1	Positive	Application costs to mirror implementation efforts are approved Application cases, description, scope, and customization are approved to create transparency on practice variations Impulse: Social practices such as systematic teambuilding are undervalued in practice
2	Positive	Impulse: Management practices are received differently by CMOs than intended by the client Impulse: The simplicity of design and parameters is paramount
3	Positive	Impulse: Management practices are customized and used differently at different relationship stages
4	Positive	Design of management practice profiles is approved Practice sensitivity as a signal to the discussion is approved

Therefore the artifact answers RQ_1 by providing a frame for successful adaption of management practices based on design requirements drawn from CMR across four industries. Finally, the toolbox includes practices adapted for use in or developed within CMRs and therefore emphasizes the unique nature of managing CMRs.

5.2 Assessment of Management needs in Contract Manufacturing Relationships

Against the backdrop that many CMRs are not meeting their performance targets, proper assessment of management needs is critical for client companies. The empirical results suggest two elements of CMR management needs assessment: first, client companies seek to standardize the allocation of essential management practices for operational control through segmentation to create transparency and reduce operating costs. Second, targeted relationship development is an essential concern in CMRs, but is not systematically captured in current management evaluation processes and therefore is not reflected in the choice of management practices. Therefore, to answer RQ_2, this chapter presents a 'CMR *management needs assessment guide*' that addresses the requirements derived in Section 4.3. The artifact distinguishes two steps in the assessment process:

1. *Stage 1:* The assessment of the CMR's operations and supplier management needs serves the relative evaluation of the CMR concerning other CMRs in the client's portfolio to allocate resources efficiently and can therefore be done unilaterally.
2. *Stage 2:* Assessment of the CMR's relationship management and development needs requires the alignment of goals, expectations, and perceptions of the client and CMO and must be conducted jointly.

In addition, due to the ongoing dynamics of the relationship, it may be necessary to perform the management assessment repeatedly throughout the relationship, requiring the applicability of the artifact to new and existing CMRs. The commercial contract and existing manufacturing agreements build the frame of reference to measure the management needs.

Supplier segmentation is an SCM method in which selected suppliers are classified based on specific segmentation criteria to develop targeted management strategies (Rezaei & Ortt, 2012). However, the sheer number of existing segmentation approaches underscores the complexity of developing universally practical segmentations. Häkkinen (2008) provides an overview of existing CMR segmentation approaches, which are limited in terms of the assessment process's granularity and recommendations concerning management practices. Rezaei and Ortt (2012) distinguish three types of segmentation approaches: Process, portfolio, and involvement.

- *The process method* by Parasuraman (1980) represents one of the oldest and least frequented approaches to supplier segmentation in literature. It stands out by not specifying variables and segments but instead providing a procedure by which practitioners can identify segments.
- *The portfolio method* pioneered by Kraljic (1983) offers an easy-to-use two-variable approach based on the attributes of the supply item.
- *The involvement method* extensively reviewed by Tangpong et al. (2015) focuses on the bonds between client company and supplier, offering a variety of variables and segments.

In recent decades, portfolio and involvement methods have been increasingly combined to provide truthful and meaningful distinctions of supplier relationships based on supply item and relationship characteristics. By providing predefined variables and segments, these approaches have found broad appeal among practitioners and have visibly influenced the management assessment within client companies' CMR portfolios. However, the empirical results of this dissertation suggest that the contemporary challenges in the first phase of management assessment are rooted in a lack of process understanding in adapting portfolio and involvement segmentations to the client's organization. For example, the adaption or development of portfolio method segmentations frequently fails in CMRs due to the prevalence of multi-product relationships. Furthermore, due to the diversity of the client's CMR objectives, subcontracted activities, and industry specifics, it is not viable to define a generalizable set of variables and segments that can be operationalized straightforwardly and beneficially. Moreover, even though standardization is envisaged in the first stage of management assessment, the ability of segmentation methods with predefined variables and segments to make meaningful recommendations about relationship development paths and supportive management practices is limited.

Therefore, this dissertation uses the process approach based on observed deficiencies to develop a management assessment guide. The artifact's purpose is consistent with DSR's pursuit of utility and helps practitioners develop, tailor, and refine their custom CMR segmentations. Furthermore, the process approach is most suitable for appropriately integrating the CMO's perspective in the assessment procedure regarding CMR's relationship management and development needs. The CMR management assessment guide is developed in the following sections using the process approach along the two assessment stages. The methodology defines the sequence of activities, the selection of meaningful criteria, and the output format of the artifact for each stage.

5.2.1 Assessment of Operations and Supplier Management needs

This chapter deals with the first stage of the integrated management needs assessment focusing on operations and supplier management needs. Parasuraman's (1980) original process approach to supplier segmentation followed the sequential identification of key customer segment factors, critical supplier characteristics, supplier segmentation variables, and supplier segments. However, for this dissertation, the process approach will be used to build an artifact that allows for a high degree of standardization and direct estimation of CMR management needs rather than being limited to segments.

Therefore, the dissertation proposes a five-step procedure that covers rigorous development and implementation of the management needs assessment procedure. Explicitly addressing the frequent shortcomings in practice, the first three steps of the procedure provide systematic support for the setup, validation, and refinement of the artifacts adoption to specific client companies' business environments. Once significant variables for evaluating a CMR's fit with particular segments and management practices are in place, client companies can directly skip the setup steps and measure variable values for management assessment. Finally, a refinement of variables through revisiting should be conducted judiciously to compare CMRs based on a standardized assessment procedure.

a. **Procedure setup: Assignment criteria definition**

In practice, individual and segment-based evaluations of CMR management needs can be found. Although clients utilizing segmentation tend to take a more mature CMR management approach, an individual evaluation may make more sense for smaller companies based on their CMR portfolio size. A segment-based approach builds on a higher level of abstraction, making it particularly useful for large CMR portfolios where the approach's transparency, comparability, and standardization are essential. On the other hand, individual assessments allow a much more precise fit of management practices but also require excellent transparency about the available management practices and their characteristics. Therefore, this artifact is designed to equally support the setup of a relationship-based and segment-based evaluation procedure for attributing management practices.

The first setup step is identifying the assignment criteria that lead the client to adopt certain management practices or assign a CMR to a particular segment. For example, if the customer chooses a segment-based approach, inclusion criteria must be established for each segment. Alternatively, for individual assignment of management practices to CMRs, assignment criteria must be determined for the management practices directly. In order to illustrate the application of the management assessment guide, the perspective of an individual assignment based on the profiles given in the management practice toolbox presented in Section 5.1 is assumed in the following steps.

Consistent with the applied TCE frame of this research question, the relevant assignment criteria presented can be matched with the profile dimensions of the management practice toolbox: Application costs, cases, and sensitivity (see Table 5.1). While the mutual relationship gap analysis covers application sensitivity in the second stage of the management assessment, the remaining criteria build the basis for deriving the management practice's assignment criteria. For example, management practices with high application costs are only applied if a CMR shows substantial investment attractiveness. Likewise, the application case of safeguarding is fulfilled when a CMR poses significant risks to the client company. Furthermore, performance management practices are used when the client organization believes that significant performance potential can be leveraged by controlling or supporting CMO activities. Finally, CMRs employ practices for operational alignment when there is need for synchronization or integration of processes. Consequently, in this instance, investment attractiveness, risk profile, performance potential, and synchronization and integration needs constitute the assignment criteria of the management practices against which CMRs characteristics must be matched in the next step.

b. **Procedure setup: CMR characteristics identification**

Next, the CMR needs to be evaluated to whether it fits the assignment criteria to warrant the deployment of individual management practices. Therefore meaningful CMR characteristics which match the management practice's assignment criteria or the segments inclusion criteria need to be defined for measurement. CMR characteristics can be structured and derived from the captured transaction characteristics displayed in Figure 4.5.

For example, investment attractiveness relates to a CMR's strategic transaction value, volume, and scope, implying the client's willingness to invest in the relationship. In addition, the risk profile is determined by the shared investments, the integration level, the stability of the partner and its value contribution, and the balance of power in the CMR, which reflects the likelihood and severity of a CMO's withdrawal or misconduct. Performance potential can be divided into CMR characteristics such as performance risk, opportunism risk, and appropriability risk, which require additional control. Furthermore, it includes performance and evaluation complexities that benefit from goal alignment and support practices. Finally, CMR's synchronization and integration needs are defined by the product life cycle stage, the technology novelty, the market volatility, and competitiveness that must be mitigated by effective communication routines and flexible material flow structures.

In this example, the four assignment criteria result in seventeen CMR characteristics. Clients tend to consider as many relationship characteristics as possible relevant to create a comprehensive picture. However, since each CMR characteristic must be measured, the complexity of the assessment quickly increases. Therefore, portfolio and involvement approaches in literature usually rely on two to three dimensions to define segments, drastically reducing the evaluation process's complexity at the cost of accuracy. Hence, it is recommended to include a validation cycle to avoid redundant characteristics with low relevance. Methodologically, the reduction of variables in the validation cycle should be supported by visualization, for example, through Venn diagrams (Verdinelli & Scagnoli, 2013) and Cognitive maps (Kitchin, 2001), to detect intersections.

Furthermore, transparent thresholds must be established to show when a characteristic meets management practices' or segments' assignment criteria. Ordinal scales based on meaningful levels such as *'low,' 'middle,'* and *'high'* or *'criteria met'* and *'criteria not met'* are preferred for more straightforward comparability.

c. **Procedure setup: Variable definition**

The third step involves translating CMR characteristics into measurable variables for data collection. First, the goal is to define variables that are easy to measure in the evaluation of CMR. Secondly, the variables must be aggregated to quantify the fit against management practices and segments.

There are significant differences in measurability. Transaction volume, for example, can easily be quantified in terms of expected revenue, spent, or the number of orders. More abstract characteristics, such as the power balance, might not be measured quantitatively and rely on qualitative estimation. However, a reasonable qualitative estimation of the CMR characteristics conducted by an expert familiar with the topic might be more appropriate than an accurate quantitative metric that neglects relevant aspects. In the case of power balance, for example, a comparison of company sizes or revenue shares may be measured precisely but lacks aspects such as switching barriers and capabilities.

Next, variable results must be aggregated to evaluate whether a CMR's characteristics match the assignment criteria of the management practices or segments. For example, joint investments could be measured by their net value, resulting in a numerical outcome. In contrast, measuring the balance of power could return a qualitative assessment. However, since both variables contribute to the risk profile criterion, their results must be summarized. Consequently, an ordinal evaluation might be preferred for greater transparency and more accessible aggregation.

Finally, the variables must be meaningful to the assignment of practices in a given CMR or the inclusion of a CMR in a given segment. During the process of abstracting and aggregating criteria for evaluating the suitability of management practices or segments, much information is consciously and unconsciously delineated. Therefore, this dissertation proposes an actively applied validation cycle to assess the appropriateness of a variable for the management needs assessment. Validation of selected variables is an essential concern in management assessment in practice and has received little attention in the literature. Polar cases (Al-Qurtas & Zairi, 2003) and sensitivity analyses (Frey & Patil, 2002) are practical approaches to test whether the match between a CMR and a management practice or segment is affected by extreme or changing variable value. For example, Table 5.6 illustrates three examples of how extreme values for the characteristic *partner contribution* can affect the design of specific management practices. Consequently, the partner's contribution is a valid variable because the extent to which the partner is substitutive changes the focus of CMR management.

Table 5.6 Validation template of management assessment variables

Management practice	Validated variable: *Partner contribution*	
	Minimum score	Maximum score
Business reviews	Operational focus, strategic reviews	Regular meetings across management levels, strategic outlooks
KPIs	Operational KPI for performance management	Social KPI, Joint KPI for CMR guidance
Common agenda	Understanding product lifecycle and regulations	Teambuilding, understanding partner's business
...	...	...

Thus, a high or increasing value of the CMO's contribution to the CMR is meaningful for assessment because it affects the use and design of specific practices, such as KPIs. Since the selected criteria and variables are only an approximation of the actual management needs of a CMR, understanding the selected criteria and their shortcomings is essential for the successful application and refinement of the process.

1. **Procedure implementation: Variable measurement**

Fourth, after defining the variables, client companies have several options for data collection to measure their degree of fulfillment. First, questionnaires can structure and capture the required data, including the CMO, and disclose necessary information. Second, a focus group evaluation can be conducted, including the process owner and organizational interfaces with the CMO. Finally, Rezaei and Ortt (2013) tested a segmentation method based on fuzzy logic that allows the collection and aggregation of numerous variables through a high degree of automation. All approaches have specific advantages and disadvantages in different CMR environments. However, the systematic review and implementation of variable measurement allow to uncover systemic weaknesses and achieve a more robust assignment of segments and practices. Therefore the variable measurement process should be standardized within companies to achieve comparability of results among CMRs. Individual measurement by business segments or country divisions in client companies has contributed to limited transparency concerning management needs, appropriateness, and effectiveness of management practices impeding successful CMR management.

2. **Procedure implementation: Management need evaluation**

In the fifth step, the measured variable values are aggregated to analyze the CMR criteria thresholds and evaluate the management need by fulfilling the assignment criteria. In the chosen illustrative case, a CMR is evaluated based on the assignment criteria of investment attractiveness, risk profile, performance potential, synchronization, and integration needs. These are broken down into 17 CMR characteristics indicating the criteria fulfillment. Based on the measured variable values, the procedure returns how the CMR performs on the assignment criteria. In the case of a segment-based approach, the result should conclusively assign the CMR to an available segment. However, in the case of individual assessment, the results are not deterministic since a CMR can be assigned to several management practices simultaneously.

Consequently, meeting the assignment criteria, in this case, represents merely a fit between the management practice and the CMR. For example, client companies might standardize specific core practices and select other practices by individual assessment, including various experienced-based considerations that cannot be quantified. Furthermore, since the artifact proposes a second-stage analysis of management practices with the CMO, an open internal discussion of management practices and potential combinations is preferred over a deterministic assignment. Finally, it serves as a briefing and preparation for the workshops conducted with the CMO by reflecting on each practice's advantages and disadvantages in the given CMR.

In practice, it is helpful to visualize the results to compare, challenge and communicate the assignment. For assessment processes based on two assignment criteria, matrices are the norm, according to Rezaei and Ortt (2012). In contrast, assessment processes with more than two assignment criteria benefit from radar chart visualization, as outlined by Kaczynski, Wood, & Harding (2008).

Figure 5.1 summarizes the first stage of the management assessment procedure focusing on the CMR's operations and supplier management needs. The second stage will complete the artifact by focusing on the CMR's relationship management and development needs.

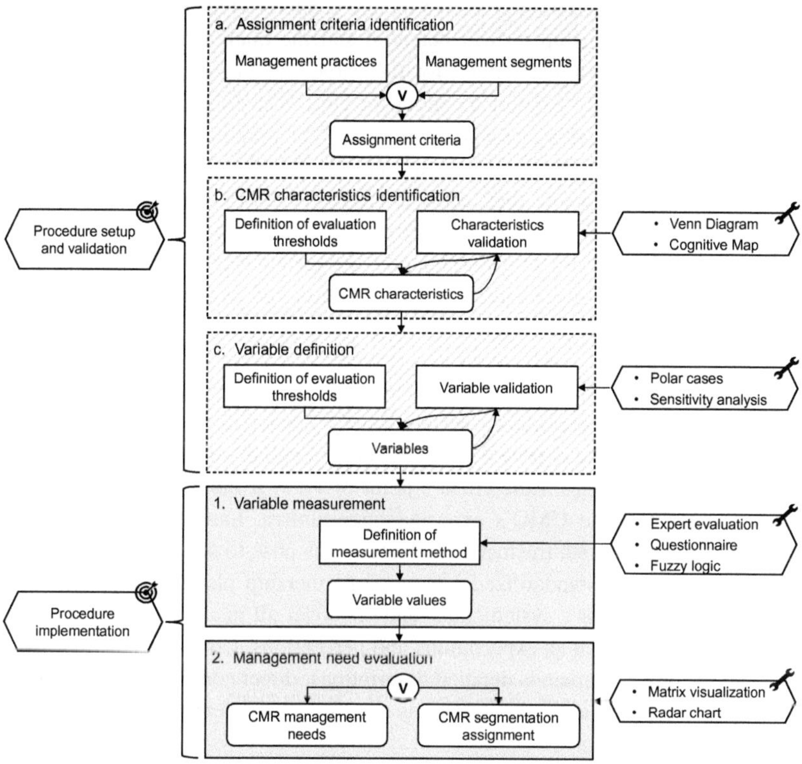

Figure 5.1 Stage one of the management needs assessment procedure

5.2.2 Assessment of Relationship Management and Development needs

This chapter deals with the second integrated management needs assessment stage, focusing on relationship management and development needs. The second stage builds on the established segments and selected management practices from the first stage. The transformation of CMOs from service providers to value creation partners enhances the need for strategic and operational alignment beyond contractually agreed conditions to enable a flexible and effective CMR. The empirical findings indicated a frequent gap in the relationship between such contractual duties and desired proactive mutual support, which is named the '*relationship gap*.' Relationship growth potential and the quality of collaboration in the CMR have been named criteria for the choice of management practice and are directly affected by existing relationship gaps. The relationship gap can be divided into an *expectation* and a *perception gap*. The relationship's growth potential refers to the compatibility of the expectations of both partners in terms of the intangible and future value they can gain from the CMR. Relationship quality results from the social fit of how the relationship is managed by both parties and affects trust and commitment. Consequently, the second stage of the management assessment procedure must address the expectation and perception gap to refine the choice of management practices to enable effective collaboration.

Bridging the expectation gap

Expectations play an important role in partner behavior in CMRs because commitment is based on the expected future benefits of collaboration (Palmatier et al., 2013). Consequently, from the client's point of view, it influences their willingness to invest and the CMO's expected opportunism. Lambert and Knemeyer (2004) recognize the risk mismatched expectations pose to supply chain relationships and propose a standardized integrated partnership planning method. They emphasize the need for a systematic agenda to cover all intangible topics that are frequently missed, such as expectations and perceptions. Consequently, assessing the relationship gap demands detailed descriptions, direct comparisons, and quantification of expectations and perceptions as a frame of reference for relationship development and quality.

Practitioners seek to clarify the partner's expectations for the CMR's future development and partner behavior to uncover potential discrepancies between expectations and synergies for growing the relationship. A distinction between the business and partner expectations is recommended in the assessment, as the former relates to future business prospects and the latter to social fit.

- *Business expectations* define the business opportunities beyond the current and agreed-upon core business that partners should actively work to exploit. The existence of business opportunities for future CMR expansion increases the growth potential of the relationship. It allows the client company to refine its choice of management practices to develop the relationship systematically, for example, by raising the CMR's investment attractiveness to the client. Conversely, severely mismatched expectations for the relationship may require more aggressive safeguard and performance management due to a lower level of CMO commitment. For example, it may be helpful for each party to outline specific criteria as to why they joined the CMR and what circumstances would lead to an exit. Each side prepares and presents its expectations for future CMR growth to assess the relationship expectation gap. The expectations must be described in detail, based on specific factors, and evaluated against an estimated timeframe for implementation and likelihood of achievement on a scale from *'unlikely'* over *'possible'* to *'likely.'*

Furthermore, the partner states the significance of the expectation for themselves, ranking it *'low'* or *'considerable.'* In return, the other side then comments on the expectations. Finally, both parties must compromise on a joint likelihood estimation—failure to compromise results in an *'unlikely'* score. The results with reasoning are then distributed and can be reevaluated in management reassessments, annual reviews, or strategic outlooks. The client company can utilize the expectation list to evaluate relationship growth potential and refine management practices by assigning numerical values to the ratings as indicators. Essentially, a relationship's growth potential exists when significant opportunities can be exploited in the future. Therefore, the values for the joint likelihood estimate and the significance of each specified expectation can be multiplied and summed up. The client companies can then set their action thresholds based on the total sum. For example, high development potential can be recorded when the score corresponds to a very likely fulfillment of a significant expectation. Table 5.7 illustrates the procedure by providing a template for the business expectation assessment.

- *Partner expectations* refer to the demands that both partners place on targeted cooperation. These expectations may include, for example, commitment to continuous improvement, corporate values, flexibility, responsiveness, transparency, and social etiquette. Behaviors or work philosophies that may indicate an underlying social fit can ease the need for control mechanisms. Unlike CMR expectations, which deal with the future expansion of CMR, knowing and meeting partner expectations are a foundation for daily work and thus actively influence the existing relationship.

  Therefore, both partners should prepare their expectations of the partner's behavior in detail, preferably with concrete examples they can share. All expectations are documented, and the partner in question can respond by accepting them, eventually suggesting amendments that the other partner must agree to or politely reject. As a result, the partners receive a list of agreed and disagreed behaviors, which they can later use in reassessing the quality of the relationship. According to Häkkinen (2008), the quality of joint activities in

Table 5.7 Template for business expectation assessment

Partner	**Relationship expectation**	**Expected time frame**	**Likelihood estimation** (unlikely, possible, likely)	**Significance declaration** (low, considerable)	**Joint likelihood estimation** (unlikely, possible, likely)	**Comments**
CMO	*Take over manufacturing responsibility for APAC*	*Eight years*	*Likely*	*Considerable*	*Possible*	*The client plans new bidding*
…	…	…	…	…	…	…

CMRs can be effectively discussed by having the client and CMO quantify and then compare their assessments. Consequently, adherence to partner expectations can be assessed in recurrent meetings by having each partner rate the other partner's perceived degree of expectation fulfillment. Finally, the client company can leverage the assessment to quantify social fit, assess relationship quality, and improve management practices to increase or decrease direct control. Therefore, each matched partner expectation should score one point, while rejected expectations receive zero points. The relative score ratio represents the social fit. What level of social fit is deemed healthy for the CMR, and what requires adjustment of management practices already selected depends on the envisaged relationship development path. Table 5.8 gives an overview of the evaluation of relationship quality and provides a template for adoption.

Table 5.8 Template for partner expectation assessment

Partner	Partner expectation	Partner acceptance (1 p.)	Partner reject (0 p.)	Comments
Client	*Permanent access to the manufacturing line*	..	*X*	*No access due to third-party contractual obligations*
...	...	...	...	...
Acceptance ratio (Social fit)		**0/1**		

Bridging the perception gap

Apart from clear expectations regarding relationship prospects and partner behavior, management practices may be received differently than intended by the CMO and may lead to undesirable side effects in the absence of transparency. Thus, a lack of understanding and empathy for the CMO's business model can jeopardize attempts to evolve the CMR beyond a based zero-sum relationship to trust-based cooperation. The empirical results showed that client companies and CMOs often have different perceptions of the appropriateness and usefulness of management practices for CMR management. For example, practices such as dedicated bundling or periodic collaboration surveys suggested by the client create a disproportionate burden on the CMO or are not perceived as sincere. In addition, the standard inclusion of CMOs in qualification, innovation, or improvement programs is often perceived as interference and distrust. However, perception gaps in CMRs can remain hidden and accumulate over time, causing the relationship to deteriorate undetected. CMOs state that the lack of sincere interest and client commitment constitutes '*a different kind of business relationship*' in which work is done strictly by contract.

Thus, to avoid harm from perception gaps, the management practices derived in the first stage of the management assessment process should be reflected jointly to determine their utility to the CMR. Of course, it is not practical for the client and CMO to agree on all management practices. However, knowing partner perceptions provides valuable insight into the quality of the relationship, indicates management practice effectiveness, and can mitigate the risk of alienation. Subsequently, client organizations can adjust certain practices based on the partner CMO or reassess management needs. Depending on the corporate culture or competitive situation, customers may be reluctant to openly discuss management practices with the CMO. The client can therefore tailor the level of transparency of the assessment. For example, a client company might exclude discussion of KPI or incentive systems but ask for feedback on the use and design of shared S&OP, team building, or innovation practices. However, the empirical results suggest that the design of perceived standard practices should be considered since they are often overlooked, and active exclusion of specific topics signals a lack of sincerity in closing the perception gap.

When conducting the assessment, client companies should present the selected management practices to the CMO, regardless of whether they are visible or invisible in daily operations, and explain the rationale for their adoption. The CMO is then asked to provide feedback to them based on their contribution to the relationship and suggest adjustments if appropriate.

Table 5.9 provides a template for documenting the assessment with a typical example from practice. In this example, based on the client's clearly described intention, the CMO can propose an adjustment to management practices to avoid an unnoticed perception gap. The client is then free to incorporate the CMO's feedback or maintain the practice for internal benefit. However, the decision and reasoning should be communicated transparently.

Process requirements

Clients and CMOs consider a quarterly to an annual assessment of relationship quality and development opportunities appropriate. Lambert and Knemeyer's (2004) approach to partnership evaluation and turnaround suggests that one-and-a-half-day workshops on neutral ground with a neutral facilitator are most effective. However, client companies are looking for a standardized and streamlined approach to conducting the assessment procedure amidst the numerous CMRs in the supplier portfolio. Clients suggest questionnaires as a streamlined

Table 5.9 Template for assessment of the management practice perception gap

Client presentation			**CMO evaluation**	
Management practice	**Description**	**Objective**	**Evaluation of contribution**	**Suggestions for refinement**
Dedicated bundling	*Bundling products A and B to compensate CMO for decreasing demand for product A*	*Reduce client's management costs and increase CMR transaction volume*	*Product B cannot be produced at the same site without costly adjustments*	*Shortening the required shelf life allows for temporal bundling and production on stock, which is more effective than the proposed dedicated bundle*
...	....	...	...	...

implementation option, while CMOs insist on face-to-face and open exchanges to allow for genuine dialogue. Nonetheless, location and facilitation are valuable design options for the assessment process, while multi-day workshops might be appropriate only in highly urgent situations or for strategic CMRs. In addition, the participants of each partner can be customized for implementation, from the CMR process owners to the strategic supervisors to the representation of all operational interfaces. For example, initial and annual relationship assessments should include broader stakeholders, while quarterly evaluations limit themselves to selected personnel. Finally, depending on the occasion or partners' integration level, it may make sense to implement a multi-level or decentralized process to reduce the operational effort.

As a result, several design options for implementing relationship management assessment exist, and implementation can be adjusted as needed. The six identified design variables shown in Table 5.10 impact the operational process and signal the client's commitment to CMR. In contrast to the first stage of management assessment, relationship management assessment allows greater design freedom for client companies. Based on the first stage assessment results, clients can determine whether the CMR should be managed at arm's length based on contract terms or whether an active build-up of commitments is required. Thus, clients can customize the second stage of the integrated assessment procedure according to the extent of their investment willingness.

Table 5.10 Design variables of the stage two assessment

Design variable	Attributes			
Recurrence	Quarterly	Bi-annually	Annually	Needs-based
Procedure	Sequential	Parallel	Integrated	
Medium	Questionnaire	Remote Workshop	Workshop in person	
Participants	Process owner	Strategic apex	Operating core	
Location	Client site	CMO site	Neutral location	
Moderation	Client	CMO	Neutral	

Artifact presentation and explanation

The presented approach to assessing CMRs' relationship management and development needs can be integrated as a second stage with the procedure developed in Section 5.2.1 to provide a holistic assessment of CMRs' management needs. Stage one addresses the operations and supplier management needs and provides the foundation for CMR management, targeting coordination, and performance management. Since the first stage of management assessment is significantly more mature in literature and practice, the process focuses on frequent issues in practice, which have been particularly neglected by scholars before. As a result, the first stage of the management assessment procedure introduces method-supported validation cycles to enable practitioners to identify meaningful assessment criteria.

Stage two builds on the first evaluation and management assessment basis focusing on intangible relationship characteristics necessary for trustful collaboration. Social criteria receive increasing attention from practitioners due to the development of more strategic CMR, yet systematic relationship assessment and management are lacking. However, systematic relationship assessment and development are used sparingly because of the effort involved. Therefore, in contrast to the standardized approach at the first stage of management assessment, a scalable approach is necessary for stage two. Stage two provides a structured yet flexible approach that tailors the discussion and assessment of expectation and perception gaps to refine chosen management practices.

Furthermore, quantification in the second stage supports the evaluation of expectations. Although the proposed values for these scores cannot accurately measure intangible expectation gaps, they are intended to compel practitioners to explain their statements in detail. The constraint of quantifying statements and assessments requires a focus and evaluation of all relevant considerations, leading to more precise results. This approach is recommended because expectation gaps are not objectively verifiable, making it difficult to have a transparent discussion without a frame of reference. The quantification approach, therefore, addresses the 'irrational side' of the CMR, supporting the systematic assessment of the social relationship layer.

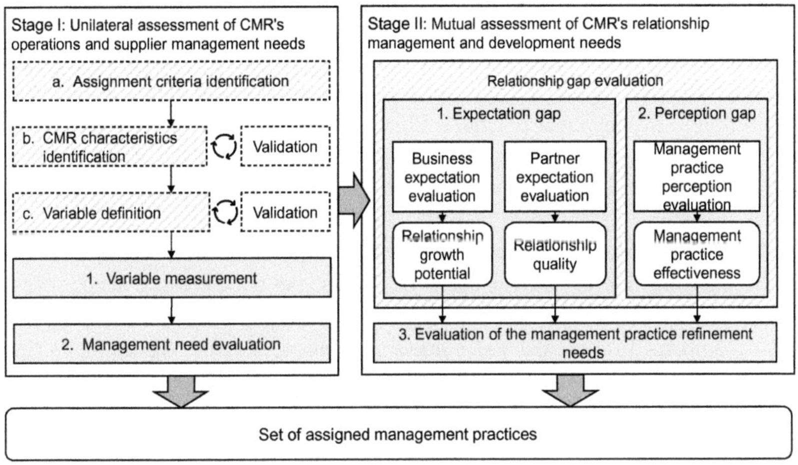

Figure 5.2 Artifact 'CMR management needs assessment guide'

The integration of the first and second stage procedures, as shown in Figure 5.2, completes the artifact called the *'CMR management needs assessment guide.'* An integrated implementation of stages one and two is recommended, as a comprehensive application covers all assessment criteria presented in Figure 4.5. However, stages one and two can also be applied separately, depending on the customer's perceived CMR relevance or the reason for the assessment. For example, a new CMR formation could proceed sequentially through stages one and two, with the design of stage two corresponding to the client's perceived importance of the CMR. In addition, the second stage can be undergone separately regularly, as requested by customers and CMOs, to monitor the quality of the relationship. It is assumed that the first step will be applied uniformly across CMRs and can be done separately if the overall management approach and evaluation criteria are adjusted.

Artifact evaluation and contribution to RQ_2

The developed artifact builds on a process approach to supplier segmentation to increase the likelihood of successful transfer and assignment of management practices in CMRs, amid heterogeneous industry and business requirements. By purposely addressing execution gaps caused by shortcomings in literature through validation cycles, practitioners can assign targeted management practices and segments to individual CMRs based on more effective selection criteria. The artifact builds on a TCE framework that captures the practitioner-named criteria for management assessment. Furthermore, it expands the scope of existing management assessment approaches by introducing the concept of relationship gaps and their connection to management practices. Finally, in line with the chosen process and DSR approaches, the artifact provides a tangible guideline encompassing validation cycles, templates, design, and methodology options for the effective adoption of the procedure.

Thus, by covering all artifact requirements empirically derived in Section 4.3 and recognizing the distinctive needs of CMRs, the management needs assessment guide provides a comprehensive answer to RQ_2. In addition, development was accompanied by regular focus group evaluation asserting the artifact's rigor and usefulness. The concept of relationship gaps as an integral part of management assessment and a workshop approach to address them systematically was presented in detail in the second focus group. Participants considered the concept and methodological approach for the relationship gap extremely valuable, as it supported systematic management of social aspects that had yet not been captured by existing approaches. In addition, the introduction of methods for validating assessment and segmentation approaches in acknowledgment of the heterogenic standards across participants was supported. Finally, the templates for both stages were welcomed as tangible impulses to adapt the artifact in practice. Table 5.11 summarizes the focus group evaluation and design impulses received from the participants.

5.3 Strategy Cycles of Contract Manufacturing Relationships

Relationship dynamics are a central issue in the successful management of CMRs due to the duration and close entanglement between the client company and the CMO. Moreover, the empirical results reveal numerous dynamics affecting the CMR from outside and within. However, to understand the impact of these relationship dynamics on CMR management adjustment, it is more viable to focus

Table 5.11 Focus evaluation of 'CMR management needs assessment guide'

Focus group (No.)	Utility evaluation	Participant feedback
1	n.a.	Impulse: Mismatch of expectations creates management needs, but soft CMR criteria are underexplored Impulse: Trust bridges formal management gaps and should be institutionalized in CMR management Impulse: Assessment criteria used in practice are often ambiguous and partly misleading Impulse: Universal segment definitions are of limited operational use due to their high degree of abstraction
2	Positive	Relationship gaps which include expectation and perception gaps, are approved Impulse: Relationship gap assessment must be conducted regularly, jointly, in person, and allow for open discussion Impulse Conflicting perceptions between clients and CMO concern specific management practices Impulse: Scalability of management needs assessment is important
3	Positive	Impulse: Limited openness to talk about goals in relationship gap assessment indicates CMR commitment
4	Positive	The first process stage focusing on methodological support of segmentation was approved The second process stage focusing on the relationship gaps was approved

on the outcomes of the relationship dynamics rather than their causes. For example, some dynamics, regardless of their source, lead to such severe changes that they require monitoring techniques, resilient structures, and flexible responses to adapt CMR management to permanently altered circumstances. Other dynamics, however, cause minor changes that can be handled in a standardized temporary manner and only require permanent adjustment of CMR management when they occur frequently or when there are definite trends. Such dynamics need ongoing monitoring to determine the right time to adjust CMR management practices.

Consequently, a meaningful visualization of CMR relationship dynamics for answering RQ_3 needs to structure the relevant relationship dynamics according to their relevance for adjustment of management practices. The identified CMR relationship dynamics are characterized by abrupt, gradual, or partly both types of occurrences. However, their relevance for CMR management is measured by their effect on management practice adjustment. Therefore, the form in which the relationship dynamic triggers the event of a management adjustment is crucial to visualize the relevant relationship dynamics for CMRs. In SCM, impact and frequency are the primary dimensions for clustering the occurrence of specific events (Heckmann et al., 2015).

The dynamicity impact on CMR describes whether relationship dynamics permanently or temporarily alter the relationship and the business environment or leave it untouched. However, various dynamics do not unfold their effect on management following a one-time event but gradually change the relationship through the accumulation of minor deviations. Therefore, their relevance to CMR management is defined by the frequency of the deviations they produce until they change the business environment to require a management response. Hence, the identified relationship dynamics are clustered using the dimensions of dynamicity impact and frequency.

Figure 5.3 shows the three emerging clusters for CMR relationship dynamics of *strategic*, *operational,* and *incremental* dynamics, which are elaborated on in the following paragraphs. The relationship dynamics presented are considered equally relevant by practitioners, but because of their different modes of action, they require different management approaches. The relationship between the three clusters was illustrated in the fourth focus group. One participant proposed that inflation is a typical gradual dynamic to which little attention is devoted. However, the actual situation with significant inflation at the time the focus group was held has brought this dynamic to management's attention. Thus the dynamic moved up between the clusters because it had accumulated considerable impact. Consequently, participant companies evaluated whether current high inflation would mean temporary or permanent interference with supply chain operations, making operational or strategic measures necessary.

Types of relationship dynamics in CMRs

- *Strategic dynamics:* Strategic dynamics owe their name to the expected permanent change in the relationship they create, requiring a strategic reassessment of relationship management. Strategic reassessment encompasses the perceived opportunities, risks, and alternative options associated with the

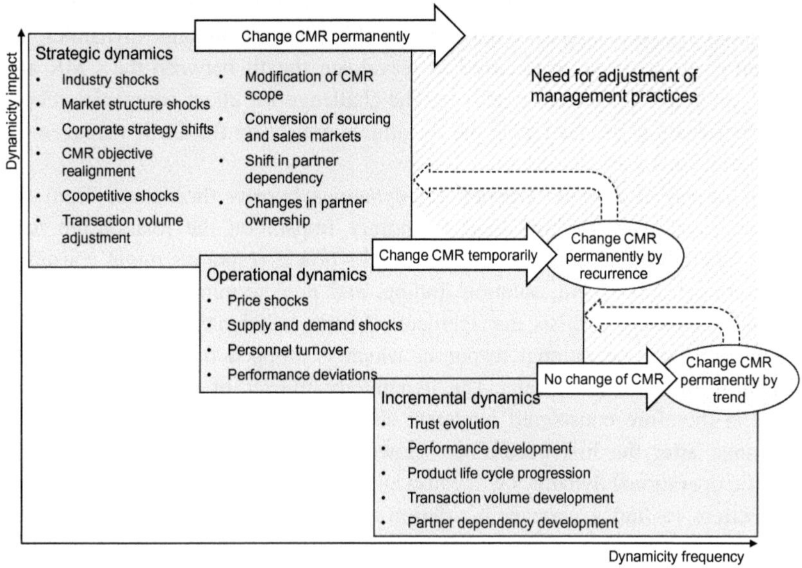

Figure 5.3 Impact-oriented clustering of CMR dynamics

relationship and forms the basis for investment readiness and the CMR's management needs. Consequently, strategic dynamics are characterized by significant dynamicity impact. Furthermore, the effects of strategic relationship dynamics are expected to establish a new equilibrium of management requirements in the relationship that lasts until new dynamic changes alter the CMRs trajectory in such a way that a new reassessment is necessary. Therefore within such an equilibrium, strategic dynamics are considered one time-events with low dynamicity frequency.

When observing the assigned dynamics, it is noticeable that strategic dynamics primarily arise within the relationship. For example, coopetitive shocks caused by the CMO's competitive behavior trigger an immediate reassessment of the CMR's security risks. As a result, they can lead to restricting knowledge transfer activities and revoking data access. This modification of management practices will continue until a discontinued competition or other dynamics allow for a relaxation of safeguards or require more stringent means. An example of external strategic dynamics in the CMR environment is industry shocks that require stricter control based on new regulations.

Hence, new regulatory compliance practices must be installed as long as the regulations are in place. Therefore, in the event of strategic dynamics, an immediate response is required to reevaluate the fit between the CMR and the applied management practices. The challenge for client companies relates to anticipating and analyzing the dynamic's impact on the CMR management requirements.

- *Operational dynamics:* Operational dynamics borrow their name from the operational response that their temporary impact on the relationship triggers. For example, when a machine breaks down, responses might constitute situational assessment, solution finding, and predetermined routines such as troubleshooting or crisis management. Operational dynamics should be mitigated by the operational response, which is stopped once the relationship returns to its former state. The dynamicity impact of operational dynamics is therefore considered moderate since it does not warrant a permanent change after the first occurrence. However, the repeated occurrence of the same operational dynamics will cause client companies to rethink management practices to find a permanent solution that eliminates the need for periodic operational responses. Thus, operational dynamics can also permanently adjust CMR management practices when they often emerge within one relationship equilibrium. Hence, the dynamicity frequency of operational dynamics is moderate. Both relationship dynamics within the CMR and the environment can cause operational dynamics.

  For example, individual price shocks may trigger a suspension of cost targets. However, regular price shocks will challenge the validity of the remuneration schemes or target values and trigger new permanent cost-saving measures, alternate targets, or metrics to monitor performance. Similarly, personnel turnover in crucial positions might be met with increased attention to performance development and dedicated onboarding routines to mitigate adverse effects during the familiarization phase. Nevertheless, frequent personnel turnover can be viewed as a strategic risk to the performance and stability of the partnership, leading to a reduction in business or a restriction in the CMO's ability to self-govern. Subsequently, operational dynamics require immediate action to overcome the temporal interference with established relationship routines through individual or standardized responses. In addition, the frequency of occurrence must be monitored to assess the appropriateness of permanent management adjustment. The challenges of operational dynamics, therefore, lie in preparation for an operational response on the one hand and in accurately assessing the threshold of recurring events that warrant a strategic reassessment of the CMR.

- *Incremental dynamics:* Incremental dynamics earn their name from the gradual change they cause, which initially does not entail any change in management practice. Therefore, incremental dynamics score low concerning dynamicity impact. However, their relevance to CMR management lies in their high dynamicity frequency, resulting in an accumulation of small changes in management requirements until a reassessment of the relationship's status quo is imperative. Incremental dynamics are often neglected because their gradual effects usually do not cause visible disruptions but result in hidden opportunity costs due to a mismatch between the relationship and the management approach used. In that sense, incremental dynamics are exceptional because they need to be monitored until a definite trend materializes to uncover the need for action. However, when to start monitoring and when a trend is robust enough to activate management response is fuzzy. Performance development is probably the most mature incremental dynamic from a management perspective since it is well monitored and defined thresholds for action are widespread. For example, CMOs' continued positive performance trends induce clients to re-evaluate the partner's capabilities and allow for greater self-management or upgrading of the relationship by expanding the transaction volume, value, or scope. Despite their recognized importance, other incremental dynamics, such as trust or transaction volume development, are less integrated into CMR management. The evolution of trust, for example, is considered a prerequisite for awarding strategically relevant activities or products, but it is rarely actively monitored or managed. This example emphasizes the main challenge of incremental dynamics in CMR management. Client companies must decide on, invest in, and set thresholds for action for dynamics with little management visibility since they pose no immediate risk of obstructing CMR operations. Thus, the investment willingness into management practices for incremental dynamics is limited due to challenging verifiable return on investment. The incremental relationship dynamics identified in this dissertation can be used to stimulate the practitioner's efforts in this context.

Toward a comprehensive model for CMR relationship progression
Considering the effect of the relationship dynamics on CMR, it is apparent that they have the power to alter the relationship's trajectory. This finding leads to the question of the relationship's trajectory or the equilibrium phases in which CMR management requirements are supposed to be stable. Hence, a comprehensive visualization must capture the envisaged and continuous progression of the relationship. The literature recognizes several evolutionary concepts such as

relationship life cycles and, more prominently, product life cycles. However, participants rejected these models as inadequate in the focus group evaluation. Product life cycle-based approaches from the literature, such as Birou et al. (1997), were not considered applicable because CMR takes a partner-centric management approach contrary to category management. Furthermore, CMRs often include multiple products whose product life cycles overlap and cause dynamic interactions in relationship management.

Existing relationship life cycle concepts in supplier management, such as those from Trumpfheller and Hofmann (2004), are more suitable since they focus on relationship intensity for model progression. Relationship intensity captures the degree of management attention a supplier relationship receives from the client side by combining qualitative and quantitative indicators such as openness, decision participation, or investment and interaction frequency (Trumpfheller & Hofmann, 2004). However, relationship life cycles were still deemed too deterministic and generic to visualize the dynamics relevant to CMR management adequately. Doz (1996) notes that even the underlying continuous relationship dynamics are only partially deterministic, and their direction and speed are influenced by management activities and decisions of the partner firms.

Therefore, based on the metric of relationship intensity, a temporal bracketing approach, similar to Pernot and Roodhooft (2014), was applied to derive CMR strategy cycles. Temporal bracketing divides the duration of a CMR into nonconsecutive periods with similar trajectories of relationship intensity due to client companies' implemented strategies. Interfering relationship dynamics can change the default trajectory accounting for the non-deterministic progression of CMRs. Following this approach, five strategy cycles of CMR were developed, characterized by a predictable progression of relationship intensity. The term 'cycle' suggests that the individual relationship phases are repeated multiple times throughout the CMR, similar to natural business cycles. The beginning and end of relationships are unique to individual CMRs. However, they are relived repeatedly by the client and the CMO across multiple CMRs, and sometimes sequential collaborations, which promotes an understanding of how to execute these phases properly.

Strategy cycles indicate the speed and direction of continuous relationship progression. However, contrary to life cycle models, CMR strategy cycles are not bound to a deterministic sequence but occur due to management responses to relationship dynamics. The relationship dynamics presented in this chapter trigger a strategic reassessment of the CMR, which in turn can end and initiate a strategy cycle, changing the course of the relationship. Therefore, strategy cycles are a non-deterministic concept of CMR development that considers ongoing relationship evolution and the effects of emergent relationship dynamics, whether of gradual, disruptive, external or internal nature. The five strategy cycles for *onboarding, anchoring, expansion, consolidation,* and *resolution* are explained below.

CMR strategy cycles

- *Onboarding cycle*: The onboarding cycle in CMRs is unique since it is the only phase without a predecessor. The onboarding cycle encompasses all activities necessary to establish the CMR to generate the envisaged value. Each CMR passes the onboarding cycle only once, but it may be repeated between the same client and CMO when a new CMR is established after a previous agreement has been fully terminated. The definitive decision to engage a CMO and establish a relationship triggers the onboarding cycle, which encompasses the entire legal, financial, operational, and social CMR setup. When not interrupted by relationship dynamics, it transitions into the anchoring cycle of collaboration after all project activities for the setup have ceased. The mutual adjustment of interfaces and production preparation usually requires extensive interaction in the form of a time-limited project organization. Therefore, the onboarding cycle is characterized by a significant increase in relationship intensity, which slowly subsides when the various setup activities are completed. Due to the long payback period and the necessary operational setup of the CMR, there is a fundamental willingness to invest during the onboarding cycle to lay the foundation for efficient and effective collaboration. However, further investments may be tied to the development of the relationship.

  Consequently, management requirements in the onboarding cycle are primarily operational alignment to enable rapid setup and efficient future production, as well as the establishment of safeguards for future collaboration. Performance management, by comparison, receives less attention as the relationship has yet to find its productive balance. In addition, the onboarding cycle is a susceptible phase of the collaboration, as the relationship is based on a leap of faith. Both partners' business cultures and routines are still unknown, making the CMR vulnerable to misunderstandings, misconceptions, and cultural discrepancies, which are temporarily masked by initial enthusiasm, and can have a delayed impact on the relationship.
- *Anchoring cycle*: The anchoring cycle represents the targeted equilibrium of collaboration in CMR and is revisited after each change in trajectory. It

encompasses all activities necessary to support the manufacturing of the subcontracted products. Thus, while the four remaining strategy cycles represent a transition between changing strategies, the anchoring cycle primarily concerns strategy implementation. Thus it stands out among the CMR strategy cycles as it is the most stable and typically most extended cycle. Except for the resolution cycle, all cycles not interrupted by the relationship dynamics merge into it, while the anchoring cycle remains and only discontinues with the emergence of relationship dynamics. The intensity of the relationship remains stable at a defined level during this phase. However, it usually declines slowly over time as management attention is lost to routine and the desire to increase efficiency.

Investment readiness is limited in the anchoring cycle because the appropriate operational infrastructure for production has been prepared in previous cycles. Consequently, mainly replacements, renewals, or individual technical innovations are reasons for new investments with the unchanged expected output. Similarly, the leading management requirement in the anchoring cycle is performance management. The foundations for collaboration have been laid beforehand and must be implemented successfully. Working conditions and safety risks are stable in this phase, which makes an additional focus on operational alignment or safeguards at the predefined level of secondary relevance. The anchoring cycle is characterized by little active change in the collaboration over an extended period, allowing the relationship to spill over into a routine. Routine is a chance and risk in CMR management since it reduces the likelihood of misunderstandings but increases the peril of losing track of the partner's expectations and conceptions. The CMR can benefit from the routine through increased efficiency but must also deal with the relationship potentially drifting apart due to lack of attention.

- *Expansion cycle*: The expansion cycle represents a transition phase, moving the CMR to an operational state with a greater scope of activities, transaction volume, or knowledge transfer. Triggers for expansion cycles can be new products, competitor behavior, or gradually increased trust or transaction volumes occurring multiple times throughout the relationship. The expansion cycle transitions into an anchoring cycle once the adjustments necessary to extend collaboration, such as new product launches or technology transfers, are in place. In multiproduct CMRs, expansion cycles cover multiple project streams deepening collaborations simultaneously. Comparable to the onboarding cycle, the expansion is implemented through various customization projects that run parallel to the already established activities. Therefore, the intensity of relationships increases steadily in the expansion phase, with adaptation projects initially attracting management attention and resources and then being replaced by extended operational cooperation after finalization.

Investment readiness tends to be highest in the expansion cycles of a CMR. In addition to the need to adapt relationship structures for increased collaboration, expansion builds on the proven trust through prior engagement, reducing the investment concerns that exist in the onboarding cycle. Primary management requirements during expansion are adaptation and safeguarding, while performance losses due to a focus shift must be minimized. The deepening of the CMR beyond the initial contract demonstrates trust and allows forms of cooperation and practices to be addressed that were previously too sensitive in the relationship.

- *Consolidation cycle*: The consolidation cycle reduces the scope of the CMR and transitions into an anchoring cycle characterized by a reduced extent of activities, transaction volumes, and products. Consolidation is triggered by the withdrawal of products, emerging competition, or unsatisfactory performance and ends when the necessary adjustments have been made. After a short spike due to the coordination of the adjustment, relationship intensity sinks steadily in the consolidation cycle as activities and management practices are scaled back or discontinued. Hence, investment willingness is low in this phase since the reduced operations diminish envisaged returns. As a result, management focus shifts to operational alignment to enable effective low-level collaboration and then to performance management and safeguarding to detect and mitigate any negative impacts from CMO behavior due to opportunism or reduced engagement. Consolidation is a critical phase in CMRs because it reveals the company's declining commitment and limits its bargaining power. As a result, the CMO may scale back its operational and strategic efforts in favor of more profitable arrangements, leading to a decline in performance or even a deterioration of the relationship. Consequently, the consolidation cycle must address the challenge of stabilizing the relationship at the new level to enable continued profitable collaboration for both partners.
- *Resolution cycle*: The resolution cycle of a CMR is similar to the onboarding cycle in several ways, in that it has a fixed position at the end of a CMR with no successor and can occur only once during a CMR. However, the limitation within a CMR does not extend to partners, as the client company and CMO may begin and end multiple consecutive CMRs. The impetus for ending the relationship may come from the client, CMO, or institutional parties due to strategic realignments, missed expectations, or regulatory and financial constraints. The resolution cycle is particularly challenging as it demands

significant management attention and effort with no prospect of returns. Consequently, the intensity of the relationship increases as the factual and temporal disentanglement of the client and the CMO are coordinated, then sharply decreases until it reaches zero. Some CMRs may experience an extended phase-out period with low relationship intensity after production ceases. The CMO continues to provide sporadic customer services such as spare parts and returns in such an extended phase-out. A lack of investment readiness characterizes the resolution cycle as both partners set their resources onto new prospective projects.

Conversely, residual financial values and claims arising from the relationship, for example, for stocks and joint investments, must be clarified. As a result, safeguarding and performance management are paramount to maintaining a coordinated termination of the relationship with minimal disruption to business operations and solid confidence for future collaborations. Especially since there are no future adverse effects to fear, the dissolution phase can tempt opportunism. However, since CM involves highly specialized services, reputational damage or future business relationships for lack of alternatives or personnel changes are possible. Consequently, a sensitive approach must be taken to CMR dissolution.

Application of the CMR strategy cycles

Figure 5.4 visualizes the CMR dynamics and progression and their interplay, presenting the CMR strategy cycles as the developed DSR artifact to answer RQ_3. The artifact depicts and structures the relationship dynamics and trajectories in CM. However, besides the informative visualization for scholars, they can be applied in practice to support CMR management. For example, the artifact can be used as a framework for cooperative relationship planning with the CMO, setting goals, and adapting management practices for specific cycles. Furthermore, it can serve as a guideline for developing capabilities to monitor and respond to various relationship dynamics efficiently.

Artifact evaluation and contribution to RQ_3

The artifact addresses the empirically derived requirement of comprehensive visualization of the relationship dynamics based on their effect on CMR management. Among the various dynamics prevalent in the business relationship between client companies and CMOs, it depicts those relevant for adjustment of management practices. Based on the empirical foundation, the artifact clusters the dynamics according to their impact and frequency, contributing to a deeper understanding

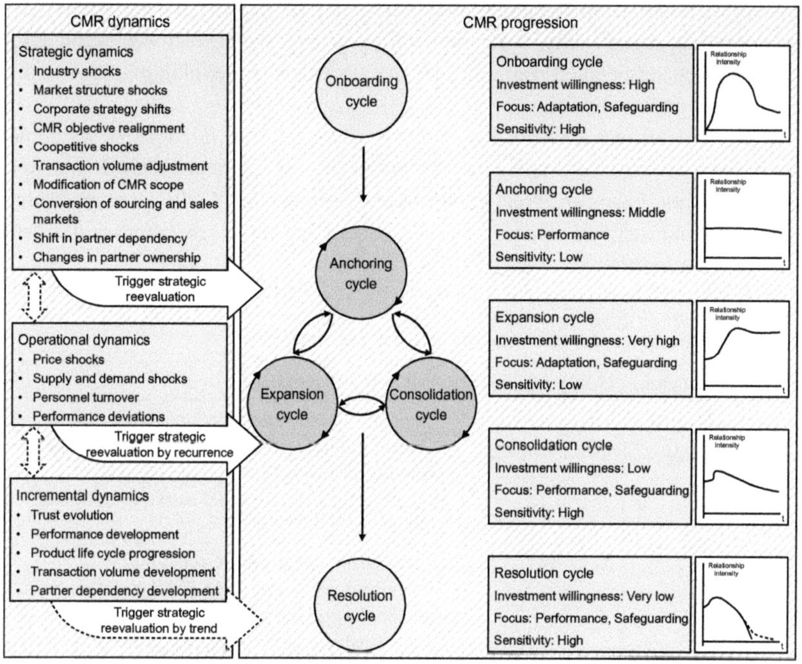

Figure 5.4 Artifact 'CMR strategy cycles'

of the relationship dynamics and enabling a meaningful management response. Finally, the artifact sets CMR relationship dynamics in context with planned relationship progression and identifies management requirements for the strategy cycles. The interplay between the strategically set phases and interfering dynamics allows a better understanding of CMRs' heterogenic trajectories. Consequently, it provides scholars with insights into the challenges of managing CMRs in practice.

Table 5.12 shows how the artifact was evaluated and refined by practitioners through focus group evaluation. A cumulative, product lifecycle-oriented version of the artifact was first explicitly tested for usefulness in the second focus group and rejected by participants. As a result, the non-deterministic cycle concept was developed and discussed in the third focus group. Then, following acceptance of the 'CMR strategy cycles,' the artifact was further refined by developing the individual cycle's characteristics and phase transition mechanics. Next, the three clusters of relationship dynamics were integrated to explain diverse relationship development paths. Finally, in the fourth focus group, the artifact was evaluated in its final form and deemed useful during the evaluation for explaining relationship progression and dynamics.

Hence the artifact answers RQ3 depicting the relevant relationship dynamics that trigger reassessment and possibly permanent adjustment of CMR management practices. From an effect-centered perspective, the 'CMR strategy cycles' encompass industry turbulences and relationship age and stage, offering a holistic view of relationship dynamics in CMRs.

Table 5.12 Focus group evaluation of 'CMR strategy cycles'

Focus group (No.)	Utility evaluation	Participant feedback
1	n.a.	Impulse: Relationship dynamics can change CMR parameters permanently or temporary Impulse: CMR trajectory depends on relationship dynamics and active progression alike
2	Negative	Product life cycles are rejected due to shortcomings in capturing CMR beginning, end, and multi-product setups Relationship life cycles are rejected because CMRs are actively transitioned to different stages without deterministic trajectories Impulse: Quantitative and qualitative (business and social) progression cannot be separated Impulse: Excess routine in the operational phase deteriorates relationship; active vitalization is necessary Impuls: The CMR dissolution is critical because quality and performance usually deteriorate
3	Positive	Strategy cycles are approved to describe non-deterministic relationship progression Standby cycles outside of active manufacturing were excluded from CMR management by the focus group Impulse: Cycle transition is paramount for usefulness, cycle beginning, ending, and triggers need to be defined Impulse: Resolution cycle with high initial relationship intensity and two trajectories: immediate decline or long-term fading

(continued)

Table 5.12 (continued)

Focus group (No.)	Utility evaluation	Participant feedback
4	Positive	The relationship dynamics clusters were approved The artifact encompassing the strategy cycles and relationship dynamics clusters was approved

5.4 Integrated Management Process for Contract Manufacturing Relationships

Dynamics play a central role in CMR management as they continuously change management requirements along the relationship lifecycle and interfaces. However, because the measurability and impact of the multiple dynamics affecting CMR vary significantly, it is difficult for client companies to determine when and how to adjust management practices. The CMR strategy cycles presented in the previous chapter provide a deeper understanding of the CMR's natural progression and reaction to various types of relationship dynamics. In addition, the management practice toolbox and CMR assessment guide described in Sections 5.1 and 5.2 support the CMR's evaluation and the selection of appropriate management practices.

Still, a purely reactive adjustment of management practices to incisive events that change the CMR permanently is costly as it leads to performance degradation and misses opportunities for improvement. Consequently, answering RQ4 requires a systematic and integrative approach to guide the reassessment and reallocation of CMR management practices concerning relationship dynamics. The empirical findings indicate the role of commitment as a connecting element to enable integrated and proactive adjustment of management practices in CMRs, considering the underlying social dynamics and future expectations of the business relationship. Firm commitment supports CMR's ability to flexibly balance operational and incremental dynamics without adjusting management practices as both partners seek to maintain a profitable relationship on their own merits. It also mitigates the risk of opportunistic behavior when strategic or operational dynamics permanently or temporarily disrupt the CMR. Managing CMO commitment is thus a success factor in CMR management, reducing the need to adjust management practices and enabling focused action. To this end, commitment must be actively measured and influenced to reduce any necessary adjustment of management practices at an early stage through targeted commitment control.

The artifact *'Integrated CMR management process'* aims to systematically guide client companies in dynamically aligning their CMR management with the changing management needs of the relationship. For more comprehensive application across different industries, the artifact was developed in a broader framework, omitting restrictive industry-specific requirements of the pharmaceutical industry in which the artifact was tested. Building on the findings presented in the previous chapters, the artifact provides a design that can be applied in various CMRs of differing scopes, business environments, and industries.

The CMR strategy cycles note that CMRs are subject to planned strategic development and uncontrolled dynamics. Consequently, in CMR management, strategic development direction must be implemented through management practices in operations management and corrected as necessary. Thus, since connecting strategic aims and operational management amidst relationship dynamics is an ongoing challenge in CMRs, this dissertation proposes an integrated and cyclical process to connect the two levels of relationship dynamics to select suitable management practices. Figure 5.5 depicts the intertwining of CMR progression and operational management of relationship dynamics at the example of the expansion cycle.

The strategy cycles provide a frame of specific goals the client company sets for a portion of the whole CMR duration, which is defined by the relationship's trajectory. Within that strategic cycle, CMR management assesses, implements, and monitors operations and the relationship with the CMO. The seven steps of the integrated management process cover the *positioning* of the CMR within the strategy cycles and *assessment*, *selection*, *alignment*, *refinement*, *implementation,* and *monitoring* of management practices. The process enables transitioning between strategic cycles and adaptation of management practices based on the regular evaluation of objective fulfillment and partner alignment through meaningful metrics as triggers for action. Furthermore, in response to the limited effectiveness of oversight of external manufacturing activities, the management process actively engages CMOs to overcome expectations and perception gaps for a more substantial relationship commitment. The artifact's seven management steps are outlined in the following paragraphs.

1. **Positioning within CMR strategy cycles**

The first step operationalizes the 'CMR strategy cycles' and serves as a temporal orientation within the CMR life cycle. While each CMR begins with the onboarding cycle, CMR's expansiveness makes it likely that the artifact will

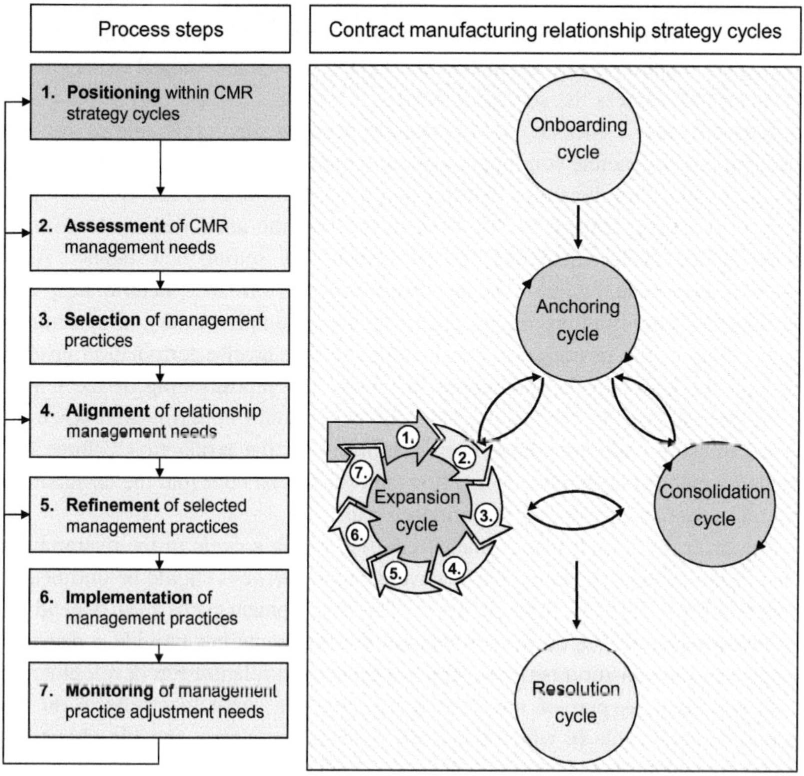

Figure 5.5 Artifact 'Integrated CMR management process'

also be adopted in existing relationships. In addition, CMRs go through individual cycles repeatedly, thus requiring initial positioning. Positioning is relevant to CMR management because each cycle is associated with specific goals and challenges. Therefore, the cycle-based management orientation enables a targeted selection of management practices to manage the complexity of CMRs. For example, high investment willingness in the expansion cycle allows more costly management practices for relationship expansion and preparation for the next cycle. In addition, the expansion cycle systematically increases the CMR's scope or transaction volume, focusing on adjusting interfaces and safeguards in line with the increasing reliance on the CMO. Consequently, the positioning step deals with the definition of cycle-specific goals, which are closely pursued through selecting and designing appropriate management practices and metrics. The selected metrics are monitored and interpreted throughout the cycle to adjust management practices and reassess the strategic course.

Complementary, focusing CMR management on one cycle allows for the development of concrete contingency plans to monitor and prepare actions against specific relationship dynamics that threaten the achievement of the cycle's objectives. In practice, strategy cycles often merge into the anchoring cycle without reviewing the cycle's activities and performance or setting new targets. As a result, management attention is lost over time, performance deteriorates, and development opportunities are missed. Therefore, complementary to systematic cycle building, the positioning step involves setting precise termination criteria that end the active cycle and prompt a review and repositioning of the CMR. In the example of the expansion cycle, the phase could be terminated when all agreed transition activities have been completed, or the production volume has reached a planned level. However, a timetable should be built into the termination criteria in case of delays and performance gaps.

Moreover, to link all management activities within a cycle to the overarching relationship strategy, potential CMR development pathways should be outlined in preparation for the next strategic cycle. The development paths may depend on the performance of the cycle and external developments but provide a decision framework for transition between strategy cycles and relationship development.

In summary, as part of the positioning step, the client first reflects on the current strategy cycle in which the CMR is located to derive specific objectives and contingencies that need to be reflected in management practices. Furthermore, criteria for the completion and transition of the strategy cycle are outlined, which form the basis for the restart of the integrated management process. Table 5.13 illustrates the positioning process with the chosen example providing a template practitioners can adapt to carry out the described activities.

2. **Assessment of CMR management needs**

The second process step relates to the first stage of the CMR management assessment artifact, fully described in Section 5.2.1, and involves the one-sided evaluation of operational and supplier management needs. The assessment uncovers the specific operational management needs and places the CMR within the client company's CMO portfolio, which typically standardizes management practices and investment levels. Complementary to the positioning step, assessment against established criteria supports efficient CMR management through operational standardization and targeted resource allocation, preventing costly

Table 5.13 Template for documenting positioning step key outcomes

1. Reviewed CMR	*CMR XYZ*	
2. Current cycle	*Expansion cycle*	
3. Cycle strategy	**Cycle goals**	**Cycle key metrics**
	• *Setting up the proprietary production line #2* • ...	• *Project delay days* • *On-time in full (OTIF)* • *Rejection rate* • ...
4. Contingency plan	**Potential risks and dynamics**	**Contingency actions**
	• *Failure to transfer technology* • *Demand development slows down* • ...	• *Secure safety stocks and try to buy line #1* • *Bundle with product C to achieve capacity utilization* • ...
5. Cycle transition	**Cycle termination criteria**	**Development paths**
	The new line has been quality approved for operation	*CMO is considered as a development partner for product X if the transfer is completed successfully*

over-adjustment of management practices. In addition, segment assessment in the context of strategy cycles contributes to a more appropriate segmentation of the CMO portfolio and more efficient use of resources overall. Several client companies interviewed stated that they aim for or already carry out a regular segment reassessment.

The assessment procedure translates the strategic evaluation outcomes from the positioning step into the set of CMR characteristics conducting a comprehensive evaluation of management needs. The second step results in a visualization of the fit between the CMR and appropriate management practices and segments, for example, using a comprehensive visualization such as the radar chart.

3. **Selection of management practices**

The third process step involves selecting management practices into a comprehensive set. A strategic cycle-oriented selection of management practices supports efficient CMR management by focusing on specific objectives whose fulfillment can be monitored more comprehensively. In addition, management practices with low cycle-specific impacts can be omitted, saving implementation resources. In practice, the degree to which segments determine management practices varies greatly. Often, a standardized base of core practices is individually complemented by other practices. However, despite efficient practice assignments, standardization limits understanding of the strengths and weaknesses of the own management approach. Therefore, this step allows for reflection and a conscious decision on a set of management practices to successfully implement practices that fit the CMR's management needs.

The management practice toolbox presented in Section 5.1 supports this step by providing detailed profiles of CMR management practices with detailed design options for customization beyond the standardized allocation. For example, the profiles provide information on the suitability of practices for sensitive CMRs, which is challenging to capture in a standardized way but can be discussed based on personal impressions within the client's management team. As the whole organization needs to implement management practices at the interface with the CMO, the selection should be made with the relevant internal stakeholders. Furthermore, the selection of management practices, including their critical discussion, serves as preparation for the fourth process step, in which the client company reflects on goals and management practices with the CMO.

4. **Alignment of relationship management needs**

The fourth process step involves the CMO in the mutual assessment of CMR's relationship management and development needs, which relates to the second stage of the assessment guide artifact comprehensively described in Section 5.2.2. As the successful management of CMRs is strongly influenced by commitment, it is necessary to involve the CMO systematically to align the relationship management requirements from the perspective of both partners and overcome relationship gaps. The relationship gap comprises the expectation of the relationship's development, the partner's behavior, and the perception of the management practices applied. As the CMO's expectations and perceptions change over time, regular assessment of the relationship gap in strategy cycles is strongly recommended by practitioners.

Concerning the business expectation gap, the client discloses cycle goals, contingencies, and envisaged development paths defined in the positioning step based on the client's willingness. Next, the CMO presents his expectations, which leads to a discussion in which a list of common goals and rejected expectations is created. In addition, rules of conduct for the cooperation are jointly established by comparing the expectations of the partner's behavior during the strategy cycle. For example, the CMO might expect the client not to conduct quality audits during the expansion cycle due to the additional effort required to set up the new production line. Finally, the client company discloses the planned management practices to support relationship management and receives feedback on their suitability from the CMO. At this point, the CMO could, for instance, disclose that he will appoint a new project manager to expand the product line and propose team-building measures on his initiative.

Consequently, the fourth step of the integrated management process documents critical aspects of the CMO's engagement management by providing transparency on objectives, rules for collaboration, and feedback on management practices. However, it must be assumed that neither partner is willing to share all expectations and perceptions openly and that the process step cannot guarantee complete coverage of the relationship gap. Nevertheless, the deliberate adherence to or neglect of the CMO's expectations and perceptions throughout the cycle must be monitored to manage commitment. Details on conducting the mutual assessment with the CMO and templates for documenting the results of this step can be found in Section 5.2.2.

5. **Refinement of selected management practices**

The fifth step conducts an internal evaluation of the CMO's feedback and potential refinement of the selected management practices based on the perceived relationship quality and future collaboration prospects from the fourth step. Again, direct involvement and open exchange with the CMO allows for a more accurate assessment of the CMO's sensitivity. In the consolidation phase, for example, when the volume of business decreases, the CMO's commitment may decrease in favor of other profitable customer relationships. Consequently, based on the exchange of business expectations and exit criteria, it may be determined that development paths must be adjusted, and more safeguarding against CMO opportunism is needed. Conversely, practitioners find that targeting expectations can uncover future business opportunities, increasing the client company's willingness to invest in development paths and related management practices and reducing the CMO's willingness to act opportunistically.

Consequently, resources might be reallocated from safeguarding practices to the operative alignment of interfaces, creating more substantial exit barriers for both companies. The client company is not obliged to adopt the CMO's feedback. Nevertheless, thorough analysis and communication are recommended, as the CMO's reception of client behavior influences the quality of the relationship and, thus, the success and stability of the CMR. Consequently, the client should inform the CMO about considering the CMO's specific feedback and suggestions in a transparent and reasoned manner.

As a result of the fifth step, the client can derive an appropriate set of management practices that consider the cycle's strategic needs, operational coordination needs, and the CMO's expectations and mindset.

6. **Implementation of management practices**
In the sixth step, the refined management practices are implemented, which may call for substantial internal and inter-firm implementation efforts. For example, some management practices, such as IT integration, require a more complex setup that involves briefing and onboarding previously uninvolved personnel. In addition, some practices or cycle-specific needs may require an adjustment of the organizational interfaces with the CMO. For example, during the expansion cycle, it may be necessary to set up a temporary project team to support the CMO in setting up a new production line. In addition, the responsibility for CMR management may change to a key account or executive position, reflecting the increase in business volume. Consequently, the sixth process step coordinates the implementation of management practices and the adjustment of organizational structures, including roles, responsibilities, and communication routines.

Furthermore, the CMO must be informed of implementation schedules and changes in contact persons. In the case of expansive practices such as joint S&OP or dedicated bundling, the CMO needs to be integrated into practice design, implementation, and the adjustment of organizational structures. In practice, using RACI[1]-matrices has proven to be effective in documenting and communicating organizational restructuring within the client companies and with the CMO.

However, even with minor organizational adjustments, reviewing management structures and stakeholders' internal alignment is vital for successfully implementing refined management practices. The refined management practices recognize the CMO's stance as a central success factor for managing the CMR. Because failure to deliver on commitments is a significant source of dissatisfaction, the goals, expectations, and collaboration rules agreed upon in step four must be disseminated within the organization to enable coordinated cooperation across all interfaces. Therefore internal briefings are recommended to ensure effective management routines are established through implementing the management practices.

[1] RACI is an acronym made up of the four main responsibilities Responsible, Accountable, Consulted, and Informed.

7. **Monitoring of management practice adjustment needs**
Finally, the variables that determine the choice of management practices need to be continuously monitored to allow for targeted adjustment of management practices. As the decision to adopt certain management practices is driven by the cycle goals, strategic objectives, and CMO commitment, these dimensions must be reflected in the monitoring procedure through appropriate metrics.

The first step in the process is to define the key objectives and KPIs for the current strategy cycle. For cycle steering, monitoring a smaller number of meaningful KPIs is advisable instead of tracking different metrics with less informative value about the strategy cycle's primary goals. For example, adherence to the set-up schedule and stability of quality and delivery may be more critical in the expansion cycle than cost, which determines the choice of management practices in the subsequent production phase. Another approach could be to set joint KPIs to reflect mutual responsibility for technology transfer during expansion and to drive project performance. Furthermore, in addition to selecting the proper KPIs, thresholds for action must also be envisaged. For example, cost, delivery, and quality targets could be measured with greater tolerance during technology transfer to reflect operational work on the line than in the actual production phase. Reconciliation of target fulfillment with the CMO usually occurs in regular business reviews. Failure to meet cycle targets may, depending on the severity of the failure, trigger a simple adjustment, e.g., through additional audits in step five or a reassessment of management practices through process steps two to four.

In addition, the strategic opportunities and risks need to be monitored to revise the strategy cycle. To this end, the main contingencies of the cycle were documented in the positioning step. For example, the KPIs could detect a non-critical project delay but include an assessment that the technology transfer will continue to fail. Consequently, a repositioning of the entire strategy cycle would be required to derive new goals and activities. In this instance, the expansion could be halted to rethink it or switch to buying the existing line, which fundamentally changes the need for management practices. However, other contingencies may not arise directly from the CMR and must be derived from sources other than key performance indicators. In the expansion cycle example, a slowdown in demand growth that justifies the investment poses a strategic risk. Thus the sales or product management department could monitor this contingency's occurrence by assessing competitors' behavior or internal product development activities. Since strategic contingencies require a more vital interpretation of the measured values due to the degree of abstraction, a regular internal discussion of strategy development is recommended. Strategic development is then discussed regularly with the CMO in strategic outlooks.

Confining monitoring to the contingencies of the strategy cycle under consideration allows the client companies to focus on dynamics that can be averted through CMR management. For example, cycle-specific contingencies can be proactively addressed by adjusting cycle targets or switching between cycles as part of CMR management. The distinction between dynamics that can be mitigated and those that cannot be prepared for is seen by practitioners as a success factor for the efficient allocation of management resources in CMR management. Commitment is deemed an appropriate safeguard to react to dynamics which cant' be mitigated by contingency plans as it supports collaboration outside of standardized frames.

Consequently, the relationship quality needs to be monitored and, if necessary, promoted through targeted management adjustments to maintain a strong commitment from the CMO. However, monitoring commitment is exceptionally challenging because it is an abstract concept experienced differently by stakeholders. As derived from the RVP in Section 3.2.4 and confirmed in the empirical results, commitment is determined by investment, communication, and trust capabilities. Investment capacity is about reciprocity and investment payback, while communication capacity is concerned with the openness and effectiveness of communication. Finally, trust is built through perceived fairness and shared understanding.

Figure 5.6 Development of commitment metrics to monitor commitment

Furthermore, in the fourth process step client and CMO have aligned on business and partners' expectations and management practices through the second stage of the management assessment guide developed in Section 5.2.2. Compliance with the alignment is supposed to ensure the relationship's growth potential, quality, and effectiveness of management practice. Consequently, considering the theoretical background of RVP and the findings from RQ_2, five commitment metrics are derived for monitoring CMO engagement. Figure 5.6 briefly presents the approach and the derived commitment metrics.

The commitment metrics are outlined in the following paragraphs.

1. *Economic satisfaction* relates to the CMR's profitability for the client company and CMO as a requirement for investments.
2. *Relationship growth potential* estimates the CMR's future business prospects and future investment capabilities.
3. *Communication* covers the openness of communication and the effectiveness of communication routines.
4. *Collaboration quality* assesses the trustful interaction across interfaces, the perceived fairness, and the adherence to rules of conduct.
5. *Management practice effectiveness* rates the strength of organizational coordination and the usefulness of the established management routines.

The derived metrics provide a framework for monitoring commitment. When applying the commitment metrics in practice, referring back to the established rules of conduct through an explicit mention or additional inclusion is advisable. For example, the client and CMO might explicitly agree on verbal advance notice of last-minute orders in step four. Compliance with this arrangement will consequently influence the CMO's trust and commitment and needs to be monitored.

Regarding the measurement of commitment metrics, Häkkinen (2008) notes that personal assessments between clients and CMO often diverge due to misleading descriptions and trigger discussions. While Häkkinen (2008) tries to avoid discrepancies in his research through more precise descriptions, personal and open discussions are conducive to closing the relationship gap for evaluating commitment metrics. Consequently, a comparative relative assessment of the commitment metrics based on the personal perception of clients and CMOs was presented in the focus groups. Respondents found the relative assessment of commitment metrics beneficial. They indicated that broad terminology quickly leads to misunderstandings and is particularly beneficial in measuring commitment because it triggers open and detailed discussions about the partner's perceptions. In addition, the emerging discussions must be well documented, capturing the reasons for perception gaps to guide responsive actions.

Therefore, this dissertation proposes a regular, joint perception-based commitment assessment between the client company and the CMO. It is recommended to measure commitment with the CMO on a quarterly to annual basis to obtain meaningful assessments. For communication and collaboration quality metrics, a monthly reconciliation is also suited in the case of intensive collaboration. Questionnaires can support measurement through a scoring system by breaking down commitment metrics and aggregating different perceptions within collaborating companies.

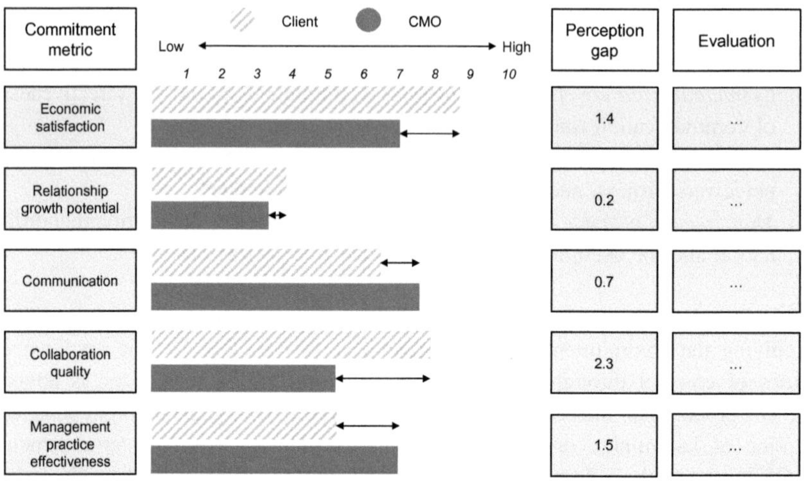

Figure 5.7 Perception-based evaluation of commitment through metrics

Figure 5.7 visualizes the monitoring procedure through an illustrative example. In the example shown, the low estimated growth potential of the CMR is noticeable. However, since the perception gap is small and both sides attest to CMR's robust profitability, the relationship risk can be considered low. Nevertheless, improving the CMOs' profitability or exploring new business opportunities through appropriate practices is recommended. Conversely, despite a fundamentally higher rating, the discrepancy in the perceived quality of the collaboration indicates a significant misalignment that could lead to an unexpected loss of commitment. Therefore, preemptive refinement of management practices or, in this case, a realignment of the relationship gap is advisable.

Thus, the monitoring step produces metrics and routines to control intra-cycle business objectives, strategic contingencies, and CMO commitment. As the final sequential process step in the cyclical management process, the monitoring step transitions to the process steps already presented, depending on the values of the monitored metrics. First, once the criteria for completing the strategy cycle are met, or contingencies require repositioning, the monitoring step moves to the positioning step. Second, missing cycle targets leads to a reassessment of management needs by going through the process again from step two. Third, relationship management is realigned from step four onwards when significant perception gaps are identified that jeopardize commitment. Finally, if there is little need for adjustment, at the discretion of the relationship manager, a direct adjustment of management practices can be made through step five. Figure 5.8 summarises the integrated management process and shows the key outcomes of each step and the CMO's involvement using a RACI description.

Process steps	Key outcomes	CMO involvement
1. **Positioning** within CMR strategy cycles	• Current strategy cycle • Cycles goals and metrics • Contingency plan and actions • Cycle termination criteria and development path	*Not involved*
2. **Assessment** of CMR management needs	• Assignment of CMR to segment • Recommended set of core management practices	*Not involved*
3. **Selection** of management practices	• Assigned set of management practices	*Not involved*
4. **Alignment** of relationship management needs	• List of goals and expectations • Rules of conduct • Feedback on management practices	Consulted
5. **Refinement** of selected management practices	• Aligned set of management practices	Informed
6. **Implementation** of management practices	• Adopted management routines	Consulted / Informed
7. **Monitoring** of management practice adjustment needs	• Cycle-oriented KPI assessment routine (ongoing) • Strategic evaluation routine (ongoing) • Commitment assessment routine (monthly to quarterly)	Consulted / Informed

Figure 5.8 Operational view of the 'Integrated CMR management process'

Effective alignment with the CMO is a critical success factor for managing dynamic CMRs. Assessing and facilitating relationship commitment allows for early modification of management practices and reduced control and adaptation efforts. Practitioners recommend performing steps one to six at least once a year to evaluate the strategy cycle, uncover business opportunities or inconsistencies and adjust management practices to gradual changes throughout the year. During the year, cyclical KPIs and strategic contingencies should be monitored on an ongoing basis, while commitment as a social factor requiring CMO involvement is recommended monthly to quarterly.

Artifact evaluation and contribution to RQ_4

A comprehensive answer to RQ_4 relies on a thorough understanding of the CMR management practices, dynamics, and adaptability as presented in the research gaps. Therefore, the developed artifact includes the findings and artifacts from Sections 5.1 to 5.3 and considers the additional requirements from Section 4.5 in the context of an integrated management approach. Embedded in the theoretical lenses of TCE and RVP, the artifact provides a tangible approach to identifying strategic, operational, and social changes and guiding appropriate action. Furthermore, the integrated management process considers the CMO's role in relationship management, given the substantial exit barriers and strong dependency on CMO capabilities. Consequently, the CMO is actively involved in designing and evaluating management practices to compensate for the client's limited control capabilities through aligned collaboration.

During the evaluation of the artifacts addressing RQ_1 to RQ_3, focus group participants called for the results to be operationalized to enable a continuous management process that includes monitoring relationship quality and recommending management action. The artifact incorporated these demands and presented the concept of measuring relationship quality through commitment metrics in focus group two. It was well received and later stated by one participant to be adapted in their operations. In focus group three, the strategy cycles were added and approved as a temporal frame for assessing management needs and focusing on management efforts. Finally, the integrated approach was presented in the fourth focus group iteration, where the participants approved it. The participants stressed that the process provides a beneficial systematic approach to reducing complexity of dynamicity and management adjustment in CMRs. However, the participants also noted that, despite useful simplification, the procedure requires further individualization to be implemented in practice. This limitation is acknowledged within the DSR methodology's scope and will be discussed in Section 6.3. In addition, focus group participants suggested that the responsibilities of both parties in the integrated management process should be anchored in the contract, which would position relationship management as a shared responsibility in CMRs. However, since detailed contract design was not a focus of this dissertation, the impetus was documented but could not be incorporated into the developed artifact without limiting adaptability. Table 5.14 outlines the evaluation process and covers the participants' evaluations and impulses

Table 5.14 Focus group evaluation of the 'Integrated management process'

Focus group (No.)	Utility evaluation	Participant feedback
1	n.a.	Impulse: Regular CMR evaluation is necessary because parameters change over time Impulse: Intangible metrics such as expectations and trust must be measured the same way as cost and quality
2	Positive	Commitment KPIs to track CMR development and social risks are approved Commitment monitoring based on each partner's perception is approved Impulse: Heterogeneity limits standardization; thus, relationship and partner understanding must be fostered Impulse: The management approach must allow for customization to particular CMR segments
3	Positive	Orientation in relationship cycles as a temporal frame for tailored management is approved Impulse: Positioning, terminating, and transitioning cycles is paramount for adjusting management
4	Positive	The components of the integrated management process (strategy cycles, assessment, practice toolbox) were approved The cyclical integrated management process as a whole, including social monitoring, was approved Impulse: Responsibility for the integrated management process could be anchored in the contract

Conclusion

6

Subsequent to the development, presentation, and practical evaluation of the artifacts, this chapter analyses the findings from Chapters 4 and 5 from a scientific perspective and evaluates them against the research objectives RO_1 to RO_4 stated in section 1.3. Section 6.1 first discusses the contribution of this dissertation to filling the research gaps derived in Section 2.7 by answering the four research questions to expand the knowledge base. Then, against the background of the distinctiveness of CMRs compared to other IORs, Section 6.2 considers the management implications of the thesis. Finally, Section 6.3 discusses the limitations of the thesis and highlights the need for further research.

6.1 Contribution

This dissertation addresses two significant theoretical shortcomings in the field of CMR management. First, TS_1 established that research on CMR focuses on the strategic issues of preconditions, outcomes, and transfer during outsourcing, lacking a relationship management perspective. Complementary, TS_2 noted that CMR management is attributed to IOR management without a dedicated research stream in literature systematically advancing the knowledge base. The literature, therefore, assumes that the high failure rates of CMR in practice are due to execution gaps between the knowledge base and its application in practice.

Contribution to the delineation of CMR management

A significant obstacle to targeted research on CMR is the remarkable heterogeneity and dynamic development of practice concepts with different scopes, blurring

T. Brandl, *Managing Contract Manufacturing Relationships*, Supply Chain Management, https://doi.org/10.1007/978-3-658-41359-0_6

the boundaries between supply relationship concepts. Therefore as part of this dissertation's knowledge base, a delimitation of manufacturing service concepts was first derived and visualized in Figure 2.2 to create transparency on the research object. Then, in response to the theoretical weight of CMR research described by Busi and McIvor (2008), a rich empirical base from different CMRs was investigated to verify the execution gap assumed by scholars.

The dissertation's empirics show that client companies are building their CMR management approaches on established IOR management practices that they continuously adapt to meet the management requirements of CMRs. However, adopting IOR management practices has not contributed to overcoming the challenges of CMR management, leaving managers dissatisfied and often restructuring CMR management. In addition, many interviewees stated that their current practices do not meet the scientific standard or best practices but have grown over time without deliberate development.

The main obstacles to CMR management not addressed by established IOR management approaches are the extensive collaboration scope and the inevitable lock-in effect weakening client's power position. SRM, as the most frequently applied methodology in CMRs, has structural weaknesses in this context, as it focuses on avoiding strong supplier dependency but does not adequately address relationship management. In addition, SRM is based on a position of client power, focusing on developing and controlling the supplier according to its requirements. Contrary to CMR practice, SRM assumes that value creation takes place within the company and thus does not cover the targeted coordination of collaborative value creation. Empirical evidence from interviews in the food and pharmaceutical industries underlines that the SRM approach in CMR often divides partner companies into customers and suppliers, which makes flexible cooperation outside of standardized processes difficult and contributes to transactional business relationships.

While SAs, JVs, and outsourcing relationships are faced with integrating processes to create shared value, their relationship management approaches fail to meet CMR's challenges. CMRs are characterized by asymmetries in strategic alignment, which are not replicated in other integrated IORs. In CMRs, clients and CMOs create value collaboratively by integrating their capabilities. As a result, many client companies view the result as a *'joint product,'* acknowledging the CMOs' contribution. However, as the rightful owners of the design, the clients benefit disproportionately from the increase in value. In contrast to JDM, CMOs do not partake in value creation through financial participation or branding. Instead, they strive for standardization and economies of scale. Thus, client companies depend more on the CMR, as the value they derive from the CMO's complementary skills is greater than the replaceable production volume CMOs receive. The difference in dependency is reflected in the goals each partner in the CMO pursues. Focus group participants enumerated client and CMO goals, indicating that the client's goals are often strategic while the CMO's goals are opportunistic. As a result, the imbalance in value capture limits the ex-post bargaining power of the client and leads to different priorities being pursued in CMR management.

It could be argued that the CM development towards shared value creation in combination with volume-based remuneration schemes is inherently unstable when aligning the objectives of both partners. However, in practice, there are plenty of mutually attractive CMRs in which the CMO's valuation of the transaction volume matches the client's valuation of the capability contribution. Still, with the progressive specialization of CMOs through forward and backward integration, clients' bargaining power and CMOs' competitive pressure decrease (Denicolai et al., 2015). At the same time, the gradualness of the shift in the scope of CMR is precarious for client companies, as established SRM practices slowly lose effectiveness as reliance on CMOs progresses.

On the network level, the dissertation's findings provide a new perspective on supply chain integration. Formerly CM has been associated with outsourcing and disintegration of supply chains. However, examples such as Flextronics are increasingly relevant in various industries and show a systematic integration of operations, including manufacturing, sourcing, and logistics. At the same time, brand-leading companies focus on intangible value creation through business models and product design. The emergence of CM can thus be interpreted as a shift in supply chains based on the co-specialization of product and operations management, leading to a change in preferred corporate boundaries. Naturally, this development causes tension regarding the degree of individualization and standardization of CMR operations. Thus, CMR management requires enormous flexibility in processes and relationship management, which can only be implemented through solid trust and mutual commitment.

Consequently, this dissertation contributes to the supply chain literature by addressing the aforementioned theoretical shortcomings of TS_1 and TS_2 and creating a deeper understanding of CMR and the dynamics that influence its management. The findings show that CMR management differs significantly from the management of other IORs since it must enable cross-organizational value creation amid divergent business interests of client companies and CMOs, limited client power, and profound relationship dynamics. Therefore, this dissertation can invalidate the assumption of an execution gap and confirm the CMR management research gap.

In addition to supporting CMR management as an emerging research field in SCM, the thesis addresses the research gap directly by answering the overarching RQ_0 of how CMRs can be managed against the background of relationship dynamics. For this purpose, the overall research gap was divided into three subsidiary research gaps, RG_1 to RG_3, which focus on CMR management practices, assessment, and adaptability. The research gaps are closed by answering the detailed research questions, RQ_1 to RQ_4. Furthermore, by aggregating the results of the four research questions, the overarching research question RQ_0 was answered, and a contribution to the management of CMRs made. The following paragraphs outline the particular research question's contribution.

Contribution to the research questions

- RQ_1 concerned the identification and successful implementation of management practices used in CMRs. First, the empirical results showed the specificity of CMR management by revealing unique management practices and reinterpretations of established practices. Furthermore, the findings uncovered a strong practitioner focus on best practices as means for competitive advantage as proposed by PBV (Bromiley & Rau, 2014). However, the results also showed that the definitions of management practices against the background of customization are vague, and their definite purpose is often unknown to the users. Therefore the dissertation developed an artifact containing the thirty discovered CMR management practices and included meaningful profiles to support the targeted application. The management practice profiles are rooted in TCE and encompass four descriptive fields, including a detailed description of application variants and relations to TCE governance problems. Furthermore, application costs are included drawing on transaction frequency as a mediating variable for investment willingness in CMRs. Finally, according to CMR's need for alignment of client companies and CMOs, the management practices' effect on partner reception was operationalized and included through the criterion of application sensitivity. Thus, the research's findings contribute to a deeper understanding of management practice adoption and implementation in practices and associated shortcomings.
- RQ_2 dealt with the targeted assessment of the CMRs management needs amidst heterogeneous relationship scopes to identify supportive management practices. The empirical findings show that management practice assignment in CMRs is either conducted individually or standardized through uniform segments. Additionally, it becomes apparent that transaction frequency is a

key criterion for the use of practices to enable efficient resource allocation between CMRs. However, the practice transfer of various segmentation approaches from literature often fails due to limited validation of assignment criteria. The research findings indicated that management needs assessment could be considered a two-stage process, considering commercial aspects first and requiring joint assessment of social relationship criteria with the CMO second. In this context, the dissertation introduces the concept of the relationship gap, which describes undisclosed differences in expectations towards business development and partner behavior and management practice perceptions, which undiscovered can deteriorate CMR performance. Finally, in response to the empirical findings, the thesis contributes to the literature by presenting a TCE-based artifact encompassing the two stages of management assessment. Stage one explicitly addresses the quality control of business-criteria-based assessment through a segmentation process. Additionally, stage two operationalizes the relationship gap, thus contributing to understanding CMR failure and enabling successful collaboration. Moreover, the relationship gap also indicates TCE's shortcomings in covering all relevant for CMR management assessment and implementation.

- *RQ3* explored relationship dynamics to provide transparency on the different triggers for adjusting management practices. The results show that practitioners consider the relationship dynamics within the CMR as highly relevant for CMR management, as they trigger a permanent change in the relationship that requires management intervention. In addition, dynamics can be distinguished according to whether their impact on CMR management is permanent or temporary. Permanent changes require individual solutions finding, while temporary changes can be overcome by flexible, trust-based cooperation and contingency plans. An accumulation or a discernible trend of temporary disruptions may, in turn, recommend permanent management adjustment. Furthermore, the thesis finds that CMR progress is characterized by frequent changes in relationship strategy and scope that are not deterministically predictable. Therefore, the dissertation developed a comprehensive CMR relationship dynamics model that distinguishes between different types of dynamics and includes strategy-guided relationship progression. The concept of strategy cycles is based on the incompatibility of CMR life cycles with product-centered and deterministic life cycle concepts such as the RVP's relationship stage and age (Palmatier et al., 2013). Consequently, the artifact contributes to understanding relationship dynamics in CMRs by systematically creating transparency and reducing complexity by clustering dynamics by management relevance.

- *RQ_4* was dedicated to how management practices can be systematically adjusted to dynamically changing management requirements. Complementary to RQ_3, the research question targeted the research gap of adaptability of management practices (RG_3). The thesis concludes that management commitment is central in aligning management practices with CMR requirements by focusing monitoring efforts on fundamental aberrations affecting CMR performance and stability. In addition, commitment has been shown to strengthen CMR's resilience to turbulence or gradual change, as both parties act in CMR's interest even outside of contractual obligations. The findings contribute to understanding relationship dynamics and open a perspective of targeted management responses. Based on TCE and RVP, an artifact was designed to guide practice assignment and adjustment amid relationship dynamics. The artifact operationalizes commitment management by developing commitment metrics from RVP's commitment drivers and aligning them with the relationship gap. Thus, the resulting artifact provides a broader perspective on CMR management, integrating and operationalizing the findings of RQ_1 to RQ_3 through the commitment construct to answer RQ_0.
- Finally, *RQ_0*, as an overarching research question, addressed how CMRs can be managed considering their broad coordination needs and constant dynamic change. The dissertation answers the research question, thus filling the related research gaps in literature through empirically grounded artifacts that enable successful CMR management. Additionally, the thesis provided insights into the industry characteristics of CMR (see section 4.6), creating transparency on the limits of transferability of management practices. In summary, the findings on CMR characteristics, delineation of relationship dynamics, and success factors increase the visibility of CM as a research field in literature. The artifacts developed throughout chapter 5 encompass detailed descriptions and templates that allow their adoption in practice. However, as the requirements for CMR management differ considerably across industries, the artifacts are set at a level of abstraction that requires individual adaptation of artifacts for practical use.

Contribution to management of IORs

The artifacts of the thesis were developed explicitly for CMR, but as commonalities and differences between IORs are known, the underlying concepts can be adapted across IORs. First, in response to the limited understanding of management practice application, the dissertation proposed a management toolbox including TCE-based practice profiles. Management practices are frequently investigated across IORs but rarely documented in detail, considering their application cases, costs, boundaries, customizing options, and impact on partner behavior. Therefore the results from RQ_1 can support the emerging practice-based view of IORs (Bromiley & Rau, 2014).

Furthermore, the empirical results of the dissertation have revealed widespread adaptation of partner segmentation in CMRs but weak implementation due to a limited understanding of constructs. Therefore, considering the dominant prevalence of portfolio and involvement approaches in the literature, the artifact developed in section 5.2.1 introduces a process approach including methodologically supported validation mechanisms. Consequently, the dissertation proposes a revival of the process approach to segmentation to develop validated and practice-relevant partner typologies in IORs.

Furthermore, the concept of a relationship gap, which encompasses the mismatch between expectations and perceptions, has excellent potential for application beyond CMR. In particular, SA and JV research relies heavily on strategic alignment, and relationship management with powerful suppliers is underrepresented in SRM. This dissertation developed and operationalized an approach to aligning business partners at strategic and operational levels based on TCE and RVP. In this context, the concept and methods for bridging and monitoring the relationship gap can be applied in different areas of the IOR literature.

Finally, the clustering of CMR relationship dynamics by management impact in RQ_3 provides an alternative perspective that can support research into relationship dynamics in IORs. The developed artifact allows a more transparent representation of the dynamics overlap and enables the targeted development of management responses, which will benefit different research areas in IORs.

Contribution to applied theories

Finally, the dissertation contributes to the theories applied in it. First, it raises new perspectives on the ongoing discussion about the operationalization of TCE by making a convincing case for transaction frequency as a mediating variable for management practice choice. While transaction frequency has long been contested due to its limited demonstrable impact on supply chain design decisions, the dissertation's empirical results show that it is a primary factor in choices of CMR management practices (Cuypers et al., 2021). Transaction frequency, volume, scale, and strategic value determine investment willingness in terms of implementation costs of management practices. In the food industry, specific regulatory management requirements, such as the need for certifications and audits, are imposed based on transaction frequency and, if necessary, exempted due to limited financial proportionality.

Furthermore, the dissertation contributes to RVP by identifying application areas and limitations in operationalizing theory constructs. For example, the thesis showed that the construct of commitment drivers and the concept of commitment velocity could be operationalized to enable dynamic relationship management through targeted monitoring routines. However, the RVP characterization of dynamics by relationship stage, age, and industry turbulence does not capture turbulence resulting from business partner behavior. This shortcoming is relevant as the originators of the dynamics can be assigned, and their impact on commitment is much more substantial. For example, if the client significantly enhances audit frequency, the same dynamic will impact commitment differently than if regulatory changes require increased auditing. Consequently, the RVP's constructs on dynamics and their impact on commitment need to be refined for operationalization. Therefore, this dissertation's categorization of relationship dynamics according to their impact could provide another perspective for understanding relationship dynamics.

Moreover, TCE has long been challenged as a static theory that lacks a dynamic perspective (Cuypers et al., 2021). For this reason, several scholars have advocated the eclectic combination of TCE with RVP to increase the explanatory power of both theories (Chmielewski-Raimondo et al., 2022; Seggie et al., 2013). To the author's knowledge, the research framework of this thesis is the first to successfully integrate both theories and align their constructs by linking commitment to the three governance problems of TCE. From the TCE perspective, commitment poses the long-term governance problem of the partner's reception of the business behavior, which determines the willingness to participate in transactions in the future, adding a dynamic perspective to the theory. At the same time, TCE complements the RVP's lack of focus on the limits of commitment as the RVP's only relationship management construct by considering transaction costs and safeguarding against opportunism. Thus, the integration of TCE and RVP contributes to research on dynamic relationship management and shows that the theories complement each other and provide valuable insights by explaining and balancing short-term and long-term supply chain relationship goals.

6.2 Managerial Implications

This chapter discusses the dissertation's managerial implications. MC_1 to MC_3 emphasized the relevance of CM for global supply chains and client companies in section 1.1. Section 2.4 looked in more detail at the challenges of CMR management, highlighting the coordination and alignment needs coupled with the heterogeneity of CMR objectives, scope, and relationship dynamics. From a management perspective, the dissertation addressed these managerial challenges along the research gaps RG_1 to RG_3: First, assessing management coordination and alignment needs; second, selecting appropriate management practices; and third, adjusting management to dynamically changing requirements.

Building on a DSR methodology, in chapter 5, four artifacts address these managerial challenges. Artifact development was grounded in the empirical findings presented in chapter 4 and the theoretical foundations of TCE and RVP. Subsequently, the artifacts were evaluated for usefulness by practitioners in focus groups and refined. The following paragraphs are structured according to the developed artifacts and describe how the managerial challenges are addressed.

CMR Management Practice Toolbox (RQ_1)

The CMR Management Practice Toolbox addresses the challenge of low transparency of CMR management practices. Due to the lack of a unified knowledge base, practitioners primarily take cues from SRM and adapt them to the needs of CMRs. As a result, CMR's individually derived management practices are diverse, and client companies are constantly seeking to compare management practices and gain new impetus. A lack of understanding of the operating conditions of benchmarked management practices hinders the successful adoption and diffusion of management practices among client companies. The artifact addresses this management challenge related to RG_1 and contributes to easier adoption and adaptation of management practices in two ways: First, the dissertation captured thirty CMR management practices from four industries, providing a comprehensive overview of management practices that practitioners can adapt to their needs. Second, the artifact includes profiles of management practices that describe the dimensions necessary to successfully select practices based on application, cost, and adaptation criteria. In this context, the profiles explicitly address aspects of the application of management practices that, according to the empirical analysis, are not considered sufficiently in practice.

On the one hand, individual interpretations of specific management practices differ significantly between and even within companies, leaving valuable impulses invisible to practitioners. Therefore, in addition to a brief description, the artifact also includes a section identifying levers for customizing individual management practices. On the other hand, the developed profiles consider the need for an agreement with the CMO by providing guidance on the partner's uptake of the practice and application scopes. Consequently, the thesis recommends that practitioners systematically organise management practices to identify application and improvement potentials through transparency. The developed artifact supports the recommendation by providing an overview of standard practices and a systematic, application-oriented template for describing them.

CMR Management Needs Assessment Guide (RQ_2)

The second artifact related to RG_2 addresses the management challenge of assigning management practices to CMRs according to their individual management needs. The empirical results have shown that in CMRs, the commercial and social relationship levels need to be managed appropriately. Furthermore, assessing the commercial relationship level is driven by the need to reduce complexity through segmentation. On the other hand, relationship quality and prospects are rarely analyzed and constitute the primary challenge for practitioners in CMR management needs assessment. The artifact addresses this need by presenting a flexible two-stage management assessment process that sequentially covers the commercial and social relationship levels. The first stage of the process concerns the evaluation of operations and supplier management needs. Given widely used segmentation approaches, the first stage explicitly supports practitioners in developing and improving company-specific solutions. The first stage guides practitioners in successfully designing and implementing the process before the actual realization. Hence, the artifact setup phase includes validation cycles supported by concrete methods to address shortcomings of company-specific approaches frequently observed in the empirical results.

The second stage introduces the concept of the relationship gap as a means to understand and actively foster CMO commitment. In this capacity, it provides concrete implementation guidance that practitioners can use to develop the social level of the relationship in a targeted way by aligning expectations and perceptions. Focus group evaluation underscored the value and applicability of the relationship gap to address the challenge of covering the social CMR layer. The dissertation results thus support clients in the targeted development of collaborative CMRs that reflect their strategic value through a targeted analysis of commercial and social management needs. In particular, the focused closing of the relationship gap allows the clients to reduce the control effort in CMR management and achieve more effective coordination.

CMR Strategy cycles (RQ_3)

Managing dynamics and disruptions is a significant concern in supply chains. However, CMRs are particularly vulnerable to dynamic change due to the close integration of partners, high dependency, and high switching barriers. As a result, clients must constantly reassess management needs and adjust management practices, as described in RG_3. The CMR strategy cycles help to understand the need to adapt management practices by transparently clustering relationship dynamics according to their impact on CMR trajectories and management. The artifact visualizes different relationship dynamics in the CMR relevant to management changes and illustrates their impacts so that practitioners can define monitoring thresholds and management responses. Three categories of relationship dynamics are distinguished, with 19 empirically assessed examples according to their frequency and impact on CMR management. In addition, the course of the relationships is presented in five strategy cycles of CMR management.

Hence, in contrast to deterministic models, the artifact explains alternative relationship development paths based on recurrent strategy cycles and their interplay with external dynamics. These insights enable practitioners to allocate management resources efficiently through CMR's temporal breakdown and the strategy-guided management practices selection. According to the empirical findings, this is a valuable insight for clients because the management of long-term CMRs becomes increasingly reactive over time, leading to a gradual deterioration in performance potential. However, systematic reinvigoration of CMRs through orientation to strategy cycles can counteract this development through focused management attention and adaptation of practices. Thus, the artifact creates transparency on the effects of relationship management and offers points of reference for response to concrete relationship dynamics and the implementation of long-term strategies.

Integrated CMR management process (RQ_4)

Finally, the fourth artifact combines the findings of the previous ones providing practitioners comprehensive guidance in selecting and adjusting management practices along the CMR's life cycle. The artifact comprises seven steps covering strategic positioning within strategy cycles, assessing management needs holistically, implementing management practices, and monitoring routines for future adjustment. Consequently, it facilitates practitioners' purposeful application of the dissertation's findings through a systematic management process. In this capacity, it proposes regular re-assessment of strategic goals, exit criteria, and relationship quality to enable proactive adjustment of management practices or redefinition of strategy.

Based on the empirical findings, the dissertation argues for targeted relationship development to bridge minor gaps between relationship control needs and applied management practices. Targeted relationship development by addressing relationship gaps and monitoring commitment enables lean control structures and effective CMR coordination. In addition, practitioners see commitment as a safeguard against disruptive dynamics, as it promotes effective CMO self-management outside contractual routines.

To this end, the artifact operationalizes commitment to overcome the practical challenge of the vagueness of the social CMR level. As a result, commitment is broken down into five metrics and a tangible measurement procedure that allows client companies to monitor relationship quality. The relationship quality is directly related to compliance with the agreements regarding the partners' expectations and perceptions of the cooperation. In this way, the process supports the ability of client companies to purposefully develop CMRs or identify dissent and intensify their management efforts preemptively.

Furthermore, the integrated management process and all entailed procedures are set at an abstraction level that allows for simple adoption and adaptation to individual practitioners' needs. Finally, the dissertation results have high practical value by applying the DSR methodology, which focuses on the usefulness of the artifacts and the frequent recursive evaluation through focus groups. The focus group participants confirmed the value of the dissertation's managerial implications and implied their incorporation into their CMR management approaches. Thus, the research provides tangible implications for client companies to overcome the challenges of managing CMRs.

6.3 Limitations and Further Research

The dissertation applied several measures to ensure the rigor of the research's results. First, the research gap is specified through a thorough delineation of CMR management from adjacent research directions in SCM, considering their explanatory impulses and shortcomings. Second, grounded in TCE and RVP, the dissertation draws on theories with considerable explanatory power for the unit of analysis. While TCE is well-established and fundamental to understanding SCM, RVP is an innovative and recognized theoretical lens for relationship dynamics. Finally, the chosen DSR methodology addresses Busi and McIvor's (2008) call for more inductive thinking in CMR research by designing a rigorous abductive research process.

Nevertheless, the research approach is still subject to limitations that affect the explanatory power of the research findings. The following sections will outline the limitations of the author's methodological choices and assumptions. Consequently, there are opportunities for further research, for which suggestions are provided below.

Limitations related to the research perspective

Firstly, due to the theoretical shortcomings concerning the observation unit, the dissertation applies a broad perspective to comprehensively capture the challenges of CMR management. The holistic and exploratory perspective was chosen to identify particular drivers of the frequent failure across CMRs and systematically delineate adjacent IOR management concepts. As a result, the dissertation is set at a substantial level of abstraction to cover CMRs across industries and value propositions. For example, the adoption of TCE governance problems for practice selection aggregates coordination and management needs so that a deep understanding of structural complexity at the operational level cannot be provided within the scope of the dissertation. Consequently, according to DSR, the research findings need to be understood as designs that allow for flexible adaptation but rely on targeted adaptation to unfold their impact on managing individual CMRs (Hevner et al., 2004). Therefore future research on the operationalization of individual concept elements and artifacts is recommended.

Given the heterogeneity of CMR scopes and goals, the dissertation takes an overarching perspective. The artifacts emphasize the challenges posed by developing collaborative value creation concepts in CMRs, which constitute the primary research and practitioner interests. As a result, CMRs without collaborative value creation (e.g., through outsourcing) are covered by the research findings yet not addressed in detail since they are well explained in the literature. Thus, CMRs with low value-added potential could still be managed preferentially based on administrative efficiency, making systematic development of the social relationship layer impractical for cost reasons. However, the corresponding artifact recognizes such preferences through flexible adaptation of the second process stage.

Moreover, CMRs with low-value propositions remain mainly managed opportunistically. Therefore management decisions are strongly driven by quantitative data. However, since the dissertation adopted a qualitative approach, the artifact development process focused on effectiveness over quantifiable management efficiency. The proposal of commitment-supported relationship management is indicated to reduce operational effort, but financial efficiency is still vague. Consequently, practitioners could be reluctant to rely on commitment in low-margin CMRs. Therefore a complementary quantitative perspective to the application and adjustment of management practices in future research could provide further insights.

Finally, the choice of theory influences the research findings by changing the perspective on the unit of analysis. Hence, the research findings are ultimately limited by the choice of TCE and RVP as a theoretical lens. Section 3.1

explored the contributions of alternative theories. By choosing PBV, the dissertation could have developed more significant explanatory potential regarding operational implementation and the costs of management practices. However, applying RBV and RV to the research phenomenon could provide insight into balancing disproportionate value capture in CMRs.

Limitations related to the methodology

Regarding methodological limitations, it should be noted that using semi-structured interviews and focus groups only allowed an indirect capture of relationship dynamics from interviewees' perceptions and memory. The relationship dynamics listed in section 4.4. are therefore not measured but based on the assessments of the interview partners. This methodological approach aimed to capture possible relationship dynamics based on their relevance to management. Nevertheless, the recorded management practices are therefore not to be considered exhaustive, as they are derived from the management attention of the interviewees.

Overall, the applied DSR methodology creates solid synergies with the exploratory research environment of the dissertation. For example, the pragmatic stance of the DSR methodology allows for subjective interpretation of the literature and design decisions for artifacts to develop valuable solutions. However, the structural aim of the methodology to achieve the usefulness of artifacts makes it vulnerable to subjective bias by the researcher and the evaluation control group. Researcher bias is a typical limitation in qualitative research and affects the interpretation of literature in Chapter 2 and data collection and analysis in Chapter 4. Although several evaluation cycles were conducted with focus groups, the dissertation's results should be challenged to validate and enrich them. Furthermore, expert bias can be mitigated by the systematic design of the empirical sample. However, since the complete exclusion of personal bias in qualitative research cannot be guaranteed, the results of the dissertation do not claim completeness and universality of findings.

Limitations related to the empirical sample

Finally, the empirical sample leads to limitations in the results of this research. The empirical design comprises a sample of 50 industry experts from different industries that have been approached for data collection. However, due to the high sensitivity of CM in industries with solid brand competition, only 21 semi-structured interviews could be conducted. Consequently, the empirical sample is strongly influenced by the participant's willingness, which causes the brand-competitive clothing and consumer electronics industries to be significantly underrepresented in relation to their global CM volume. However, as the consumer electronics industry is well documented in the literature as a pioneer of the CM business model, the lack of empirical insights can be mitigated in favor of under-researched industries.

Nevertheless, due to an evident industry bias, the dissertation does not claim representativeness. Therefore, to mitigate the industry bias, the industry specifics were analyzed in Section 4.6, and constituent characteristics were established. Based on the industry analysis, similarities and differences in CMR management requirements could be identified using the TCE transaction characteristics to ensure cross-industry applicability in artifact development. However, as only one industry was involved in the focus group's assessment of the artifacts, further assessment and field testing are recommended.

Furthermore, as 19 of the 21 interviewees and the focus group participants were based in Europe, a geographical bias can be assumed. The semi-structured interviews discussed differences in the business culture of CM in Europe and the US. Since the management of the social CMR layer can be influenced by cultural characteristics, the applicability of the artifacts should be explored in other cultures.

Future research opportunities

On the other hand, the intensive exchange with practitioners through the DSR methodology and the development of CM also provided impulses for future research directions concerning CMR.

The focus group participants confirmed the concept of the relationship gap and its usefulness for CMR management. In addition, focus group participants expressed support for integrating the assessment of cultural fit and commitment into the CMO selection phase. While the selection process was explicitly excluded from the scope of this dissertation, future research on the systematic analysis of cultural fit prior to relationship initiation may have a critical impact on the success of CMRs.

At the same time, the CMR resolution cycle is of great concern to practitioners. Since the dissolution of relationships and the termination of contracts must be announced in advance, commitment inevitably wanes in the resolution cycle, affecting relationship quality and encouraging opportunism. While the operational and functional aspects of supplier switching management have been explored by Kirst (2008), the literature still lacks an understanding of maintaining a productive collaborative relationship during dissolution.

Furthermore, the degree of integration and scope of coordination of CMRs requires efficient structural and operational organization. The empirical findings showed that efficient organizational design of interfaces is crucial for successful alignment and collaborative value creation. Considering the transition between CMR strategy cycles and varying relationship intensity, the targeted adjustment of permanent and temporary organizational structures could, thus, enable more targeted utilization of management resources. In this context, the empirical findings revealed frequent reorganization of CMR management in client companies due to unsatisfactory structural and operational organization as future research orientation.

Next, the dissertation found great practitioner interest in benchmarking management practices but limited oversight of applied practices. As a result, standards, systematic development, targeted application, and acquisition of management practices are lacking, leaving the potential for effective relationship management underutilized. Thus, there is an opportunity to explore the systematic organization of management practices contributing to the discussion on the PBV.

Finally, disproportionate value capture from CMRs was deduced as a structural management challenge. Against this background, a comparison of CMR management against other manufacturing service concepts is attractive. For example, JDM is characterized by financial sharing, whereas ODM involves a strict separation of value creation. Therefore, a comparative analysis of management concepts of different manufacturing service concepts could reveal whether the management of CMRs can be improved through targeted value sharing.

Beyond the research opportunities related to the unit of analysis, the eclectic integration of TCE and RVP in supply chain research should be further explored. The successful integration of the two theoretical lenses in this dissertation has contributed to explaining the dynamic governance of CMR. However, further research is recommended to increase the rigor and better understand managing dynamic supply chain relationships.

References

Accenture LifeSciences (2019). *Dare to be different.: It's time to revamp collaboration in life sciences contract manufacturing*. Retrieved from https://www.accenture.com/_acnmedia/PDF-98/Accenture-Life-Sciences-Dare-to-Be-Different-Contract-Manufacturing.pdf

Adams, W. (2010). Conducting Semi-Structured Interviews. In J. S. Wholey, H. P. Hatry, & K. E. Newcomer (Eds.), *Handbook of Practical Program Evaluation, 3rd Edition* (3rd ed., pp. 365–377). John Wiley & Sons.

Agarwal, S., Aggarwal, V., & Singh, H. (2015). Partnering in a Haze: Interdependence Misspecification and Firm Performance in Strategic Alliances. *Academy of Management Proceedings*, *2015*(1). t

Aggarwal, V. A., Siggelkow, N., & Singh, H. (2011). Governing collaborative activity: interdependence and the impact of coordination and exploration. *Strategic Management Journal*, *32*(7), 705–730. https://doi.org/10.1002/smj.900

Al-Qurtas, M., & Zairi, M. (2003). Enhancement of the effectiveness of case studies as a research method through the selection of polar cases. *Journal of Advances in Management Research*, *1*(1), 41–47. https://doi.org/10.1108/97279810380000357

Argyres, N., Mahoney, J. T., & Nickerson, J. (2019). Strategic responses to shocks: Comparative adjustment costs, transaction costs, and opportunity costs. *Strategic Management Journal*, *40*(3), 357–376. https://doi.org/10.1002/smj.2984

Asanuma, B. (1989). Manufacturer-supplier relationships in Japan and the concept of relation-specific skill. *Journal of the Japanese and International Economies*, *3*(1), 1–30. https://doi.org/10.1016/0889-1583(89)90029-4

Barney, J. (1991). Firm Resources and Sustained Competitive Advantage. *Journal of Management*, *17*(1), 99–120. https://doi.org/10.1177/014920639101700108

Beal Partyka, R. (2021). Supply chain management: an integrative review from the agency theory perspective. *Revista De Gestão*. Advance online publication. https://doi.org/10.1108/REGE-04-2021-0058

Birou, L., Fawcett, S. E., & Magnan, G. M. (1997). Integrating Product Life Cycle and Purchasing Strategies. *International Journal of Purchasing and Materials Management*, *33*(4), 23–31. https://doi.org/10.1111/j.1745-493X.1997.tb00022.x

T. Brandl, *Managing Contract Manufacturing Relationships*, Supply Chain Management, https://doi.org/10.1007/978-3-658-41359-0

Bloomberg L.P. (2022). Global Supply Chain Data. SPLC function for Apple Inc.

BMC (2020). *Private Label Beverages and Contract Packing in the U.S. 2020 edition.* New York.

Boston Consulting Group (2018, September 10). *Creating More Powerful Partnerships in Pharma Manufacturing.* Retrieved from https://www.bcg.com/publications/2018/how-to-make-pharma-manufacturing-partnerships-more-strategic

Boston Consulting Group (2019, November 14). *Getting a Grip on COGS in Generic Drugs* (BCG's 2019 Generics COGS Benchmark). Retrieved from https://www.bcg.com/publications/2019/getting-a-grip-on-cogs-in-generic-drugs

Boulaksil, Y., & Fransoo, J. C. (2010). Implications of outsourcing on operations planning: findings from the pharmaceutical industry. *International Journal of Operations & Production Management, 30*(10), 1059–1079. https://doi.org/10.1108/01443571011082526

Bowen, D. E., & Jones, G. R. (1986). Transaction Cost Analysis of Service Organization-Customer Exchange. *Academy of Management Review, 11*(2), 428. https://doi.org/10.2307/258470

Brady, P., Seidman, S., & Morris, J. (2009). *Choosing and Using a Co-Packer* (Research Reports and Research Bulletins). Retrieved from https://scholarworks.uark.edu/aaesrb/14

Brandl, T. (2021). *Managing contract manufacturing relationships : An explorative research framework* (Proceedings of the Hamburg International Conference of Logistics (HICL)). epubli. https://doi.org/10.15480/882.3958

Briggs, R. O., & Schwabe, G. (2011). On Expanding the Scope of Design Science in IS Research. In H. Jain, A. P. Sinha, & P. Vitharana (Eds.), *Lecture Notes in Computer Science. Service-Oriented Perspectives in Design Science Research* (Vol. 6629, pp. 92–106). Berlin, Heidelberg: Springer Berlin Heidelberg. https://doi.org/10.1007/978-3-642-20633-7_7

Bromiley, P., & Rau, D. (2014). Towards a practice-based view of strategy. *Strategic Management Journal, 35*(8), 1249–1256. https://doi.org/10.1002/smj.2238

Bromiley, P., & Rau, D. (2016). Operations management and the resource based view: Another view. *Journal of Operations Management, 41*(1), 95–106. https://doi.org/10.1016/j.jom.2015.11.003

Bryson, J. R., Sundbo, J., Fuglsang, L., & Daniels, P. (2020). *Service Management.* Cham: Springer International Publishing. https://doi.org/10.1007/978-3-030-52060-1

Busi, M., & McIvor, R. (2008). Setting the outsourcing research agenda: the top-10 most urgent outsourcing areas. *Strategic Outsourcing: An International Journal, 1*(3), 185–197. https://doi.org/10.1108/17538290810915263

Caniëls, M. C., & Gelderman, C. J. (2007). Power and interdependence in buyer supplier relationships: A purchasing portfolio approach. *Industrial Marketing Management, 36*(2), 219–229. https://doi.org/10.1016/j.indmarman.2005.08.012

Carter, C., Kosmol, T., & Kaufmann, L. (2017). Toward a Supply Chain Practice View. *Journal of Supply Chain Management, 53*(1), 114–122. https://doi.org/10.1111/jscm.12130

Casula, M., Rangarajan, N., & Shields, P. (2020). The potential of working hypotheses for deductive exploratory research. *Quality & Quantity*, 1–23. https://doi.org/10.1007/s11135-020-01072-9

Chakkol, M., Selviaridis, K., & Finne, M. (2018). The governance of collaboration in complex projects. *International Journal of Operations & Production Management*, *38*(4), 997–1019. https://doi.org/10.1108/IJOPM-11-2017-0717

Chan, M. F., & Chung, W. W. (2002). A framework to develop an enterprise information portal for contract manufacturing. *International Journal of Production Economics*, *75*(1–2), 113–126. https://doi.org/10.1016/S0925-5273(01)00185-2

Chao, G. H., Iravani, S. M. R., & Savaskan, R. C. (2009). Quality Improvement Incentives and Product Recall Cost Sharing Contracts. *Management Science*, *55*(7), 1122–1138. https://doi.org/10.1287/mnsc.1090.1008

Chen, X., Wang, X., & Xia, Y. (2019). Production Coopetition Strategies for Competing Manufacturers that Produce Partially Substitutable Products. *Production and Operations Management*, *28*(6), 1446–1464. https://doi.org/10.1111/poms.12998

Chmielewski-Raimondo, D., Shamsollahi, A., Bell, S., & Heide, J. (2022). When the Honeymoon Is Over: A Theory of Relationship Liabilities and Evolutionary Processes. *Journal of Marketing*, 1–18. https://doi.org/10.1177/00222429211062247

Collins, J. A., & Fauser, B. C. J. M. (2005). Balancing the strengths of systematic and narrative reviews. *Human Reproduction Update*, *11*(2), 103–104. https://doi.org/10.1093/humupd/dmh058

Cooper, M. C., & Gardner, J. T. (1993). Building Good Business Relationships: More than Just Partnering or Strategic Alliances? *International Journal of Physical Distribution & Logistics Management*, *23*(6), 14–26. https://doi.org/10.1108/09600039310044876

Cox, A. (2001). Understanding Buyer and Supplier Power: A Framework for Procurement and Supply Competence. *Journal of Supply Chain Management*, *37*(1), 8–15. https://doi.org/10.1111/J.1745-493X.2001.TB00094.X

Cropanzano, R., Anthony, E. L., Daniels, S. R., & Hall, A. V. (2017). Social Exchange Theory: A Critical Review with Theoretical Remedies. *Academy of Management Annals*, *11*(1), 479–516. https://doi.org/10.5465/annals.2015.0099

Cropanzano, R., & Mitchell, M. S. (2005). Social Exchange Theory: An Interdisciplinary Review. *Journal of Management*, *31*(6), 874–900. https://doi.org/10.1177/0149206305279602

Cropper, S., Ebers, M., Huxham, C., & Ring, P. S. (2009). *Introducing Inter-organizational Relations*. Oxford University Press. https://doi.org/10.1093/oxfordhb/9780199282944.003.0001

Cuypers, I. R. P., Hennart, J.-F., Silverman, B. S., & Ertug, G. (2021). Transaction Cost Theory: Past Progress, Current Challenges, and Suggestions for the Future. *Academy of Management Annals*, *15*(1), 111–150. https://doi.org/10.5465/annals.2019.0051

Dachs, B., Kinkel, S., Jäger, A., & Palčič, I. (2019). Backshoring of production activities in European manufacturing. *Journal of Purchasing and Supply Management*, *25*(3). https://doi.org/10.1016/j.pursup.2019.02.003

Daft, R. L. (2010). *Management* (9th ed.). Mason, Ohio: South-Western Cengage Learning.

Das, K. (2009). Relationship marketing research (1994-2006). *Marketing Intelligence & Planning*, *27*(3), 326–363. https://doi.org/10.1108/02634500910955236

Defee, C., Williams, B., Randall, W., & Thomas, R. (2010). An inventory of theory in logistics and SCM research. *The International Journal of Logistics Management*, *21*(3), 404–489. https://doi.org/10.1108/09574091011089817

Dekker, H. C. (2004). Control of inter-organizational relationships: evidence on appropriation concerns and coordination requirements. *Accounting, Organizations and Society, 29*(1), 27–49. https://doi.org/10.1016/S0361-3682(02)00056-9

Deloitte (2016). *Third party governance and risk management: Global survey 2016.*

Denicolai, S., Strange, R., & Zucchella, A. (2015). The Dynamics of the Outsourcing Relationship. In R. van Tulder, A. Verbeke, & R. Drogendijk (Eds.), *Progress in International Business Research. The Future of Global Organizing* (Vol. 10, pp. 341–364). Emerald Group Publishing Limited. https://doi.org/10.1108/S1745-886220150000010026

Denscombe, M. (2010). *The Good Research Guide: For Small Scale Social Research Projects* (4th Edition). Berkshire: Open University Press.

Denyer, D., & Tranfield, D. (2009). Producing a systematic review. In D. A. Buchanan (Ed.), *Organizational research methods* (pp. 671–689). Los Angeles: SAGE.

Doz, Y. (1996). The Evolution of Cooperation in Strategic Alliances: Initial Conditions or Learning Processes? *Strategic Management Journal, 17*(Special Issue: Evolutionary Perspectives on Strategy), 55–83.

Durach, C. F., Kembro, J., & Wieland, A. (2017). A New Paradigm for Systematic Literature Reviews in Supply Chain Management. *Journal of Supply Chain Management, 53*(4), 67–85. https://doi.org/10.1111/JSCM.12145

Dyer, J., & Singh, H. (1998). The Relational View: Cooperative Strategy and Sources of Interorganizational Competitive Advantage. *The Academy of Management Review, Vol. 23*(No. 4), 660–679. Retrieved from https://www.jstor.org/stable/259056

Dyer, J., Singh, H., & Hesterly, W. (2018). The relational view revisited: A dynamic perspective on value creation and value capture. *Strategic Management Journal, 39*(12), 3140–3162.

Eccles, R. G. (1981). The quasifirm in the construction industry. *Journal of Economic Behavior & Organization, 2*(4), 335–357. https://doi.org/10.1016/0167-2681(81)90013-5

Eggert, A., Böhm, E., & Cramer, C. (2017). Business service outsourcing in manufacturing firms: an event study. *Journal of Service Management, 28*(3), 476–498. https://doi.org/10.1108/JOSM-11-2016-0306

Eisenhardt, K. M. (1989). Agency Theory: An Assessment and Review. *Academy of Management Review, 14*(1), 57–74. https://doi.org/10.5465/AMR.1989.4279003

Embleton, P. R., & Wright, P. C. (1998). A practical guide to successful outsourcing. *Empowerment in Organizations, 6*(3), 94–106. https://doi.org/10.1108/14634449810210832

Emerson, R. (1976). Social Exchange Theory. *Annual Review of Sociology*. (2), 335–362.

Engel, C., & Ebel, P. (2019). Data-Driven Service Innovation: A Systematic Literature Review And Development Of A Research Agenda. In *Proceedings of the 27th European Conference on Information Systems (ECIS).*

Essig, M., Hofmann, E., & Stölzle, W. (2013). *Supply Chain Management*. Vahlen. https://doi.org/10.15358/9783800647132

Fayezi, S., O'Loughlin, A., & Zutshi, A. (2012). Agency theory and supply chain management: a structured literature review. *Supply Chain Management: An International Journal, 17*(5), 556–570. https://doi.org/10.1108/13598541211258618

Ferretti, I., Mazzoldi, L., Zanoni, S., & Zavanella, L. E. (2017). A joint economic lot size model with third-party processing. *Computers & Industrial Engineering, 106*, 222–235. https://doi.org/10.1016/j.cie.2017.01.014

Foerstl, K., Kirchoff, J. F., & Bals, L. (2016). Reshoring and insourcing: drivers and future research directions. *International Journal of Physical Distribution & Logistics Management, 46*(5), 492–515. https://doi.org/10.1108/IJPDLM-02-2015-0045

Fredriksson, A. (2011). *Materials supply and production outsourcing.* Zugl.: Göteborg, Univ., Diss., 2011. *Doktorsavhandlingar vid Chalmers Tekniska Högskola: N.S., 3237.* Göteborg: Chalmers Univ. of Technology.

Frey, C., & Patil, S. (2002). Identification and Review of Sensitivity Analysis Methods. *Risk Analysis, 22*(3), 553–578. https://doi.org/10.1111/0272-4332.00039

Friedli, T. (2006). *Technologiemanagement.* Berlin/Heidelberg: Springer-Verlag. https://doi.org/10.1007/3-540-29971-8

Gerring, J. (2017). Qualitative Methods. *Annual Review of Political Science, 20*(1), 15–36. https://doi.org/10.1146/annurev-polisci-092415-024158

Geyskens, I., Steenkamp, J.-B. E. M., & Kumar, N. (2006). Make, Buy, or Ally: A Transaction Cost Theory Meta-Analysis. *Academy of Management Journal, 49*(3), 519–543. https://doi.org/10.5465/AMJ.2006.21794670

Gibson, M., & Arnott, D. (2007). The Use of Focus Groups in Design Science Research. *ACIS 2007 Proceedings.* (14). Retrieved from http://aisel.aisnet.org/acis2007/14

Gioia, D. A., Corley, K. G., & Hamilton, A. L. (2013). Seeking Qualitative Rigor in Inductive Research. *Organizational Research Methods, 16*(1), 15–31. https://doi.org/10.1177/1094428112452151

Glowik, M. (2017). *Global Strategy in the Service Industries.* Routledge. https://doi.org/10.4324/9781315682167

Gray, J. V., Tomlin, B., & Roth, A. V. (2009). Outsourcing to a Powerful Contract Manufacturer: The Effect of Learning-by-Doing. *Production and Operations Management, 18*(5), 487 505. https://doi.org/10.1111/j.1937-5956.2009.01024.x

Gregor (2006). The Nature of Theory in Information Systems. *MIS Quarterly, 30*(3), 611. https://doi.org/10.2307/25148742

Gregory, T. (2011). Transaction Cost Economics and Directions for Relational Governance Research Transaction Cost Economics and Directions for Relational Governance Research. *SAIS 2011 Proceedings 22.*

Grover, V., & Malhotra, M. K. (2003). Transaction cost framework in operations and supply chain management research: theory and measurement. *Journal of Operations Management, 21*(4), 457–473. https://doi.org/10.1016/S0272-6963(03)00040-8

Häkkinen, K. (2008). *Managerial approach to subcontract manufacture co-operation in the metal industry: Common Agenda as a management tool between parties* (Dissertation). Helsinki University of Technology, Helsinki.

Han, C., Porterfield, T., & Li, X. (2012). Impact of industry competition on contract manufacturing: An empirical study of U.S. manufacturers. *International Journal of Production Economics, 138*(1), 159–169. https://doi.org/10.1016/j.ijpe.2012.03.015

Handley, S., & Angst, C. (2015). The impact of culture on the relationship between governance and opportunism in outsourcing relationships. *Strategic Management Journal, 36*(9), 1412–1434. https://doi.org/10.1002/smj.2300

Handley, S., & Benton, W. (2012a). The influence of exchange hazards and power on opportunism in outsourcing relationships. *Journal of Operations Management, 30*(1–2), 55–68. https://doi.org/10.1016/j.jom.2011.06.001

Handley, S., & Benton, W. (2012b). Mediated power and outsourcing relationships. *Journal of Operations Management, 30*(3), 253–267. https://doi.org/10.1016/J.JOM.2011.11.004

Handley, S., & Gray, J. (2013). Inter-organizational Quality Management: The Use of Contractual Incentives and Monitoring Mechanisms with Outsourced Manufacturing. *Production and Operations Management, 22*(6), 1540–1556. https://doi.org/10.1111/j.1937-5956.2012.01351.x

Handley, S., & Gray, J. (2015). Managing Quality in a Heterogeneous Contract Manufacturing Environment. *Decision Sciences, 46*(6), 1011–1048. https://doi.org/10.1111/deci.12147

Hayes, R. H., Wheelwright, S. C., & Clark, K. B. (1988). *Dynamic manufacturing: Creating the learning organization.* New York, London: Free Press; Collier Macmillan.

He, L., Yang, R., & He, Y. (2018). Does social exchange relationship impair audit committee effectiveness? *Journal of Management and Governance, 22*(2), 219–249. https://doi.org/10.1007/s10997-017-9385-5

Heckmann, I., Comes, T., & Nickel, S. (2015). A critical review on supply chain risk – Definition, measure and modeling. *Omega, 52*, 119–132. https://doi.org/10.1016/j.omega.2014.10.004

Hevner, March, Park, & Ram (2004). Design Science in Information Systems Research. *MIS Quarterly, 28*(1), 75. https://doi.org/10.2307/25148625

Hevner, A. (2007). A Three Cycle View of Design Science Research. *Scandinavian Journal of Information Systems, 19*(2), 87–92.

Hobbs, J. (1996). A transaction cost approach to supply chain management. *Supply Chain Management, 1*(2), 15–27.

Homans, G. C. (1958). Social Behavior as Exchange. *American Journal of Sociology, 63*(6), 597–606. https://doi.org/10.1086/222355

Huang, Y., & Wilkinson, I. F. (2013). The dynamics and evolution of trust in business relationships. *Industrial Marketing Management, 42*(3), 455–465. https://doi.org/10.1016/j.indmarman.2013.02.016

Hunt, S. D. (2014). *Marketing Theory: Foundations, Controversy, Strategy, and Resource-advantage Theory.* Routledge. https://doi.org/10.4324/9781315702537

Hussain, K., Jing, F., Junaid, M., Shi, H., & Baig, U. (2020). The buyer–seller relationship: a literature synthesis on dynamic perspectives. *Journal of Business & Industrial Marketing, 35*(4), 669–684. https://doi.org/10.1108/JBIM-09-2018-0280

Imrie, R. (1994). 'A strategy of the last resort'? Reflections on the role of the subcontract in the United Kingdom. *Omega, 22*(6), 569–578. https://doi.org/10.1016/0305-0483(94)90048-5

IQ4I Research (2019). *Pharmaceutical Contract Manufacturing Global Market – Forecast To 2025.*

Isidor, R., Steinmetz, H., Schwens, C., & Kabst, R. (2014). Linking transaction cost and social exchange theory to explain strategic alliance performance: a meta-analytic structural equation model. *International Journal of Strategic Business Alliances, 3*(2/3), 140–167. https://doi.org/10.1504/IJSBA.2014.062333

Ittner, C. D., Larcker, D. F., Nagar, V., & Rajan, M. V. (1999). Supplier selection, monitoring practices, and firm performance. *Journal of Accounting and Public Policy, 18*(3), 253–281. https://doi.org/10.1016/S0278-4254(99)00003-4

Jarzabkowski, P., Kaplan, S., Seidl, D., & Whittington, R. (2016). On the risk of studying practices in isolation: Linking what, who, and how in strategy research. *Strategic Organization, 14*(3), 248–259. https://doi.org/10.1177/1476127015604125

Jensen, M. C., & Meckling, W. H. (1976). Theory of the firm: Managerial behavior, agency costs and ownership structure. *Journal of Financial Economics, 3*(4), 305–360. https://doi.org/10.1016/0304-405X(76)90026-X

Johnson, P. F., Klassen, R. D., Leenders, M. R., & Awaysheh, A. (2007). Utilizing e-business technologies in supply chains: The impact of firm characteristics and teams. *Journal of Operations Management, 25*(6), 1255–1274. https://doi.org/10.1016/j.jom.2007.01.005

Johnson, R. (2005). *Optimal Contract Appraisal for Fine Chemicals Contract Appraisal for Fine Chemicals Contract Manufacturing Organisations* (Dissertation). Imperial College London, London.

Juntunen, M., & Lehenkari, M. (2021). A narrative literature review process for an academic business research thesis. *Studies in Higher Education, 46*(2), 330–342. https://doi.org/10.1080/03075079.2019.1630813

Just Food (2019, June 26). Should Europe's food majors make more use of co-manufacturing? *Just Food.*

Kaczynski, D., Wood, L., & Harding, A. (2008). Using radar charts with qualitative evaluation. *Active Learning in Higher Education, 9*(1), 23–41. https://doi.org/10.1177/1469787407086743

Kaiser, F., & Obermaier, R. (2020). Vertical (Dis-)Integration and Firm Performance: A Management Paradigm Revisited. *Schmalenbach Business Review, 72*(1), 1–37. https://doi.org/10.1007/s41464-020-00083-1

Kamminga, P. E., & van der Meer-Kooistra, J. (2007). Management control patterns in joint venture relationships: A model and an exploratory study. *Accounting, Organizations and Society, 32*(1–2), 131–154. https://doi.org/10.1016/j.aos.2006.03.002

Kang, M., Wu, X., Hong, P., & Park, Y. (2012). Aligning organizational control practices with competitive outsourcing performance. *Journal of Business Research, 65*(8), 1195–1201. https://doi.org/10.1016/j.jbusres.2011.07.004

Kang, M., Wu, X., Hong, P., Park, K., & Park, Y. (2014). The role of organizational control in outsourcing practices: An empirical study. *Journal of Purchasing and Supply Management, 20*(3), 177–185. https://doi.org/10.1016/j.pursup.2014.02.002

Kao, P.-J., Pai, P., & Tsai, H.-T. (2020). Looking at both sides of relationship dynamics in virtual communities: A social exchange theoretical lens. *Information & Management, 57*(4), 103210. https://doi.org/10.1016/j.im.2019.103210

Kauffman, R., & Pointer, L. (2021). Impact of digital technology on velocity of B2B buyer-supplier relationship development. *Journal of Business & Industrial Marketing.* Advance online publication. https://doi.org/10.1108/JBIM-07-2020-0326

Kelly, L., & Cordeiro, M. (2020). Three principles of pragmatism for research on organizational processes. *Methodological Innovations, 13*(2), 205979912093724. https://doi.org/10.1177/2059799120937242

Kembro, J., Selviaridis, K., & Näslund, D. (2014). Theoretical perspectives on information sharing in supply chains: a systematic literature review and conceptual framework. *Supply Chain Management: An International Journal, 19*(5/6), 609–625. https://doi.org/10.1108/SCM-12-2013-0460

Ketokivi, M., & Mahoney, J. T. (2020). Transaction Cost Economics As a Theory of Supply Chain Efficiency. *Production and Operations Management*, *29*(4), 1011–1031. https://doi.org/10.1111/poms.13148

Khalid, S., & Ali, T. (2017). An integrated perspective of social exchange theory and transaction cost approach on the antecedents of trust in international joint ventures. *International Business Review*, *26*(3), 491–501. https://doi.org/10.1016/j.ibusrev.2016.10.008

Kim, B. (2003). Dynamic outsourcing to contract manufacturers with different capabilities of reducing the supply cost. *International Journal of Production Economics*, *86*(1), 63–80. https://doi.org/10.1016/S0925-5273(02)00473-5

King, N. (2004). Using Interviews in Qualitative Research. In C. Cassell & G. Symon (Eds.), *Essential Guide to Qualitative Methods in Organizational Research* (pp. 11–22). 1 Oliver's Yard, 55 City Road, London EC1Y 1SP United Kingdom: SAGE Publications Ltd. https://doi.org/10.4135/9781446280119.n2

Kinkel, S. (2014). Future and impact of backshoring—Some conclusions from 15 years of research on German practices. *Journal of Purchasing and Supply Management*, *20*(1), 63–65. https://doi.org/10.1016/j.pursup.2014.01.005

Kirst, P. (2008). *Supplier Switching Management: An empirical analysis of supplier switching activities in an industrial context* (Dissertation). Universität St. Gallen.

Kitchin, R. (2001). Cognitive Maps. In *International Encyclopedia of the Social & Behavioral Sciences* (pp. 2120–2124). Elsevier. https://doi.org/10.1016/B0-08-043076-7/02531-6

Knight, G., & Greenberg, J. (2002). Promotionalism and Subpolitics. *Management Communication Quarterly*, *15*(4), 541–570. https://doi.org/10.1177/0893318902154002

KPMG (July 2020). *Third Party Risk Management outlook 2020* (No. 137087-G).

Kraljic, P. (1983). Purchasing must become supply management. *Harvard Business Review*, *61*(5), 109–117.

Kroes, J., & Ghosh, S. (2010). Outsourcing congruence with competitive priorities: Impact on supply chain and firm performance. *Journal of Operations Management*, *28*(2), 124–143. https://doi.org/10.1016/j.jom.2009.09.004

Krueger, R., & Casey, M. (2010). Focus Group Interviewing. In J. S. Wholey, H. P. Hatry, & K. E. Newcomer (Eds.), *Handbook of Practical Program Evaluation, 3rd Edition* (3rd ed., pp. 378–403). John Wiley & Sons.

Lambe, C. J., Wittmann, C. M., & Spekman, R. E. (2001). Social Exchange Theory and Research on Business-to-Business Relational Exchange. *Journal of Business-to-Business Marketing*, *8*(3), 1–36. https://doi.org/10.1300/J033v08n03_01

Lambert, D., & Knemeyer, M. (2004). We're in this together: Collaboration and Teams. *Harvard Business Review*, 1–15.

Lamminmaki, D. (2008). Accounting and the management of outsourcing: An empirical study in the hotel industry. *Management Accounting Research*, *19*(2), 163–181. https://doi.org/10.1016/j.mar.2008.02.002

Leußer, W., Hippner, H., & Wilde, K. D. (2011). CRM – Grundlagen, Konzepte und Prozesse. In H. Hippner, B. Hubrich, & K. D. Wilde (Eds.), *Grundlagen des CRM* (pp. 15–55). Wiesbaden: Gabler. https://doi.org/10.1007/978-3-8349-6618-6_1

Lillis, A. M. (1999). A framework for the analysis of interview data from multiple field research sites. *Accounting and Finance*, *39*(1), 79–105. https://doi.org/10.1111/1467-629X.00018

Liu, F. H., Chen, L.-J., & Chen, H.-H. (2011). Sustaining Client Relationships in the Contract Manufacturer Own-Brand Building Process: The Case of a Smartphone Firm. *International Journal of Business and Management*, *6*(7). https://doi.org/10.5539/ijbm.v6n7p59

Lohtia, R., Brooks, C. M., & Krapfel, R. E. (1994). What constitutes a transaction-specific asset? *Journal of Business Research*, *30*(3), 261–270. https://doi.org/10.1016/0148-2963(94)90056-6

Luo, Y., Liu, Y., Zhang, L., & Huang, Y. (2011). A taxonomy of control mechanisms and effects on channel cooperation in China. *Journal of the Academy of Marketing Science*, *39*(2), 307–326. https://doi.org/10.1007/s11747-010-0198-1

Lüthje, B. (2002). Electronics Contract Manufacturing: Global Production and the International Division of Labor in the Age of the Internet. *Industry and Innovation*, *9*(3), 227–247. https://doi.org/10.1080/1366271022000034471

Malmi, T., & Brown, D. A. (2008). Management control systems as a package—Opportunities, challenges and research directions. *Management Accounting Research*, *19*(4), 287–300. https://doi.org/10.1016/j.mar.2008.09.003

Mandjak, T., Szalkai, Z., Hlédik, E., Neumann-Bodi, E., Magyar, M., & Simon, J. (2021). The knowledge interconnection process: Evidence from contract manufacturing relationships. *Journal of Business & Industrial Marketing*, *ahead of print*(ahead of print).

March, S. T., & Smith, G. F. (1995). Design and natural science research on information technology. *Decision Support Systems*, *15*(4), 251–266. https://doi.org/10.1016/0167-9236(94)00041-2

Marshall, D., McIvor, R., & Lamming, R. (2007). Influences and outcomes of outsourcing: Insights from the telecommunications industry. *Journal of Purchasing and Supply Management*, *13*(4), 245–260. https://doi.org/10.1016/j.pursup.2007.07.001

Mayring, P. (2010). Qualitative Inhaltsanalyse. In G. Mey & K. Mruck (Eds.), *Handbuch Qualitative Forschung in der Psychologie* (pp. 601–613). Wiesbaden: VS Verlag für Sozialwissenschaften. https://doi.org/10.1007/978-3-531-92052-8_42

Meira, J., Kartalis, N. D., Tsamenyi, M., & Cullen, J. (2010). Management controls and interfirm relationships: a review. *Journal of Accounting & Organizational Change*, *6*(1), 149–169. https://doi.org/10.1108/18325911011025731

Mentzer, J. T., DeWitt, W., Keebler, J. S., Min, S., Nix, N. W., Smith, C. D., & Zacharia, Z. G. (2001). Defining Supply Chain Management. *Journal of Business Logistics*, *22*(2), 1–25. https://doi.org/10.1002/j.2158-1592.2001.tb00001.x

Miles, M., & Huberman, M. (1994). *Qualitative Data Analysis: An Expanded Sourcebook* (2nd Edition). Thousand Oaks, London, New Dehli: Sage Publications.

Miles, R. E., & Snow, C. C. (2007). Organization theory and supply chain management: An evolving research perspective. *Journal of Operations Management*, *25*(2), 459–463. https://doi.org/10.1016/j.jom.2006.05.002

Mordor Intelligence (2021a). *Global Contract Packaging Market (2021–2026)*. Hyderabad.

Mordor Intelligence (2021b). *Global Electronics Manufacturing Service Market (2021–2026)*. Hyderabad.

Morgan, D. (1996). Focus Groups. *Annual Review of Sociology*, *22*, 129–152.

Morgan, R. M., & Hunt, S. D. (1994). The Commitment-Trust Theory of Relationship Marketing. *Journal of Marketing*, *58*(3), 20–38. https://doi.org/10.1177/002224299405800302

Morschett, D. (2003). Formen von Kooperationen, Allianzen und Netzwerken. In Zentes, J.: Swoboda, B. & D. Morschett (Eds.), *Kooperationen, Allianzen und Netzwerke: Grundlagen – Ansätze – Perspektiven* (1st ed., S. 387–414). Gabler Verlag.

Morschett, D., & Donath, A. (2011). Die Globale Strategie von Flextronics – Contract Manufacturer als Outsourcing-Partner international tätiger Industrieunternehmen. In J. Zentes, B. Swoboda, & D. Morschett (Eds.), *Fallstudien zum Internationalen Management* (pp. 211–228). Wiesbaden: Gabler Verlag. https://doi.org/10.1007/978-3-8349-6793-0_13

Morsy, H. (2017). Buyer-Supplier Relationships and Power Position: Interchaning. *International Journal of Supply and Operations Management (IJSOM)*, *4*(1), 33–52.

Nag, R., Hambrick, D. C., & Chen, M.-J. (2007). What is strategic management, really? Inductive derivation of a consensus definition of the field. *Strategic Management Journal*, *28*(9), 935–955. https://doi.org/10.1002/smj.615

Narayanan, S., & Narasimhan, R. (2014). Governance Choice, Sourcing Relationship Characteristics, and Relationship Performance. *Decision Sciences*, *45*(4), 717–751. https://doi.org/10.1111/deci.12090

Nassimbeni, G. (1998). Network structures and co-ordination mechanisms: A taxonomy. *International Journal of Operations & Production Management*, *Vol. 18*(No 6.), 538–554.

New Venture Research (June 2021). *The Worldwide Electronics Manufacturing Services Market 2021 Edition.* Nevada City.

Noonan, J., & Wallace, M. (2003). Complementors: fellow travellers in contract manufacture. *Supply Chain Management: An International Journal*, *8*(1), 26–31. https://doi.org/10.1108/13598540310463332

Noonan, J., & Wallace, M. (2004). Building responsive contract manufacturers through value-focused strategies. *Supply Chain Management: An International Journal*, *9*(4), 295–302. https://doi.org/10.1108/13598540410550046

Noonan, J., & Wallace, M. (2006). Improved optimisation through advanced relationship planning. *Supply Chain Management: An International Journal*, *11*(6), 483–490. https://doi.org/10.1108/13598540610703873

Nordigården, D., Rehme, J., Brege, S., Chicksand, D., & Walker, H. (2014). Outsourcing decisions – the case of parallel production. *International Journal of Operations & Production Management*, *34*(8), 974–1002. https://doi.org/10.1108/IJOPM-06-2012-0230

Onwuegbuzie, A. J., Dickinson, W. B., Leech, N. L., & Zoran, A. G. (2009). A Qualitative Framework for Collecting and Analyzing Data in Focus Group Research. *International Journal of Qualitative Methods*, *8*(3), 1–21. https://doi.org/10.1177/160940690900800301

Palmatier, R. W., Houston, M. B., Dant, R. P., & Grewal, D. (2013). Relationship Velocity: Toward a Theory of Relationship Dynamics. *Journal of Marketing*, *77*(1), 13–30. https://doi.org/10.1509/jm.11.0219

Papas, N., O'Keefe, R. M., & Seltsikas, P. (2012). The action research vs design science debate: reflections from an intervention in eGovernment. *European Journal of Information Systems*, *21*(2), 147–159. https://doi.org/10.1057/ejis.2011.50

Parasuraman, A. (1980). Vendor segmentation: An additional level of market segmentation. *Industrial Marketing Management*, *9*(1), 59–62. https://doi.org/10.1016/0019-8501(80)90035-8

Penrose, E. (1959). *The Theory of the Growth of the Firm.* Oxford: Basil Blackwell.

Pernot, E., & Roodhooft, F. (2014). The impact of inter-organizational management control systems on performance: A retrospective case study of an automotive supplier relationship. *International Journal of Production Economics, 158*(1), 156–170. https://doi.org/10.1016/j.ijpe.2014.07.029

Picot, A., Reichwald, R., Wigand, R. T., Möslein, K. M., Neuburger, R., & Neyer, A.-K. (2020). *Die grenzenlose Unternehmung.* Wiesbaden: Springer Fachmedien Wiesbaden. https://doi.org/10.1007/978-3-658-28565-4

Pollak, P. (2011). *Fine Chemicals: The Industry and the Business* (2nd Edition). Hoboken, NJ, USA: John Wiley & Sons, Inc. https://doi.org/10.1002/9780470946404

Prat, N., Comyn-Wattiau, I., & Akoka, J. (2015). A Taxonomy of Evaluation Methods for Information Systems Artifacts. *Journal of Management Information Systems, 32*(3), 229–267.

Rao, P. (2003). *The Economics of Transaction Costs: Theory, Methods and Application* (1st ed. 2003). London: Palgrave Macmillan UK; Imprint; Palgrave Macmillan.

Revilla, E., & Villena, V. (2012). Knowledge integration taxonomy in buyer–supplier relationships: Trade-offs between efficiency and innovation. *International Journal of Production Economics, 140*(2), 854–864. https://doi.org/10.1016/j.ijpe.2012.07.002

Rezaei, J., & Ortt, R. (2012). A multi-variable approach to supplier segmentation. *International Journal of Production Research, 50*(16), 4593–4611. https://doi.org/10.1080/00207543.2011.615352

Rezaei, J., & Ortt, R. (2013). Supplier segmentation using fuzzy logic. *Industrial Marketing Management, 42*(4), 507–517. https://doi.org/10.1016/j.indmarman.2013.03.003

Rigby, D., & Bilodeau, B. (2015). *Management Tools & Trends 2015.* Boston.

Rindfleisch, A., & Heide, J. B. (1997). Transaction Cost Analysis: Past, Present, and Future Applications. *Journal of Marketing, 61*(4), 30–54. https://doi.org/10.2307/1252085

Roth, A. V. (2007). Applications of Empirical Science in Manufacturing and Service Operations. *Manufacturing & Service Operations Management, 9*(4), 353–367. https://doi.org/10.1287/msom.1070.0197

Rumer, K. (1994). Geschäftsmöglichkeiten von Unternehmen mit dem/im Ausland. In K. Rumer (Ed.), *Internationale Kooperationen und Joint Ventures* (pp. 21–30). Wiesbaden: Gabler Verlag. https://doi.org/10.1007/978-3-663-07879-1_3

Sampson, S., & Froehle, C. (2006). Foundations and Implications of a Proposed Unified Services Theory. *Production and Operations Management, 15*(2), 329–343. https://doi.org/10.1111/j.1937-5956.2006.tb00248.x

Sanders, N. R., Locke, A., Moore, C. B., & Autry, C. W. (2007). A Multidimensional Framework for Understanding Outsourcing Arrangements. *Journal of Supply Chain Management, 43*(4), 3–15. https://doi.org/10.1111/j.1745-493X.2007.00037.x

Saunders, M., Lewis, P., & Thornhill, A. (2007). *Research methods for business students* (4th ed.). Harlow: Financial Times/Prentice Hall.

Saunders, M., Lewis, P., & Thornhill, A. (2020). *Research methods for business students* (Eighth Edition). Harlow: Pearson.

Schmidt, C. G., & Wagner, S. M. (2019). Blockchain and supply chain relations: A transaction cost theory perspective. *Journal of Purchasing and Supply Management, 25*(4), 1–13. https://doi.org/10.1016/j.pursup.2019.100552

Seawright, J., & Gerring, J. (2008). Case Selection Techniques in Case Study Research: A Menu of Qualitative and Quantitative Options. *Political Research Quarterly*, *61*(2), 294–308.

Seggie, S., Griffith, D., & Jap, S. (2013). Passive and Active Opportunism in Interorganizational Exchange. *Journal of Marketing*, *77*(6), 73–90. https://doi.org/10.1509/jm.11.0529

Selviaridis, K., & Spring, M. (2007). Third party logistics: a literature review and research agenda. *The International Journal of Logistics Management*, *18*(1), 125–150. https://doi.org/10.1108/09574090710748207

Shahzad, K., Ali, T., Takala, J., Helo, P., & Zaefarian, G. (2018). The varying roles of governance mechanisms on ex-post transaction costs and relationship commitment in buyer-supplier relationships. *Industrial Marketing Management*, *71*, 135–146. https://doi.org/10.1016/j.indmarman.2017.12.012

Shaw, S., Grant, D. B., & Mangan, J. (2021). A supply chain practice-based view of enablers, inhibitors and benefits for environmental supply chain performance measurement. *Production Planning & Control*, *32*(5), 382–396. https://doi.org/10.1080/09537287.2020.1737977

Silva, F., Souza, R., & Machado, I. (2020). Taming and Unveiling Software Reuse opportunities through White Label Software in Startups. In *46th Euromicro Conference 2020* (pp. 302–305). https://doi.org/10.1109/SEAA51224.2020.00057

Silva, M., Fritz, M., & El-Garaihy, W. (2022). Practice theories and supply chain sustainability: a systematic literature review and a research agenda. *Modern Supply Chain Research and Applications.* Advance online publication. https://doi.org/10.1108/MSCRA-01-2021-0001

Simon, A., Scheidl, H., Campos, R. S., & Matana, G. (2021). Performance management in logistics outsourcing: a study on sugar-energy industry. *International Journal of Productivity and Performance Management*, *70*(7), 1772–1792. https://doi.org/10.1108/ijppm-05-2019-0216

Skowronski, K., Benton, W. C., & Hill, J. A. (2020). Perceived supplier opportunism in outsourcing relationships in emerging economies. *Journal of Operations Management*, *66*(7–8), 989–1023. https://doi.org/10.1002/joom.1123

Slack, N., Brandon-Jones, A., & Johnston, R. (2013). *Operations management* (7th edition). Harlow (England), London, New York: Pearson.

Sonnenberg, C., & vom Brocke, J. (2012). Evaluations in the Science of the Artificial – Reconsidering the Build-Evaluate Pattern in Design Science Research. In D. Hutchison, T. Kanade, J. Kittler, J. M. Kleinberg, F. Mattern, J. C. Mitchell, … B. Kuechler (Eds.), *Lecture Notes in Computer Science. Design Science Research in Information Systems. Advances in Theory and Practice* (Vol. 7286, pp. 381–397). Berlin, Heidelberg: Springer Berlin Heidelberg. https://doi.org/10.1007/978-3-642-29863-9_28

Sousa, R., & Voss, C. A. (2007). Operational implications of manufacturing outsourcing for subcontractor plants. *International Journal of Operations & Production Management*, *27*(9), 974–997. https://doi.org/10.1108/01443570710775829

Spina, G., Caniato, F., Luzzini, D., & Ronchi, S. (2016). Assessing the use of External Grand Theories in Purchasing and Supply Management research. *Journal of Purchasing and Supply Management*, *22*(1), 18–30. https://doi.org/10.1016/j.pursup.2015.07.001

Stebbins, R. (2001). *Exploratory Research in the Social Sciences.* 2455 Teller Road, Thousand Oaks California 91320 United States of America: SAGE Publications, Inc. https://doi.org/10.4135/9781412984249

Stölzle, W. (1999). *Industrial Relationships.* De Gruyter. https://doi.org/10.1515/9783486801620

Stölzle, W., & Brandl, T. (2021). Praktiken zur Steuerung und Kontrolle von Contract-Manufacturing-Dienstleistern in der Supply Chain. In R. Bogaschewsky (Ed.), *ZfbF-Sonderheft. Einkauf und Supply Chain Management* (76/21, pp. 197–221). Wiesbaden: Springer Fachmedien Wiesbaden. https://doi.org/10.1007/978-3-658-32895-5_8

Stouthuysen, K., Slabbinck, H., & Roodhooft, F. (2012). Controls, service type and perceived supplier performance in interfirm service exchanges. *Journal of Operations Management, 30*(5), 423–435. https://doi.org/10.1016/j.jom.2012.01.002

Stouthuysen, K., Slabbinck, H., & Roodhooft, F. (2017). Formal controls and alliance performance: The effects of alliance motivation and informal controls. *Management Accounting Research, 37*, 49–63. https://doi.org/10.1016/j.mar.2017.03.002

Stump, R. L., & Heide, J. B. (1996). Controlling Supplier Opportunism in Industrial Relationships. *Journal of Marketing Research, 33*(4), 431–441. https://doi.org/10.1177/002224379603300405

Takeishi, A. (2001). Bridging inter- and intra-firm boundaries: management of supplier involvement in automobile product development. *Strategic Management Journal, 22*(5), 403–433. https://doi.org/10.1002/smj.164

Tangpong, C., Michalisin, M. D., Traub, R. D., & Melcher, A. J. (2015). A review of buyer-supplier relationship typologies: progress, problems, and future directions. *Journal of Business & Industrial Marketing, 30*(2), 153–170. https://doi.org/10.1108/JBIM-10-2012-0193

Teece, D. J., Pisano, G., & Shuen, A. (1997). Dynamic capabilities and strategic management. *Strategic Management Journal, 18*(7), 509–533. https://doi.org/10.1002/(SICI)1097-0266(199708)18:7<509::AID-SMJ882>3.0.CO;2-Z

Tescari, F., & Brito, L. (2018). The Relational View: Future challenges for a non-confirmed expectation. *Review of Business Management, 20*(3), 461–487. https://doi.org/10.7819/RBGN.V20I3.3541

Thompson, J. (1967). *Organizations in Action.* Routledge. https://doi.org/10.4324/9781315125930

Tremblay, M. C., Hevner, A. R., & Berndt, D. J. (2010). Focus Groups for Artifact Refinement and Evaluation in Design Research. *Communications of the Association for Information Systems, 26.* https://doi.org/10.17705/1CAIS.02627

Trumpfheller, M., & Gomm, M. (2004). Gestaltungsoptionen des Supply Chain Relationship Managements. In H.-C. Pfohl (Ed.), *Netzkompetenz in Supply Chains* (pp. 301–318). Wiesbaden: Gabler Verlag.

Trumpfheller, M., & Hofmann, E. (2004). Supply Chain Relationship Management: Beziehungsmanagement als konstitutives Element der Netzkompetenz in Supply Chains. In H.-C. Pfohl (Ed.), *Netzkompetenz in Supply Chains* (pp. 67–91). Wiesbaden: Gabler Verlag.

Tsay, A. (2014). Designing and Controlling the Outsourced Supply Chains. *Foundations and Trends® in Technology, Information and Operations Management, 7*(1–2), 1–160. https://doi.org/10.1561/0200000030

Tsay, A., Gray, J., Noh, I., & Mahoney, J. T. (2018). A Review of Production and Operations Management Research on Outsourcing in Supply Chains: Implications for the Theory of the Firm. *Production and Operations Management*, *27*(7), 1177–1220. https://doi.org/10.1111/poms.12855

Ülkü, S., Toktay, L. B., & Yücesan, E. (2007). Risk Ownership in Contract Manufacturing. *Manufacturing & Service Operations Management*, *9*(3), 225–241. https://doi.org/10.1287/msom.1060.0141

Van Aken, J. E., & Romme, A. G. L. (2012). A Design Science Approach to Evidence-Based Management. In D. Rousseau (Ed.), *The Oxford Handbook of Evidence-Based Management* (pp. 43–57). Oxford University Press. https://doi.org/10.1093/oxfordhb/9780199763986.013.0003

Van den Bogaard, M. A., & Speklé, R. F. (2003). Reinventing the hierarchy: strategy and control in the Shell Chemicals carve-out. *Management Accounting Research*, *14*(2), 79–93. https://doi.org/10.1016/S1044-5005(03)00020-9

Van Weele, A. J., & Eßig, M. (2017). Beschaffung, Corporate Social Responsibility und Integrität. In A. J. van Weele & M. Eßig (Eds.), *Strategische Beschaffung* (pp. 455–501). Wiesbaden: Springer Fachmedien Wiesbaden. https://doi.org/10.1007/978-3-658-08491-2_15

Varoutsa, E., & Scapens, R. W. (2018). Trust and control in evolving inter-organisational relationships. *Accounting, Auditing & Accountability Journal*, *31*(1), 112–140. https://doi.org/10.1108/AAAJ-02-2013-1218

Venable, J., Pries-Heje, J., & Baskerville, R. (2016). FEDS: a Framework for Evaluation in Design Science Research. *European Journal of Information Systems*, *25*(1), 77–89. https://doi.org/10.1057/ejis.2014.36

Verdinelli, S., & Scagnoli, N. I. (2013). Data Display in Qualitative Research. *International Journal of Qualitative Methods*, *12*(1), 359–381. https://doi.org/10.1177/160940691301200117

Vita, G. de, Tekaya, A., & Wang, C. L. (2011). The Many Faces of Asset Specificity: A Critical Review of Key Theoretical Perspectives. *International Journal of Management Reviews*, *13*(4), 329–348. https://doi.org/10.1111/j.1468-2370.2010.00294.x

Vom Brocke, J., Simons, A., Riemer, K., Niehaves, B., Plattfaut, R., & Cleven, A. (2015). Standing on the Shoulders of Giants: Challenges and Recommendations of Literature Search in Information Systems Research. *Communications of the Association for Information Systems*, *37*. https://doi.org/10.17705/1CAIS.03709

Walsham, G. (1995). Interpretive case studies in IS research: nature and method. *European Journal of Information Systems*, *4*(2), 74–81. https://doi.org/10.1057/EJIS.1995.9

Wang, H. (2014). Theories for competitive advantage. In H. Hassan (Ed.), *Being Practical with Theory: A Window into Business Research* (pp. 33–43). Wollongong: THEORI.

Wang, Y., Niu, B., & Guo, P. (2013). On the Advantage of Quantity Leadership When Outsourcing Production to a Competitive Contract Manufacturer. *Production and Operations Management*, *22*(1), 104–119. https://doi.org/10.1111/j.1937-5956.2012.01336.x

Watson, R. T., & Webster, J. (2020). Analysing the past to prepare for the future: Writing a literature review a roadmap for release 2.0. *Journal of Decision Systems*, *29*(3), 129–147. https://doi.org/10.1080/12460125.2020.1798591

Weber, A. (2003). Outsourcing's Alphabet Soup. Retrieved from https://www.assemblymag.com/articles/82852-outsourcing-s-alphabet-soup

Webster, M., Alder, C., & Muhlemann, A. P. (1997). Subcontracting within the supply chain for electronics assembly manufacture. *International Journal of Operations & Production Management), 17*(9), 827–841. https://doi.org/10.1108/01443579710171055

Wieland, A., & Wallenburg, C. M. (2013). The influence of relational competencies on supply chain resilience: a relational view. *International Journal of Physical Distribution & Logistics Management, 43*(4), 300–320. https://doi.org/10.1108/IJPDLM-08-2012-0243

Wiengarten, F., Pagell, M., & Fyness, B. (2013). The importance of contextual factors in the success of outsourcing contracts in the supply chain environment: The role of risk and complementary practices. *Supply Chain Management: An International Journal, 18*(6), 630–643.

Williamson, O. (1979). Transaction-Cost Economics: The Governance of Contractual Relations. *The Journal of Law and Economics, 22*(2), 233–261. https://doi.org/10.1086/466942

Williamson, O. (2008). Outsourcing: Transaction Cost Economics and Supply Chain Management.

Winter, R. (2008). Design science research in Europe. *European Journal of Information Systems, 17*(5), 470–475. https://doi.org/10.1057/ejis.2008.44

Winter, R., & Aier, S. (2016). Design Science Research in Business Innovation. In C. P. Hoffmann, S. Lennerts, C. Schmitz, W. Stölzle, & F. Uebernickel (Eds.), *Business Innovation: Das St. Galler Modell* (pp. 475–498). Wiesbaden: Springer Fachmedien Wiesbaden. https://doi.org/10.1007/978-3-658-07167-7_25

Young-Ybarra, C., & Wiersema, M. (1999). Strategic Flexibility in Information Technology Alliances: The Influence of Transaction Cost Economics and Social Exchange Theory. *Organization Science, 10*(4), 439–459. https://doi.org/10.1287/orsc.10.4.439

Zhang, M., Pawar, K., Shah, J., & Mehta, P. (2013). Evaluating outsourcing partners' capability: a case study from the pharmaceutical supply chain. *Journal of Manufacturing Technology Management, 24*(8), 1080–1101. https://doi.org/10.1108/JMTM-02-2012-0023

Zupancic, D. (2008). Towards an integrated framework of key account management. *Journal of Business & Industrial Marketing, 23*(5), 323–331. https://doi.org/10.1108/08858620810881593

Zupancic, D., & Belz, C. (2006). Controlling im Key Account Management: Plädoyer für ein KAM adäquates Review. In S. Reinecke & T. Tomczak (Eds.), *Handbuch Marketingcontrolling* (pp. 374–393). Wiesbaden: Gabler. https://doi.org/10.1007/978-3-8349-9335-9_1

MIX
Papier aus verantwortungsvollen Quellen
Paper from responsible sources
FSC® C105338

If you have any concerns about our products,
you can contact us on
ProductSafety@springernature.com

In case Publisher is established outside the EU,
the EU authorized representative is:
Springer Nature Customer Service Center GmbH
Europaplatz 3, 69115 Heidelberg, Germany

Printed by Libri Plureos GmbH
in Hamburg, Germany